PRAISE FOR *SWIMMING FOR MY LIFE*

". . . a must-read for all parents who every day leave their children in the care of others."
—DONNA DE VARONA, Olympic Gold medalist, author, broadcaster, and member of the Executive Board of the USOPC

"Kim Fairley has drawn a poignant and vivid portrait of how her eating disorder developed in the perfect storm: neglectful, demanding parenting and the harsh, grueling, pressured atmosphere of competitive swimming. This compelling book will make you squirm, pray, and applaud Kim's resilience."
—JUDITH RUSKAY RABINOR, PhD, consultant for The Renfrew Center Foundation and author of *The Girl in the Red Boots: Making Peace with My Mother*

"Thank goodness there is a writer like Kim Fairley who has the skills, talent, and heart to bring us into the world of ultra-competitive sports for children. Pulled along by her propulsive writing style, with an eye for emotionally evocative details, you experience her plight. . . . Five stars and highest praise for this page-turning book, I couldn't put it down!"
—LINDSAY C. GIBSON, PsyD, author of *Adult Children of Emotionally Immature Parents* and *Recovering from Emotionally Immature Parents*

SWIMMING FOR MY LIFE

SWIMMING FOR MY LIFE

KIM FAIRLEY

SHE WRITES PRESS

Published 2022
Printed in the United States of America
Paperback ISBN: 978-1-64742-255-4
Hardcover ISBN: 978-1-64742-295-0
E-ISBN: 978-1-64742-256-1
Library of Congress Control Number: 2022906045

For information, address:
She Writes Press
1569 Solano Ave #546
Berkeley, CA 94707

Interior design by Tabitha Lahr

She Writes Press is a division of SparkPoint Studio, LLC.

All company and/or product names may be trade names, logos, trademarks, and/or registered trademarks and are the property of their respective owners.

Since my graduation from college, allegations of sexual misconduct have been brought against Coach Paul Bergen. I do not draw from information made public many years after my time as one of his swimmers, but rather from my own memory of events.

PROLOGUE

Swimming and I were not on speaking terms.

As an adult, I tried to return to it several times, but something always stopped me. For some reason I knew that unless I was on vacation or playing sharks and minnows with my children, I needed to keep my distance from anything resembling a swimming pool.

Then one day, with two kids entering college, my marriage unraveling, and my mother calling to tell me Dad was entering hospice, I found myself—weirdly—heading to the Chelsea Wellness Center near my home in Michigan. I don't know what propelled me, because the moment I swung open those heavy glass doors and was assailed by the misty chlorine vapor, I could feel my body caving inward. Memories of my parents and swimming were so tangled up that I couldn't think of one without the other.

Get in and get this over with, I told myself. At the end of the middle lane, I bent over to rinse the inside of my cap and caught the reflection of my long legs. Just watching from the edge of the pool as other swimmers glided down their lanes, my nostrils burned from the chlorine fumes. I placed the cap on my head, spit in my goggles, then dipped my toes. Without having to think, I slipped into the familiar habit: goggles in place, a few arm circles, and a jump.

As I dropped below the surface, I could hear the familiar low-pitched thrumming. Memories—of my family, teammates, coaches—climbed over each other in fragments. The images kept coming. Toes clasping the starting block's rough pad. Legs shivering, arms shaking. Deep breathing. A voice telling me, "You've got this, Peters."

Breathe in.

Breathe out.

Slam!

Streamline.

Elbows up.

Follow through.

Another length.

Another turn.

Four hundred meters—maybe seven minutes—later, I glided off the wall, rolled over, and sculled. I saw myself as a young girl stroking through the cool water, the day's burdens riding along on my back, then one at a time dissipating. It felt so delicious to again be throwing off the cumbersome thoughts, that incessant internal monologue.

But then I touched the wall and rolled over, and there it was: the harsher reality that also informed those years. The hurled kickboards. The excessive weigh-ins. The inappropriate name-calling, pill-taking, humiliation. And then, of course, my father.

Why now, after all these years, was I still struggling with my memories of swimming?

CHAPTER 1

"You want to go for a swim?" Dad bent over and stubbed out his cigarette in the sand. "Get her ready, Beejay."

He passed Mom my bathing cap and she attached the white rubber strap beneath my chin.

"She'll be fine. Right, Butch?"

He'd called Jacquie and me "Butch" from the very beginning.

"We'll have fun," he said.

Mom glanced up. "Remember, Dick, she's only four."

It was 1961, and we were at Long Beach Island, off the Jersey Shore, where my mother had vacationed as a child. In the water, parents and young children clad in colorful bathing suits shrieked, their voices halting, as the roaring waves jostled them from side to side or knocked them over.

Dad took my hand, and before I could protest, he and I were at the edge of a thundering roll of water that surged up and covered our toes.

A part of me felt special—Dad had picked *me* to go for a swim in the ocean—but I also wanted Mom's protection. I was still anxious from the night before, when Dad and Papa—Mom's father—had burst into our beach rental, three sheets to the wind, singing "Surf City Sue" to the tune of "Sioux City Sue" and carrying a live lobster as big as a cocker spaniel. Dad had thought it was funny to allow the creature to scoot, half-crazed, across the rug and charge straight for me.

I cast my eyes furtively, searching for Mom. She sat with her legs crossed, her eyes fixed on my sister Pammy, who was seated in her lap. Jacquie sat beside her, playing in the sand.

The cold water numbed my feet and I stepped back, fluttering. "It's too cold, Daddy."

"You got nothing to worry about," he kept saying.

In the story I repeated for years, Dad took my hand and—before I could protest—hurled me into the gigantic, wintry waves to teach me to swim.

I would eventually see that this story couldn't be true. Dad and I had walked down the beach together. I remember that I shrieked as the sticky sand swirled around my legs. A moment later, we were running through a foot of water, then two, then three, Dad screaming, "I've got you, Butch. Hold on." All at once, I was horizontal. As he dragged me by one arm across the surface like a kite, a giant breaker rolled toward us and I tumbled, arms and legs akimbo. That's *really* what stayed with me. My body, horizontal. The wave. The uproar. The unholy dread.

Dad hadn't hurled me into the ocean at all. I had let go.

"Grab on," he yelled as I tried to stand. "Look out, not down!"

I couldn't grab hold. I was too numb, my hands like claws. Another wave slammed us.

"Duck under and blow through your nose," Dad shouted.

I tried to locate Mom but there were too many people, too many patches of color, too far away. Time slowed. It was as if I were looking through a camera lens—droplets of saltwater on the glass, waves sloshing, sun sparkling, salt and sand in my eyes.

Dad clasped his thick hand around my upper arm and lifted my head above the water. We stumbled out of the waves and trudged up the beach.

"You were looking down too much," Dad said. "You need to look straight out at the horizon next time." He tapped me on the back of the head and I stumbled forward. "Come on, Butch, stop crying, or you'll get me in trouble."

I was trembling, not crying.

When we reached the family, Jacquie was kneeling, her chubby knees sand-covered as she loaded her plastic pail. Mom's parents had arrived and were gushing over baby Pammy, now in Gramma's lap.

Mom's eyes darted from Dad to me. "What did you do to her, Dick? Her lips are blue!"

I stretched open my mouth—fish-like—to feel the warm blood pouring in around my frozen lips.

Dad tapped the back of my head. "What are you doing with your mouth?"

"Nothing." I stood hunched over, shivering, tucking my hands under my chin, as the adults searched for a dry towel. The ocean reverberated in my head, but when I glanced up at Dad, I saw his pride: my daughter, my oldest.

TWO YEARS LATER, RICKY WAS BORN, and during that year, to give Mom time with Ricky, Dad began driving us on weekends to the Carrousel Inn, a bustling little motel located on Reading Road, about fifteen minutes from our house in Cincinnati. We splashed around in the pool while he met customers—linen buyers and their department store associates—in the motel restaurant.

Jacquie was shorter, heavier, and bigger-boned than I was. Even though she was younger by one year, she looked more mature. Kids who arrived at the Carrousel on vacation would splash around with her in the big pool, diving under her legs, while I circled back and forth to and from the baby pool, teaching Pam how to float on her back or exhale through her nose. She was a miniature version of me, thin and pale with blond, flyaway hair. I threw pennies to her in the baby pool so she could practice swimming underwater. There was no lifeguard, and I felt comforted every time a handful of adults strolled into the pool area to watch us swim.

But near the end of summer, as the weather grew colder and our interest in swimming began to fade, Dad began to take increasingly more time for his business meetings.

On one occasion, the sun had formed deep shadows and was about to disappear behind an adjacent building. We were comparing the size of our goose bumps. "He must've forgotten us," I said as we waited alone on the deck chairs, shivering. His meeting had gone on so interminably that when Jacquie stood up, the chair left horizontal indentations on the backs of her legs.

"Where are you going?" I shouted.

"Never mind." Jacquie had a can-do attitude, even as a six-year-old. She marched straight to the two sliding glass doors of the bar, her towel over her shoulders. I followed, and Pam trailed behind me. It was so cold that Pam and I threw our soggy towels over our heads like nuns and jigged in place as Jacquie put her nose to the glass.

Within a few seconds, the door slid open to reveal an ample-breasted woman wearing a tight black dress and beehive hairdo. She bent down with her hands folded in front. "May I help you girls?"

Jacquie stepped back. "We're looking for our daddy."

"Well, who *is* your daddy?"

"Dick Peters."

"Dick Peters, huh?" She cracked a smile. "What does he look like?"

Jacquie hesitated and turned toward me.

"Kind of fat," I said.

"He's not *fat*," she said, in a tone like Mom's.

I glared at her.

The bar was lined with men in dark suits with drinks in their hands, conversing.

"Can we come in and look?" I thought Jacquie sounded so grown up.

The woman looked amused. She had long, flaming-red fingernails like those of Anne Boyle, the lady Dad had brought along on a canoe trip, and who had babysat for us a couple of times; they shimmered and snapped on the handle of the glass door. "I'm sorry, but you're not allowed in your bathing suits," she said.

"He *has* to be in there," I insisted.

"Okay, just a moment." She closed the door and disappeared. We faced away from the building, eyeing the pool deck and surrounding bushes for any sign of Dad. For about five minutes we huddled together, the wind sweeping past us, our teeth chattering.

Finally, the woman from the bar returned. She bent toward us, handing Jacquie a folded piece of paper. "You find this room number, and I'll bet he's there."

She slid the door shut as Jacquie unfolded the paper. "Go back to the pool," she said. "I'll find him." She pulled her towel tightly and began to walk away.

"Why don't we *all* go?"

"Because Dad might come and we'll be in trouble if we're not waiting."

"Fine." It bugged me that Jacquie was right, but Pam and I tiptoed back to the pool. We squatted side by side on a chair, listening to the steady hum of traffic as doors slammed and headlights pulled in and out of the parking lot.

By the time we began to worry about Jacquie, she returned. "He was up there with that lady."

My mouth dropped open. "*What* lady?"

"You know. The boat ride lady. Anne Boyle. They were doing business."

"What do you mean by *business?*"

Jacquie scowled as if I were questioning her word choice. "That's what he said. He said they were doing business."

As a seven-year-old, I didn't know what to make of that statement. It sounded like she was reporting what Dad said, but what kind of business could they be doing in a hotel room? Pam scooted closer to me as Jacquie pressed her index finger to her cheek to show she was thinking. I stretched my mouth wide open and ran my fingers along the edge of my lips to loosen them. I don't know why I'd developed such a hideous habit. Despite the shock of being cuffed on the back of my head every time my father noticed, I couldn't stop. It was as if I were gasping for words, but no words came out.

"What are you doing with your mouth?" Jacquie said.

"Shut up." I hated her comments.

Before she could respond, Dad leapt out from behind a bush and, laughing, pounced on us. Pam and I startled.

"It's not funny. Why were you with that lady?" Jacquie could be tenacious and I loved that about her.

Dad reached for a cigarette in his pocket and, with a Marlboro Man swagger, took his first puff. "I had some business matters to take care of."

"Like what?" Jacquie said.

Dad didn't answer. He perused the parking lot, lost in thought. "You kids will understand about my job when you're older," he said. And, of course, he was right. In those days, an answer like that satisfied me.

As we tiptoed along in our bare feet, careful not to step on any stones or glass, I stretched my lips unconsciously, and Dad swatted the top of my head.

"Ow!"

"Stop stretching your mouth or you'll have the biggest lips in Cincinnati."

"She was doing it earlier, too," Jacquie said.

Dad jerked his head toward Jacquie. "You mind your own business, Jacquie, okay?"

I shot her my best lip curl. As we climbed into the backseat of the Bel Air, I covered my head with my wet towel and stretched to my heart's content. I wanted to believe Dad was truthful and responsible, and was protecting me. Protecting us as a family. My body was telling me otherwise.

CHAPTER 2

Mom's voice quavered with rage. "You bastard! I hope you rot in hell."

I bolted up from my nap. Dad had disappeared that morning, right before our annual day spent canning pickles with the neighbors, and now he was home.

I sneaked down the stairwell, my heart pounding. What was Dad doing? I hardly heard him move, but Mom's determined footsteps clicked the wood floor. Peeking around the wall, I glimpsed her wiping her eyes. When I heard the name "Anne," I snapped wide awake.

"I'm sorry to put you through this, Beejay, but I can't handle the kids. She makes life easier."

"Oh really?" Mom's voice softened. It sounded like she was about to cry.

"I'm sorry, Beejay, I know this is hard, but I've asked her to marry me."

Abruptly, I crouched on the steps. *Marry* her? How did he expect to marry Anne Boyle? He was already married! I dug my fingertips into the threadbare carpet on the steps as I hid against the wall.

"You have no idea what you're doing," she said.

Dad reached for her shoulder. "Beejay . . ."

Mom shook him off. "Don't touch me, you pig. She's not going to marry you."

"I'm sorry, Beejay. We've talked. She likes the kids, and she loves me."

"She doesn't give a damn about you, Dick. Did you mention to her that we can barely pay our bills?"

"Beejay, it's not what you think."

She lunged a couple of feet toward Dad and I leaned way back, trembling. "You go ahead and marry her, Dick. I don't give a damn."

"I love her, Beejay."

"Well, she doesn't love *you*." Mom began to sob. I wanted to run down and hug her, but I heard creaking behind me. Jacquie and Pam were standing there, eyes wide.

"I think she would be willing to talk."

"With *me*? You want us to sit down and chat like friends? What would we talk about, Dick? About how you meet her at some sleazy motel? How you leave the girls to freeze in the motel pool while you're up in a room with her? Sure, I'll talk to her. Where does she live?"

"Madison Road. In an apartment."

"Well, isn't that rich." Mom disappeared from view, and I heard her tearful mumbling as she dug through the coat closet. "Yeah, I'll talk to her all right. I'll tell her what it's like to have five kids and a husband who's never around." She stepped away from the closet wearing her windbreaker, which, because of the baby weight, had become too tight to zip up the front.

"She's not going to marry you." Mom grabbed her purse and car keys and was reaching for the front doorknob when she spotted the three of us on the stairs.

"Mommy?" I stammered.

"Why don't you girls go up and lie down a little longer. I need to go with your father to see someone."

I scooted down a couple of steps. "Mommy, are you okay?"

"Look, can you handle watching the kids while we're gone?"

"No, Mommy."

"If you need anything, go next door to Mrs. Engel. She can help you out."

We loved Mrs. Engel, but she wasn't always home. "What if something happens?" I heard Ricky stirring in his crib.

Dad stood at the bottom of the stairs, his hand on the door-knob. His hair was in a quiff like James Dean's, with strands dangling around his cowlick. "You'll be okay, Butch."

The three of us listened to the muffler as Mom and Dad backed out of the driveway. We tiptoed down to the sofa in the living room.

I looked at my sisters. "Did you hear what Dad said? He's going to marry Anne Boyle."

Pam sucked on her index finger. "He can't, can he? He's married to Mom."

"I guess they'll divorce." I was unsure of what that even meant.

"If they do, I'm staying with Mom," Jacquie said immediately.

Pam rearranged her baby blanket with precision. In a barely audible voice, she said, "Me too."

The two of them returned within a couple of hours, and Mom waited with us in the living room while Dad packed his clothes. She kicked the floor and panted like someone who had run around the block. Mom wasn't a crier. She seemed to be holding back her tears.

"Where are you going?" Jacquie said as she inched toward him.

"I'm going away for a while." His voice was breathy.

Mom climbed the stairs in slow motion as Dad swung open the front door to what I assumed was his future. "Take care of your mother," he said.

Family portrait taken by Dad
around the time of the affair.

WITHIN A FEW WEEKS, DAD RETURNED to live with us as if nothing ever happened. Not long after that, Mrs. Engel arrived at the back door, wearing her apron and toting a loaf of her homemade banana nut bread, still steaming from the oven.

"Come in, come in," Mom said, and Mrs. Engel sat at our Formica table.

I loved Mrs. Engel. She was a nurse in her husband's medical practice. Short and shapely, around my maternal grandmother's age of fifty-five, she had a jagged scar on her knee and walked with a pronounced limp. She told me she'd wanted to be a professional ballet dancer but had fallen on a knitting needle as a teenager, which had ended her career.

"I never did hear what happened with that woman," Mrs. Engel said.

Mom cracked a smile as she poured tap water into the tea kettle. "I don't know where to begin, Marguerite."

Mrs. Engel grabbed a dirty knife off the table and rinsed it in the sink, then dried it on her apron, her eyes fixed on Mom.

Mom was animated. "We drove over to her apartment and she wouldn't answer. Dick could hear a man's voice behind the door and he was so angry, he raced around to the other side of her apartment and tried to climb the downspout."

"What's a downspout?" I thought Mrs. Engel might tell me.

"Honey," Mom said, "Mrs. Engel and I would like to talk. Why don't you and Jacquie go play for a while."

"What were you doing when Dick was climbing up the building?" Mrs. Engel said, cringing.

"Dad was climbing up the *building*?"

"Kimmy, *please!* Let us talk, will you?" Mom smiled at Mrs. Engel sheepishly. "I didn't know *what* to do." Mom lowered her voice as Mrs. Engel leaned in to hear her. "I hid in the bushes until the police noticed me."

"Oh, Lordie. You hid from the police?" Mrs. Engel giggled.

"Dick told the officer he was sure there was someone in the apartment, so the policeman asked if he had tried knocking first." Mom chuckled as though she were talking about someone other than Dad. I wanted to stop her but she kept going.

Mrs. Engel placed a piece of banana bread on a napkin, handed it to me, and then turned again to Mom. "So, what happened, Beejay?"

Mom looked embarrassed. "Well, Dick kept telling me to shut up, but I couldn't help myself. I told the officer everything." Mom laughed as she untied her apron and set it over a chair. This got Mrs. Engel laughing. I joined in, though I didn't know what was so funny.

The kettle whistled, and Mom prepared two cups of Lipton tea. She told Mrs. Engel the policeman said they looked like nice folks, and they could go down to the station and write it up or they could go home and pretend nothing ever happened.

Mrs. Engel nibbled her piece of banana bread. "You did the right thing, Beejay," she said.

ACCORDING TO MOM, SHE AND MY FATHER never confronted Anne Boyle, and according to Mom, Dad broke it off with her then, although I still have my doubts about that. And that might've been the end of the story. But for the rest of his life, and I'm not exaggerating, Dad told and retold the story of Anne Boyle in explicit detail. He recreated the scene for the family, his customers, his friends—and without exception, his audience sat there speechless, on the edges of their chairs, usually glancing at Mom, who occasionally added some missed detail to the already numbing story.

Sometimes I think that as a Catholic, Dad felt a need to atone for his sins—that this retelling was his confession, and he looked to us for forgiveness. Maybe he told the story so many times to remind Mom that he was desirable—that he could attract another woman and leave at any time if she didn't focus her attention exclusively on him. Or maybe it was that Dad's affair felt unresolved to him, and it bugged him so much that he couldn't hold back. Though he and Mom started their lives over, Dad never understood why Anne had abandoned him. And whatever the reason, he seemed unaware that he was reopening the trauma every time he told the story.

Years later, Mom said she didn't excuse Dad's actions, but she understood them. She claimed Dad had been made by his parents to feel inadequate for most of his life, and that Anne had taken advantage of his vulnerability by luring him away from the family—which, in the end, had made him look foolish. According to Mom, he had learned his lesson and would not let this happen again.

I felt disappointed in *both* of their stories. Dad would joke that Anne had been a "hot number," and Mom would laugh as everyone else winced. Was this funny—Mom seemed to think so—or was this her attempt to show that she was unaffected? I recoiled every time she laughed about it.

If there was humor, I didn't see it. I felt embarrassed for Mom: she had trusted Dad, and he had lied to her. It chapped me that she had been forced to treat him like a child. And I hated his implication that it was our behavior that had caused the affair. *I can't handle the kids*, he'd said.

Really? *We* were unmanageable? What was there to handle? Mom did everything.

ONE THING WAS CLEAR: MY FATHER'S return marked a shift in the way Mom thought about her marriage. She told Mrs. Engel she was finished contorting herself into what Dad expected of her. She explained that she would stay with him because she was Catholic—she'd been raised Episcopalian, but had converted even before she met Dad because she found the Catholic Church more "reverent"—and because her own value system included staying married.

But I don't believe that was the only reason. Mom was competitive. She would fight to the bitter end, playing Go Fish with the toddlers. Whether she wanted my father or not mattered less than winning. "Come hell or high water," she said more than once, her lip straightening, "I intend to make this marriage work."

DAD EVENTUALLY FOUND A JOB AT Wamsutta Mills. He became kinder, less impatient, and told fewer funny stories. In some ways, he was trying too hard to please. Mom had become the badass, her uncompromising approach giving her the upper hand. At the same time, she was doing a lot of arm-crossing. She wasn't buying Dad's fawning, at least not yet. And we kids tried to stay out of her way. Her lingering hurt had piled up like dirty underwear on the living room floor, and we were stepping over it.

Dad would sometimes wink at me and say, "Kiss me, Butch," then lean over and kiss me on the mouth, and I'd think, *Yuck! Anne Boyle.* I'd wait until he faced away to wipe the slime with the back of my hand. Then I'd stretch my mouth until my lips ached.

I was too naive then to understand how the family had changed, or how Dad's affair would play out over my lifetime, but this was a decisive moment. I remember pressing my head to the glass of the school bus as I headed to school—I was in third grade—and watching Mom's figure recede through the cloudy window. Dad had disappointed us, but Mom—our lifeblood, the one with mettle, the one who was giving us our strength and spirit—was still there. I had waved good-bye to my childish notions of family, but I still believed I could count on Mom to supply the love and support we needed.

CHAPTER 3

My parents seemed mildly dumbfounded that they'd ended up with five kids by the time Mom was thirty. Doors slammed, kids yowled, crashing sounds echoed from odd corners of the house. With Dad gone all day, selling linens, and summer approaching, Mom needed some way to cope. She also, though she didn't dare say so, needed a way to keep tabs on Dad while she focused on the younger boys—Ricky (three), and David (the baby).

The day she decided on a swimming club for our family, I was nine. We were upstairs in our house on Portsmouth Avenue in Cincinnati, and Mom was perched sideways at the foot of their saggy double bed, sorting socks, with one ear on Dad's phone conversation.

"Mt. Lookout?" I said. "But you hate country clubs, Mom. You said you wouldn't join one no matter what." Mom often complained that we needed a bigger house, so it shocked me that we would join a club that would cost extra money.

"It's not a country club," she whispered. "It's a swimming club."

"But I don't understand why you say that. Don't they have a golf course?"

"No, honey, look . . ." She folded a pair of Dad's black socks. "This call is important and I have to listen." Then she added, "We need something for you kids. I don't want you—well, *some* of you— ending up as juvenile delinquents."

I was hardly the juvenile delinquent kind, so the comment stuck with me. She was suggesting that boredom created criminals. In my mind, boredom created ideas. In the middle of family projects, as we all grew tired, Dad sometimes took us on wild car rides, chasing after sirens, hoping to see houses burning down. Ricky, who was three, had recently used the side of David's crib as a ladder and climbed up and pulled the neighborhood fire alarm, which happened to be on a post in our front yard. And then there was the time Dad had taught me how to hurl ripe Osage oranges at passing cars in front of our house. Maybe Mom was referring to Dad; maybe she was afraid of behaviors we might learn from him if we had too much time on our hands.

DAD'S SHOULDERS SWUNG BACK WHEN he opened the letter congratulating us on our membership. "Your worries are over, Beejay. You made the big leagues."

Mom collapsed in a chair. "Oh, Dick, honestly. I don't know what you're talking about."

"Beejay, they don't let just *anyone* into that club."

"What do you mean?" Jacquie and I looked at him askance.

"You won't see any Jews or colored people there, Butch."

"What?" Jacquie wrinkled her nose.

This was 1965, and newspapers were filled with articles about Martin Luther King and his protests against racism. Meanwhile, Eva Henry, our Black ironing lady, worked at our house for several hours once a week and seemed like part of the family.

"I'm not lying to you," Dad said. "I doubt if they'd let Eva in even if she *had* the money. This is a fact you kids will have to adjust to." Dad handed Mom the letter as he loosened his tie.

"Why would you want to join a club like *that*?" I demanded. This was in complete contradiction to what we were learning in third grade about prejudice.

Dad backed away, stunned by my reaction. "You want to swim, don't you, Butch?"

I nodded.

"Get used to it. You'll run into this your whole life."

FROM THE START, THERE WAS SOMETHING I didn't like about Mt. Lookout. I had imagined it would be a wealthier version of the Carrousel Inn pool—quiet and cozy, with women in high heels, colorful bathing suits, and gold jewelry occasionally strolling the deck with drinks in their hands. But it was nothing like that; the pool was packed with people and seemed spacious and sprawling, intimidating even. Maybe it was the pool's size—twenty-five meters, L-shaped, with six lanes that sloped to a deep end where I couldn't touch bottom—or its twelve-foot diving well with two spring-boards. But the people at Mt. Lookout were different too. They were moneyed and well dressed, and drove wood-paneled station wagons. Even as a child I could tell we didn't fit in with them.

The first time we swam there as a family, we arrived wearing a hodgepodge of bathing suits, all sun- or chlorine-faded, and grayish towels that we used for everything from cleaning the car to soaking up water on the basement floor. Some of the mothers rubbernecked when they saw us. One group of women with dark, leathery skin wore skirt-like bathing suits and carried around stylish baskets as handbags. They looked nothing like my mother. For the life of me, I couldn't figure out what we were doing there. Were they doing this for *us*?

Dad would tell us, "You're lower upper class," which made no sense. The implication was that we belonged at Mt. Lookout because his father was a physician, and because Mom and he had both attended private high schools and then Cornell and Colgate, respectively. But in the next breath, he'd explain how he'd barely graduated from college—how, when a professor caught him cheating on his final exam Dad had circled the campus on foot several times with the professor, panicked, begging for a passing grade.

Mom always interrupted these stories, telling Dad, "If your parents hadn't been so determined to make you a doctor, maybe you would've done better." She thought part of her job as a partner was propping Dad up. And maybe she was doing the same for us by encouraging us to swim. I was supposedly the creative one in the family and would've preferred drawing lessons, but I think Dad was trying to convince his parents—and himself—of his success by doing things like joining Mt. Lookout.

Mom signed us up for lessons. To determine the proper class for our ability, we each had to swim one length—twenty-five meters, the standard pool length for summer league competition—without stopping. Somehow, I managed to finish, so they placed me with the advanced beginners. Jacquie swam doggie paddle two-thirds of the way and grabbed the side of the pool, so she landed in beginners.

With lessons, I mastered treading water, developed a decent backstroke, and learned to breathe to the right in freestyle. After each class, Jacquie and I romped around, diving for pennies or playing various forms of tag in the water. On weekends when Dad was home, he dropped the two of us off in the morning and we stayed at the pool all day, just playing.

Once Pam learned to ride a two-wheeler, Dad bought us a tandem bicycle and suggested that one of us drag Ricky on the back. I hated that they expected Jacquie and me to be responsible for getting the two younger kids to the pool safely—a journey that involved crossing busy city streets—but I thought we were up to the task. It was at the pool that the responsibility felt overwhelming. Pam was only five and couldn't tread water, and Ricky, three, only played in the baby pool. But Mom thought nothing of it. "As long as you girls keep an eye on the younger kids," she said, "nobody will notice you're there by yourselves."

I reminded Mom that Pam hadn't passed her swimming test. "How is she going to pass if she doesn't practice?"

"But what if somebody says she's too young to be there?"

"Don't be a nincompoop. If you can't swim in the deep end, don't *go* in the deep end," she said. "I don't want the lifeguards calling to say that one of the kids drowned because you older girls weren't paying attention."

She was only half joking, and I knew that, but I also figured we'd be safe under the watchful eyes of the other parents and pool staff.

So each day the four of us—wearing flip-flops, T-shirts, and shorts over our bathing suits and tucking peanut butter sandwiches into our metal baskets—hopped on our bikes, observed the signs, and pumped our pedals along the crooked sidewalk to the pool. Jacquie and I would argue about who should watch the younger kids, but we both had one eye on them whether we were floating in the shallow end or belly-flopping off the diving board.

FOR A COUPLE OF WEEKS, WE HAD no problem. Then, one late afternoon, a lifeguard called Jacquie over to his chair. Our parents had dropped us off and we had been there several hours. The lifeguard was the typical Napoleon-complex kind of guy, not much taller than Jacquie but with large, sturdy shoulders and dirty-blond hair.

"Where are your parents?"

By then, we kids were experts at steering a conversation in a different direction, and Jacquie was working the drill. "I passed the test," she said.

He stared up at Ricky, trotting around the upper-level baby pool, and Pam, who was shouting at him from the lower deck to stop running. "What about those two kids? Who do they belong to?"

Jacquie sounded nonchalant as she re-tied her pigtail. "Um, they're ours."

The lifeguard squinted. "And how old are *you*?"

"Eight."

"You're *eight*? Are you kidding me?"

Jacquie didn't answer. I noticed she looked nervous so I climbed the ladder and hustled over. "I'm nine. What's wrong?"

The lifeguard squeezed his eyes shut. "How old's your brother?"

"Where?"

He pointed to Ricky in the baby pool.

"He's three, but he acts older," I said, and we watched as Ricky dumped a pail of water on another little boy's head.

The guard set his whistle on the lifeguard chair and charged off to speak with someone in the office.

Jacquie crossed her arms. "Go tell Ricky he needs to settle down."

I ran up and clutched Ricky's hand, but he jerked away. "Get off. You're not my mother." I motioned for him to follow me to the adult pool, where Jacquie gave him a brief lecture.

The lifeguard returned and made Jacquie call home. He waited with us by the entrance, where we stood like idiots with wet, stringy hair, shivering in our dirty sneakers, as other families arrived for an evening swim. As they carried their luxurious, fresh-smelling towels past us, I felt sure they thought we were a ragtag band of orphans. Pam shivered under a skimpy towel, a red finger in her mouth. Ricky had a wide swath of snot running down his nose that nobody wiped. None of us said a word.

I was relieved when I saw our Bel Air pull up to the curb, though Mom looked embarrassed. I tried to make eye contact to show her the lifeguard was a jerk but she was giggling and girlish, as if she'd already had her evening cocktail.

The lifeguard tilted his head and glared. "Mrs. Peters, your daughter here is too young to watch three children."

Jacquie scowled at me. "He's talking about *me*," she huffed. "He thinks *I'm* the oldest because you weren't paying attention."

"Shut up. He thinks you're the oldest because you're bossy."

Mom exchanged some words with the lifeguard and then glared when she saw us shoving each other. "That's enough. Get in the car." She hit the pedal hard, kicking up gravel and fishtailing. The lifeguard watched until we rounded the corner.

"What were you kids doing? You must've been wild. I'm afraid you blew your opportunity at the pool."

Jacquie's red-hot face frowned at me like the whole thing was my fault.

"Who was watching Ricky?" Mom said. "Who? Answer me. Who was watching Ricky?"

"Pam," I said.

"Pammy? She's only five. You girls should've been watching *her*." Pam raised her eyebrows as I elbowed her in the gut.

Over the coming weeks, Mom said she was too embarrassed to send us to the pool. I judged her stress in those days by the number of tries it took her to get our names right. "Jacquie, Pammy, Ricky, David—oh, there you are," she'd sigh, and I'd know she needed a favor. "Would you and Jacquie watch the kids so I can rest a few minutes?" Then she'd lie on her bed and curl up with her *Reader's Digest*.

It sounds like I'm implying my mother couldn't handle having five kids in seven and a half years, but that's not what I mean. She believed she could do it all. Even with a husband who demanded an inordinate amount of her attention, no matter what it was—taking care of household chores, paying bills, or chasing after us—she took on more responsibilities than my father because she believed she was the only one who could handle the job. There were times she acted as if she was about to give up. But she never gave up on *us*; it was more like she momentarily gave up on herself. That she blamed herself for taking on too much.

AWAY FROM THE POOL, WE KIDS RAN helter-skelter around the neighborhood and swung like Tarzan over a muddy gully at the end of the street. One time Ricky dropped ten feet from a tire swing and practically disappeared under four feet of mud. Another time, riding bikes, Jacquie crashed into a tree and her face swelled up like a ripe tomato. Mom liked it that swimming exhausted us. It wasn't long before she suggested the three of us girls give Mt. Lookout another try.

"Be discreet, though," she said. "Don't draw attention to yourselves."

"What if the lifeguard sees Pam and wants to know where you are?" The idea sounded risky.

"Make something up," she said.

Jacquie and I traded smiles. "You want us to *lie*?"

Mom seemed tickled. "Be creative. Don't blurt out the first thing that comes to mind." This was so out of character for Mom. *Why is she telling us to lie?* I wondered. With a dad like ours, I wanted a saintly mother, one I could count on to do the right thing, but lately she wasn't making it easy to believe she was all that different from Dad.

I didn't want to be sent back to Mt. Lookout. But even at nine I could tell that my mother was in some kind of crisis. Somehow I knew that the more careless things she was saying weren't reflective of the *real* her, but instead a product of the stress of her trying to do too much.

Time is so distorted to children. It seemed like months since my dad's affair and his three-week absence from the house, but it's possible it had only been weeks. I knew that we kids were a handful—Mom was always saying as much; I thought that maybe the time of his absence had pushed her over some sort of personal edge where she'd begun to think of him as a child too. When she pressured me to take the younger kids back to the pool, she still didn't seem to recognize she couldn't do it alone, but I did.

I came to a decision: I would help her by making myself as inconspicuous and agreeable as possible, if that was what she wanted. In fact, I'd do whatever it took to allow her to be the mother I so badly wanted her to be. "But will you come get us if we get in trouble?"

"No."

"You won't come and get us?"

Mom's eyes glinted. "I won't, because you'll stay out of trouble."

"Okay, if you say so," I said, grinning.

The three of us hopped on our bikes, tucked towels into our metal baskets, and headed off for the pool.

CHAPTER 4

Mom's eyes gleamed as she pored over the *Eastern Hills Journal,* the local paper. "Kimmy, how would you like to swim on the Mt. Lookout swim team?"

It was near the end of third grade, and Mom and Dad weren't pleased at all with my report card. Somehow, in the family turmoil, I'd gone from mostly *A*s to one *C*, which happened to be in conduct. Though I'd worked hard to bring up the grade from a *C* to a *B*, Mom thought I needed more activities to occupy my time.

"Swimming on a team? Why?" It was 1966: we hadn't been pool members for a year yet, I was slow in breaststroke—I couldn't even *do* butterfly—and despite the lessons, I still wasn't the greatest at breathing to one side in freestyle. Swimming seemed like a lot of work.

"Let's see what the coach says," Mom said, and at eight thirty the following morning I was standing like a dope next to Dad on the Mt. Lookout pool deck, shivering in my green knit bathing suit. Kids splashed around me and steam rose off the surface. What they were doing looked about as much fun as swimming in a hurricane.

With his hand on the back of my head, Dad pushed me toward Bill Behrens, the coach. "Kimmy would like to swim on your team," he said, "and if you do well with her, we have four others behind her."

Bill wasn't a talker. Slouching, arms crossed, he was a few inches taller than Dad and suntanned, wearing khaki pants and a polo shirt. With his eyes on the pool, he tipped his head every couple of seconds to show he was listening as rhythmic waves of kids churned the water in front of us.

There's a certain affect that swim coaches develop in dealing with parents—a sly smile and nod with a lack of eye contact that hides judgment and conveys an immediate sense of authority. Dad must have picked up on this right away, because he spoke to Bill in a tone of ringing endorsement, as if closing a sales deal. "She's tough and can handle anything," he said.

Bill nodded toward the sea of boys and girls bobbing in the shallow end. He'd heard this before. Dad was selling me like a set of his best-quality bed linens.

Okay, I thought, *maybe, with luck, Bill will see my awkward stroke and tell him swimming is not my thing.*

"I'll take care of her," Bill said. "Jump in the middle there, Kimberly. Show me what you can do."

I tried to show my reluctance in body language, but Bill didn't seem to notice. As he whistled, six swimmers pushed off in a line, sprinting to the deep end, arms and legs thrashing. When he asked us to swim butterfly, I was four years old again, in the ocean—water rushing into my nose, choking, gasping, barely able to lift my arms. I inhaled another mouthful of water and swam freestyle to the other end of the pool. As Dad slipped away for the ensuing hour, I gagged and retched, buffeted by the waves.

THAT AFTERNOON I TRIED TO SIDLE UP TO Mom, hoping she would understand my complaints as a directive to keep me off the swim team. She was struggling to straighten the house and manage the boys, and before I could offer up my list of woes, she asked if I enjoyed swimming.

"Not much."

I could see her smiling to herself. "Well, you haven't been there long enough. I hope you're not thinking of quitting."

Well, yes, I am, I thought. *And I'll prove it to you.*

NOBODY PAID ATTENTION TO THE SKINNY boy who seemed lost in a daydream, curled up on one of the lawn chairs on the sidelines at practice. When I asked a girl how he'd gotten out, I found out he had an earache, which sounded brilliant. The next day, as soon as Dad dropped me off at the pool, I dragged myself over to Bill with a finger in my ear.

He rubbed his hands. "What's wrong, Kimberly?"

"My ear hurts."

Bill pointed to a chair. "I guess you'll have to sit and watch."

I delivered my best sickface look. "Okay," I said, fake trembling. I slid into the nearest deck chair, where I hugged my knees and squinted as the other kids sloshed around in the pool for the remaining hour.

THOSE WEEKS OF MY SO-CALLED EARACHE still haunt me as moments when I might've been able to change my life's trajectory. They were the first moments when I realized there was a world out there that wouldn't make me do something I didn't want to. *Kimmy do this, Kimmy do that*—everything at age nine was decided by my parents.

Maybe that's true for all kids, but by the side of that pool I could for once sit in peace and let my mind wander—thinking of the dark black lines on the bottom, how they swirled around like ribbons—while I listened and enjoyed the splashing of all those bodies. Bill realized I was faking, but he didn't press me, and it didn't seem like the worst type of lie. Who was I hurting? I appreciated that he was giving me a choice.

As the oldest child of a big family, you'd think I'd have been used to stating my opinion. But with five kids and Dad, there were moments when Mom had no choice but to rule over us like a dictator. She chose our books, our clothes, our food, even our friends. For one birthday party she invited twelve girls from my class, and they pushed and shoved as they crowded around to see the gifts they'd given me. I had begged Mom not to have the party. She even invited kids from the neighborhood to play with Jacquie. By the time she brought in the cake, singing "Happy Birthday" in her sweet voice, I was bawling from sheer exhaustion.

When I outgrew my clothes Mom would take me to Shillito's, a fancy department store in Kenwood, where dozens of shoppers were always prattling on about the lovely clothing. We would walk straight to the two castoff racks and she'd say, "Please, Kimmy; please try these for me," then hand me a stack of clothes in styles that nobody wore anymore. "We're not poor," she'd say, "we just don't have any money." I didn't want to wear the clothes, but I hated complaining when I knew she tried her hardest to live within our means. With both parents, I got the clear message that doing what they wanted would make my life easier.

So that's what I did with swimming. I didn't *hate* it. I just didn't *like* it. I didn't like being shoved into something for my mother's sake. I wanted her to be happy, naturally, but it didn't seem worth my continuous exhaustion. And I hated hearing her giggling to Mrs. Engel about how fantastic this swimming thing was when it felt like it had narrowed my world. It was like marveling at the hamster on the wheel, convinced the tiny cage was somehow enjoyable.

THE DAY DAD DECIDED TO TRY JACQUIE in the younger swimming group, I was sure my swimming days were finally coming to an end. Jacquie was shorter, and "chubby" by 1960s standards (though her size would be considered normal, even skinny, twenty years later). She liked to tell people she had inherited the worst of Mom and Dad's traits. For years she claimed she had Mom's bad eyes—she eventually wore glasses—and crooked teeth, needing braces—and worst of all, Dad's ugly feet and fat body. Every time she complained, I would remind her of her cooking ability, and how she got all the nice clothes and had a multitude of friends. One of the best of Jacquie's traits was her extroversion. Like Dad, she seemed comfortable with everyone, including most adults. She was the only one of the five of us with the guts to tell Dad the truth.

"You're going to hate the swim team," I told her, smirking.

Before Dad felt ready to try Jacquie for the team, he dropped by Mt. Lookout one morning, expecting a pat on the back for my great success. Instead, Bill told him there was a little problem. While the kids in the pool jumped on their toes, hugging their shoulders to stay warm, I sat curled in a fetal position, my chin on my knees, a towel draped over my arms and legs like a blanket.

Dad went ballistic; he yanked me from the deck chair—I was glad the team had their faces in the water—and dragged me to the car.

He had both hands on the wheel and his head in my face as he backed up. I can still see his unfocused gaze, wrathful and inscrutable. I'd been haunted by a memory of Mom's crying, "No!" in the middle of the night, the contents of her jewelry box scattering on the floor. I'd seen Ricky spanked so hard he'd ended up with bruises on his bottom the size of sand dollars. I figured I was next.

"You mean to tell me I have been driving you to practice and you've been lying?" Dad's face reddened as he spun the steering wheel.

I didn't answer. Saying "No thanks" to swimming was not an option. I did try, though. I fidgeted in the seat, thinking of ways to get out of it. I wanted a deal. Like, how about if I clean the basement instead of swimming? Or if I fix dinner? Mom wouldn't have to do anything. As a nine-year-old, I'd adopted some of my father's techniques in getting what he wanted.

He continued to bark, "You don't have a goddamn earache," and my stomach roiled. What was so wrong with quitting something I didn't enjoy?

"I don't *like* practice." I flung the towel over my head to blot my eyes.

"Aw, Butch, that was embarrassing to find you sitting on the bench," he said, his tone softening a bit.

"I don't like it at all," I told him. "The water's freezing cold and I hate the chlorine." It also seemed that at nine I was one of the youngest in my age group, playing catch-up with kids who'd learned to float before they could talk.

Dad's head dropped. When he lifted it, he looked dejected. I think he thought my failure would be *his* failure. "I want you to give swimming another try. You're not a quitter. This is a winning family. And you're the oldest. At least finish the season."

From that day on, I walked around with a worried look. And I'm not making this up. That look would plague me for decades to come, with random strangers stopping to ask me, "What's wrong?"— which, invariably, would bring me back to swimming. I think of the furrowed brow as muscle memory, the way a crumpled piece of paper forever shows its lines.

ONE OF SWIMMING'S GREATEST PITFALLS is that it takes up so much time that the whole family has to get involved if they ever want to see each other. Once the oldest starts, each kid falls in line like a member of a polygamous religious sect. If, by some unusual stroke of luck, you manage to leave swimming, you're an automatic outcast. You can never get together with those swimming families again. And not because they think less of you. They simply don't have time.

When I think back to that first day Jacquie joined Mt. Lookout, I can still see her rushing to the deep end and dropping into the water with the eight-year-olds like she was splashing in the bathtub. I couldn't believe my eyes. I felt like she'd betrayed me. From the pool's edge, I glimpsed Dad winking as he pointed, and I knew I had to get in. I slid into the shallow end, in one of the middle lanes, and from then on we were one of those swimming families.

EVERY OTHER THURSDAY WE HAD HOME meets, and since Mom worshiped routine, she looked forward to those nights—nights when she could hire a babysitter for the boys and then stand behind a lane with a stopwatch wrapped around her wrist, timing with the other parents. It wasn't a great social life, but it was *something*. Since she placed a high value on patience and hard work, in *her* mind, swimming offered something for all of us.

Dad, meanwhile, could be the bold entertainer, pacing the deep end, his hands on his hips, or hunched over as he judged flip-turns. He paid special attention to how we held our heads in the water and how we finished at the wall. After meets, if I'd caught my arm on a lane line or glided too long into a turn, he would pull me aside as if he were the head coach. "Next time, you'll count your strokes from the flags. You'll hit that wall dead-on and you'll win."

There's usually one parent who's more into swimming than the other, and in my case, it was my father. He paid attention to other swimmers, asked me countless questions about my stroke, and never failed to read the meet results in the newspaper, though he rarely read anything else. In high school, he'd been a better football player than he'd been a student, so I think his focus on swimming may've had to do in part with his desire to be thought of as an athlete.

As he got older, Dad had begun to look less like James Dean and more like a happy Buddha. I can still see him at Mt. Lookout in his baggy swim trunks, a bath towel around his neck, his hair dangling over his cowlick, as he psyched up for a twenty-five-meter race against Mom. Having been a smoker for so many years, he would thrash around like an injured duck and gasp so hard at the end of one length that I worried he'd suffer a heart attack. I always wished Mom would let him win at least once so he would quit trying. But she never did.

Dad had downed a few drinks and wore a shiny red glow the night he learned the season was over and Jacquie and I had failed to qualify for the semifinals. We were sitting at the dining room table, about to finish eating. Mom had been to the beauty parlor and looked elegant with her dark hair perfectly teased, not a gray hair on her head, and wearing a hammered silver necklace from our grandfather. She'd worked hard on dinner—a pork roast with mashed potatoes, lima beans, and homemade biscuits—and we'd already had conflict over Pam's aversion to lima beans. Pam had defiantly dropped them in her napkin, folded it neatly in a ball, and excused herself to use the bathroom while Ricky and David eyed their plates, stunned by her bravery.

"Jacquie needs to get her dead ass off the block faster," Dad said. He tossed his napkin on the table to signal he was finished.

Mom's eyes widened as if to send Dad a private warning: *Lay off, Dick. You're too involved. This is only the Private Pool League, not the Olympics. You'll turn them into basket cases.*

Dad wouldn't listen. "Did you beat the other girls in practice? What did Bill say about your progress?"

I glanced across the table to send an eye-roll to Jacquie.

"You kids have long legs from your mother's side, and you're both built like an ox."

Pam and Ricky stiffened as they stared at each other. Jacquie was sensitive about her weight. Sometimes strangers told us that she didn't even look like the rest of us.

Jacquie's eyes filled with tears. "I'm not an ox."

Dad seemed unaware of his insult. "Butch? What's wrong?"

"Nothing." My jaw tightened and I was unable to swallow my mouthful.

He repositioned himself in the chair. "You have a chip on your shoulder."

"I'm not hungry," I said.

Mom chucked her napkin and pushed away from the table. "Dick, I've asked you to lay off. I'm sick of it too."

He focused on Jacquie. "Maybe I was too hard on you girls, but I was only trying to emphasize that you have better genes than any of those other kids." He glanced at me for a moment. "What? Do you think I'm lying? Tell her, Beej. She thinks I'm making this up about our kids having good genes. Beej, did you hear me?"

"Yes, Dick, yes. They have better genes than the other kids."

After dinner, Mom spent a long time lecturing Dad in the kitchen. I helped with the dishes, silently hoping my parents would get into a full-blown screaming match so I could step in and say, "Just so you know, I don't really want to swim anymore." I was hoping Dad might realize that those great genes he'd passed on to us would fit another activity, like drawing, or taking photographs with that Brownie camera they'd bought me for Christmas.

But when I wandered in to say good night, Dad's red face wore a boozy grin. "You understand about swimming, don't you, Butch?"

I nodded. What I understood was that I was swimming for Dad.

CHAPTER 5

By the next summer, practice at Mt. Lookout had become routine. At ten years old, I managed to qualify for the semifinals in the 9 & 10 girls' fifty-meter backstroke, and Dad was thrilled. He would be out of town for the semifinals but promised that if I placed in the top six, he would be there for the finals.

The day of the semifinals was bitter cold. I wore my brand-new nylon yellow-and-white-striped team suit and my pigtails with rubber bands so tight my temples hurt. Mom cheered me on from behind the starting block, away from the mass of swimmers and officials.

When I climbed out, she didn't seem curious about my time or place in the heat. "Why are you crying?" She rubbed my shoulder affectionately.

"I cracked my head open on the wall," I said, wiping tears. "Didn't you see it?"

She examined the lump on the back of my head, then gave me a playful pinch. "It's a little egg. You're fine." She guided me to a chain-link fence, where handwritten cardboard posters showed the results of each race. "You're eighth, sweetie. That's great," she said. "You can swim if two people get sick or cancel." She seemed slaphappy with relief.

I suspect she was thinking, *Whew, I don't have to come back for the finals; it's only August and we're done with this swimming gig for the year.* I was pleased too—swimming was over, woohoo!—though I didn't dare say so.

Mom was rubbing my shoulder and telling me how well I'd swum when a man who reminded me of Dad—the same thick neck and giant gut—stepped forward and introduced himself as Will Keller, the women's coach of the Cincinnati Marlins. He handed Mom his business card, and she lit up with enthusiasm as she turned the card over in her hand. He explained that the Marlins was an AAU team (the Amateur Athletic Union was the forerunner of USA Swimming).

"If you're interested in winter swimming," he said, "you should bring her to the tryout."

I promptly forgot all about it.

WHEN DAD RETURNED FROM HIS TRIP, he hustled us into the Bel Air, and a few minutes later pulled us up to an attached garage three doors down from the busy corner we crossed on our way to and from Kilgour, our elementary school. The house was an imposing two-and-a-half-story structure with a central entrance and three dormer windows. Dad led us up the hill and around back, where he lifted Pam's skinny frame over a row of leggy viburnums and through an open window so she could unlock the front door and let us in.

"Slow down!" Dad's voice echoed as the boys raced from room to room, their tennis shoes squeaking on the wood floors. The place was a hollow shell, beige and drained of color, except for one thing: a menacing blue marlin hanging on the back wall of the dining room. We stopped and admired its deep blue dorsal fin and black eye.

What is this doing here? I wondered. *Did they forget to take it?*

Mom looked uncomfortable, seemingly afraid to tell us we were trespassing. "The house isn't ours until our offer is accepted," she said.

Dad grinned and reached for her, and it was one of the few times I saw them holding hands for more than a few seconds. I loved that they both seemed happy. I couldn't wait to have my own room, to shut out my sisters and brothers when they got on my nerves. There'd been so many moments with the three of us girls sharing a room when I'd wanted to hide and couldn't, with bed springs bouncing on the bunk overhead or Ricky running in and out, chasing Pam.

We explored every inch of the new house, which vibrated with our energy as we peered in closets and pulled the strings of loose-fitting lightbulbs. Dad spoke directly to Mom, but he clearly wanted us to hear. "The Albanese family who owned this house was prominent." What he meant was that they were white, undoubtedly Protestant, and had more money than we did. "I'm sure the wife was in the Junior League like you, Beej," he said.

Mom blushed. "Dick, you're too much."

"What's wrong with saying that? You *are* in the Junior League, Beej, and that's one of the reasons we belong in this neighborhood. You know, not everyone can be in the Junior League." He put his arm around Pam and she snuggled toward him. "It's better to own the worst house on the street, Pammybuster. You'll see. We'll make it as attractive as the others."

I saw the excitement in Jacquie's face, always one to prefer working as a team, the bigger the better. I think she thought the seven of us would be painting and wallpapering as a family. "How? How will you make it nice?" she asked, rubbing a tea-colored stain on the wall.

"Don't you worry," Dad said. "We'll have lots of family projects."

"Yeah, like painting, stucco, gutters, shutters . . ." Mom glanced at Dad. "How will we ever pay for repairs, Dick?"

"Think of the positive," he said. "The kids can walk to school, ride their bikes to Ault Park. Hell, they have their own private playground with the Cincinnati Observatory behind us. I promise— you're going to love this place."

Dad seemed to be saying this was another step up, like our joining Mt. Lookout. The houses were bigger on Observatory than they were on Portsmouth, and he kept referring to a higher class of people. I didn't understand what was wrong with the old class of people. Even with a fresh coat of paint, I imagined we might look like the Beverly Hillbillies, only pretending to belong and clueless about how people perceived us. But Mom and Dad seemed so proud that it was hard not to share their enthusiasm.

Our house at 3314 Observatory Avenue, Cincinnati.

THE DAY WE MOVED, I SWIRLED MY arms around like Julie Andrews in *The Sound of Music*. I'd graduated from the bottom of a squeaky bunk bed to a saggy colonial double bed that had belonged to my father's aunt Florrie. The room, located in the corner at the top of the stairs, was cavernous and airy—a huge step up from the cramped room we three girls had shared at the last house—with a window to the street and one looking into a cluster of leafy green where skittering chipmunks, squirrels, and birds were ever-present.

Lying on my back, arms above my head, clutching my pillow, I felt a warm sense of ownership—my bed, my room—and as I glanced at the scuffed beige walls, the chipped woodwork, and the window with the sunburst crack, I imagined a room in sparkling white—pictures on the walls, maybe even murals. What would I choose? I could paint anything: a landscape, a cartoon character, an abstract design. I could paint the ceiling black or the walls with hippie flowers. Mom and Dad had given me the freedom to arrange my furniture, my closet, my mementos the way I wanted. This was my new room, my new house, my new life, and the first time I'd ever been allowed to make my own choices.

The idea was so thrilling, I almost forgot I had a swimming tryout in late September hanging over my head.

THE MARLINS HAD RENTED THE DOWNTOWN YMCA pool for their one-day tryout. That Sunday, Mom sat in a set of bleachers, watching as Mr. Keller evaluated our strokes.

Somehow, I made the team.

Mom's reaction: "These are nice families. I think you'll like it."

A FEW WEEKS LATER, I WAS RICOCHETING from Aiken High School to Central High (later Courter Tech), the two pools rented by the Marlins. Mr. Keller made us stand in a single line, squished together in our nylon suits, at the corner of the deep end. There were no lane dividers. He whistled every five seconds, signaling the next kid to dive in and follow the girl in front of her for four lengths of the pool in a W pattern. The night of our first practice, I took one look at the water leaping into waves like the ocean at high tide and became religious right on the spot. I gave myself the sign of the cross, like some of the other Catholic kids at Mt. Lookout before a race, and prayed, "Jesus, I'm only ten. Please don't let me drown."

And when I returned from my first practice and Mom asked how I liked it, I told her, "Worse than canned creamed corn." She thought I was funny. Maybe I *was* trying to be funny. I was so happy at home in those days that swimming faded into the background of my life.

Despite only having part-time coaches, the Marlins had excelled to become the top AAU team in Ohio. On the national level, our swimmers were listed twenty-seven times in *Swimming World Magazine*'s "Top Five Best Times" of the year for 1967. Of course, the success was wonderful for the team's reputation, but what sticks in my mind is Will Keller's concentration on enjoyment. "When swimming stops being fun," he said, "it's time to find something else."

Compared to what came later, those early practices were effortless. At first they were three days a week, with stretching exercises beforehand, but in a short time three days increased to five, with occasional weekends at regional meets. I got stronger and faster, and when we went to swimming meets in other towns we stopped at restaurants like Perkins and Denny's and sampled foods that, to my ten-year-old palate, tasted like gourmet delicacies. My favorite nights of practice were the nights Mrs. Steele drove our carpool, and treated us to Graeters Ice Cream cones with chips the size of candy bars.

I found myself softening in my attitude toward swimming. Compared to some of the other girls, I was getting the hang of it. I'd perfected an awkward somersault flip-turn, learned to swim the butterfly, and even won a few individual ribbons in the fifty-meter backstroke.

But my change in attitude wasn't complete, as I realized a few months later when I arrived home from school to learn that Jacquie, too, would be joining the team. I found her bouncing around the house with her bathing suit neatly rolled in her towel, chattering about how much fun it would be, and let's just say I wasn't thrilled.

It wasn't jealously, exactly. More like fear. In the back of my mind, I'd always believed the swimming gig was temporary. Other girls in my group had brothers and sisters on the team with parents who were totally involved in their kids' swimming. I was afraid that once Jacquie joined, I'd be stuck on the team forever. We really would be, irreversibly, one of those swimming families.

"Too bad we don't have that marlin on our dining room wall anymore," Jacquie said.

Instantly, I tightened. "That marlin wasn't ours to begin with."

"Why are you so rude?" she said, then stomped off.

Mom looked up from her pile of bills. "Look girls, if swimming isn't enough to keep you from fighting, we'll find something else to add to your schedule." She was still pleased we'd collapsed for six hours the previous Saturday afternoon and then slept the entire night.

BUT AS I THINK BACK, IT WAS THE HOUSE that made such a difference when I was ten. It was the feeling of openness, of expansiveness. I can still hear Dad's voice in my head, saying, "You're going to love this place, Butch." It sounded like reinforcement. Some part of me believed in the change. I wanted to imagine a promising future, one where Dad made enough money to earn respect from his parents and Mom had enough space from us to be the sweet mother I knew she wanted to be.

Each night I arrived home from practice as ravenous as a bear, tossed my wet suit and towel on the kitchen steps, and joined the family for dinner, knowing that after the dishes were dried I could shut my bedroom door, curl up in my own bed, and recharge my energy. It was still too early to understand the true ramifications of having joined the Marlins.

CHAPTER 6

Will Keller was our fun-loving coach and then—poof—he was gone.

It was March or April. We were swimming indoors at Courter Tech, on the west side of Cincinnati, and everything that day was wet: the walls, the deck, the ceiling. It was one of those oppressive midwestern days when the moisture hangs in the air like a heavy curtain.

Four men in dark suits stood near the shallow end of the pool, and the only one I recognized was Charles Keating, the new president of the Marlins. A charismatic financier for American Financial Corporation and the father of six swimmers, Keating was the founder of Citizens for Decent Literature to end smut in Cincinnati and a member of President Nixon's Commission on Obscenity and Pornography. With his brother, Bill, a former judge who was now serving on the Cincinnati City Council, Mr. Keating had made it clear to the Marlin parents that he intended to make sweeping changes to our program. Nobody seemed to know precisely what that meant.

I experienced a bit of an internal freak-out the day I learned Will Keller wasn't coming back. Swimming was hard enough already. Now we were getting a coach whom the parents had lured away from his head coaching job at Kent State University.

About fifteen of us were seated on the cold concrete floor of the mezzanine before practice when our new coach arrived that first night. He was a short man, in his late twenties, with dark, wavy hair, a broad chin, and a wobbly Adam's apple. He hardly moved when he spoke, the muscles in his shoulders tense, his horn-rimmed glasses hiding dark, surveilling eyes. *Is he trying to scare us?* I wondered. Everything about him—his dark clothes, dark glasses, the whole package—intimidated. He stood flagpole straight, spouting a dry list of Marlin goals, like fostering social and emotional development and learning good sportsmanship. He told us we were to call him "Mr. Bergen."

I glanced at Connie, Kristie, and Deena—backs curled, knees hugged to their chests—and thought, *Uh-oh, this doesn't sound fun.* We were little girls between ages ten and twelve, in our bare feet and pigtails, and the way he spoke, you would've thought we were adults. When some of us whispered, he glared—"Excuse me. Are you finished?"—then went on speaking with his head down in a mono-tone, his lips barely moving. We kids didn't dare look at each other.

As Mr. Keating and the other men slipped away, Mr. Bergen said he would be turning us into elite swimmers. Until then, the boys and girls had practiced separately. Mr. Bergen explained that future prac-tices would combine boys and girls to make us more competitive.

When he glanced up from his clipboard, he saw us staring at each other, confused. "If you do what you're asked," he said, "you'll do fine. If you don't, you won't survive."

We won't survive? He sounded like my father when he wandered off on tangents about church: "You're a Catholic and you're lucky, because you're going to heaven. That's not the case for all the Prot-estants and Jews, you know."

Mom would chuckle. "Oh, Dick, honestly."

He liked to make things up as he went along.

But my first impression of Mr. Bergen was that he was clueless about kids. I didn't trust his statements regarding our future any more than I believed my father's. I only trusted his ability to instill fear. As he finished his talk, our voices sank to whispers. I stared at the still water, listening to the faint hum of rotating blades in the massive overhead box fans.

"Find a lane," he said, and we looked around, confused. *What* lane? Where? Still in elementary school, we were accustomed to lining up.

We scrambled toward the lanes; the first girl tucked her toes over the edge, and the rest of us formed a single-file line behind her. Within seconds Mr. Bergen was shouting, "Even lanes right to left. Odd lanes left to right."

We were used to swimming in a W pattern or across the width of the pool, in heats. The idea of continuous circling in all six lanes was as foreign as Mr. Bergen himself.

Instantly, it seemed, nearly every detail of our training had changed. Practice groups were structured according to talent rather than age, and since the girls' team was a bit stronger, in many cases the guys in a given practice group were two or three years older than the girls. Weight training had become "a thing" in other sports like football and wrestling, so Mr. Bergen brought in weights, and three days a week we did a half hour of circuit training, which included bench presses, tricep extensions, and bent-over rowing with barbells, in addition to swimming.

The other days we stretched and did dryland exercises. And I don't mean jumping jacks. At eleven years old, I did five sets of twenty military push-ups, five sets of twenty sit-ups, multiple squats with a teammate on my back, and concentric, isometric, and eccentric exercises with weights as well as an exergenie, a piece of equipment that was cutting-edge at the time and just beginning to be used by the NFL as a part of their training. It was a cylindrical machine the size of a bike pump, with ropes running through it and handles at the end of each rope that worked like modern Thera-Band's. Exergenies allowed us to adjust the level of resistance while modeling freestyle arm movements on dry land.

Mr. Bergen had been a mentee of Doc Counsilman, the famous swimming coach of Indiana University who coached Mark Spitz and studied swimming scientifically by measuring water flow and speed with various stroke techniques. He constantly touted Doc Counsilman's book, *The Science of Swimming*, and I believed we were learning about medicine and physiology as it related to our strokes.

There were days when my arms, legs, fingers, toes, and every muscle in my back and neck ached. I was so young that I wasn't yet wearing deodorant, shaving my arms and legs, or caring much about how I looked, and yet I was discovering muscles I didn't know I had.

When I came home from practice, exhausted, Dad—who considered argument an enjoyable sport—would ask me countless questions: "How was practice? How did you do? Talk to me, Butch." On the nights when I could hardly lift my head at the table, he would tap Mom on the arm as if to say, "See, Beej? See how beneficial this swimming thing is?"

THAT FIRST YEAR, MR. BERGEN CAME UP with the idea of swimming a mile timed trial in a different stroke every week—in other words, all-out, as if we were competing in a meet—in freestyle, backstroke, breaststroke, and butterfly. We did the mile of freestyle and backstroke first; at the end of the third week, when he gave us the mile of breaststroke, I finished at least four laps behind in my lane.

Connie was my age and she and I had joined the Marlins on the same day. As we dragged ourselves into the locker room, she moaned, "I am so sore."

"Tell me about it." I pulled down one of my straps and rubbed the red rash on the front of my armpits. My eyes, ringed in red, burned ferociously from the inside out. This was before swimmers wore goggles. The only goggles available were frog style, with wide rims that created drag and filled with water, and only one or two older guys ever wore them.

Connie yanked off her white rubber cap and tossed it on the concrete floor of the shower. She reached for the shampoo and massaged a rich lather into her chocolate-brown hair. "If he makes us swim a mile of butterfly, I'm going to quit. I can't do it. I'm not *going* to do it."

Kristie adjusted the nozzle, her lithe figure jumping back from the spit of cold water. "I'll tell him he can shove it where the sun doesn't shine."

"Yeah—right—good luck," I said, rolling my eyes.

We laughed.

Kristie and Connie both had physician fathers on the Marlin board of directors. If *they* thought a mile of butterfly was abusive, maybe we'd luck out and not have to swim it. I didn't really think this was possible, but the thought did cross my mind.

On most days, I'd come home in a chlorine-addled haze an hour or so after Jacquie. Mom and Dad would be leaning against the kitchen counters, talking about Dad's job and slugging down bourbon-and-Frescas while the kids fought upstairs and Jacquie crouched on the couch, nuzzling her book and looking traumatized. I'd list the moments I'd swallowed water and choked back vomit, and Mom and Dad would fall into hysterics.

But that night when I returned home, Mom and Dad were huddled in their bedroom office, frustratedly reviewing their finances. I could hear Mom as I climbed the stairs—"No, Dick, we paid that one. It was the damn phone bill we didn't pay."

"Hi," I said, interrupting.

"Hi, Butch," Dad grunted.

I peeked into my sister's room. "We're going to have a mile of butterfly," I said. Jacquie's 9 &10 practice group, the one down from mine, usually swam an abbreviated version of our practice, so there was some chance she might have to swim it too.

In its early days, butterfly was called the "suicide stroke" because it was so difficult and painful. It requires nearly equal amounts of strength in both arms and legs, exerted at the same time, with a rhythm as smooth and graceful as a Viennese waltz.

Jacquie lay against her twin headboard in the corner of her room with a book propped on her knees. The long, chlorine-dried tendrils of her brown hair hung limp, and her round glasses were perched at the tip of her nose. "I hope he doesn't make *us* do that," she said.

I told her about the girl on our team we knew who had a problem with swearing, whom eventually we learned must've had Tourette's syndrome. "You should've heard her after practice," I said. "She opened the car door, and said, 'Shit, shit, fuck, fuck,' and I thought, *Yep, I know exactly what you mean*."

Jacquie fixed her eyes on the book and didn't say anything at first.

Trying to get her to talk, I said, "I sure would love to see her do that rant in front of Mr. Bergen."

Jacquie's voice was flat. "That would be her last day."

"Of practice?"

"No. On earth."

THE BUTTERFLY DAY, MR. BERGEN LOOKED smug as he stood on the pool deck, watching the older kids nearly drown. His shirt was devoid of wrinkles or stains, his white gym shoes as spotless as military dress shoes. He jotted notes on his clipboard as swimmers trudged through a continuous mile—sixty-six laps in a twenty-five-yard pool—of gagging and choking on rough water.

While watching them, I considered the way my father used to give up in the middle of family projects. We would be out in the yard, raking leaves and dragging the bags to the street, and I knew if I sidled up to Dad and asked if he wanted water, he could be persuaded to sit on the porch and watch while Mom finished the job. Some part of me hoped I could tempt Darryl, our assistant coach, in the same way. He was taller and thicker than Mr. Bergen and was a gentle, happy soul with a sense of humor.

I sauntered over, trying to make eye contact, hoping for some hint of what to expect.

"If you want to win, you have to make sacrifices," Darryl said, parroting Mr. Bergen's talking points.

Did I want to *win*? I guess so. But I didn't want to drown. Swimming had started out as a place where I could go with my siblings to have fun away from my parents. Now it was a place of hard labor, of following the rules and doing what we were told, of stretching the limits of what our bodies could endure. Mr. Bergen seemed to be redefining swimming as redemption through suffering.

My best stroke was backstroke, not butterfly. When would I ever have to swim butterfly in competition? It was like making a pole vaulter do the shot put. But at age eleven, there was something exciting about Mr. Bergen's pushing us to do things that seemed unfathomable. And there was comfort in knowing that the rules applied to everyone.

I took Darryl's advice and swam the warm-up as if I were psyching up for a competition. As I waited for word of the main set, one of the guys spat huge hawkers into the gutter, making us all gag. A mass of hair and other organic matter floated toward me. I scooted back, but the glob inched closer. All at once, someone swam into the wall, a wave crashed toward me, and the dirty mass washed onto my arm. "Eew!" I flicked the glob through the air, and it hit one of the girls in the face.

As she shrieked, Mr. Bergen came up from behind and slammed a kickboard on the edge of the pool, deadening my eardrums. This was one of Mr. Bergen's signature moves. He routinely hurled kickboards, pull buoys, paddles, and, worst of all, insults at many of his strongest swimmers, but this was the first time he'd ever used it on me.

"What's the matter, Peters?" He sounded impatient, wanting a response.

"Nothing." Of course, the chunky clump *was* something. To a swimmer, the pool is a sanctuary. Without clean water, the experience is not only disgusting, it's sacrilegious. But the water quality was the least of my worries that day. In that moment, I thought of my dentist and his advice when he'd drilled into my teeth without Novocain: "Keep your eyes open and it doesn't hurt as much."

"Some of you will have to toughen up." Mr. Bergen held on to the post for the overhead flags that backstrokers used to count their strokes to the wall as we clung to the hard tiled gutter at the deep end of the pool. He pointed to the pace clock. "You know what to do: a mile of butterfly. On the top."

But then he added, "I want to see double breathing." In other words, two strokes instead of one for every breath, meaning half as much air.

I had the immediate urge to climb out. Double breathing was something I'd only managed previously for a few laps. Still, I pushed off the wall, third in line, gasping and trembling and dragging my arms through the water.

After four lengths, I wanted to give up. This was torture. Voluntary waterboarding, if you asked me. But there was no way I would give Mr. Bergen the satisfaction of knowing how brutal the workout was. *Do not resist. Do not push back.* This message was as clear to me as my reaction to my father when he paddled us as kids. I would tell myself, *This is not going to hurt.* And it didn't.

My stroke that day was more like a moth missing a wing than a butterfly, the way I flopped around. Yet, surprisingly, I didn't lose my place in line. I tried to think of only one lap at a time. For sixty-six laps, double breathing butterfly, I coughed and choked and thought I might drown. But I finished.

Years later, I heard that a guy in the older group—Jim Sheehy—quit the team the day of the mile of butterfly. He was said to have explained to Mr. Bergen, "Man was not meant to be a washing machine."

WAS THERE SOMETHING EXCITING ABOUT swimming for Mr. Bergen? Well, yes. Some part of me loved the thrill of the inherent danger. I felt overheated, lightheaded, and dead tired on most nights, unsure if my effort was sustainable. But when it was over, I felt grateful to Mr. Bergen that his raising the bar on our training had given me a sense of achievement.

There was something comforting in the structure of swimming. It left me too tired to let my parents' troubles weigh me down. The narrow focus helped. I've read that some swimmers hear songs in their head as they swim. Others memorize poems. Not me. In the water, swimming took up every inch of my brain. Maybe it was those free-wheeling stress chemicals shooting through my bloodstream that funneled my attention. I focused on maintaining my body position, making the interval with a few seconds to spare, and pleasing Mr. Bergen. Swimming was a place where I was told what to do, with no pressure to answer questions or help other people. It diverted my attention to another kind of pressure. Maybe you could call it a body awareness. It was a very directed, personal pressure that involved holding myself together.

It's a kind of meditation. You focus on your body position, and your breath. Your mind drifts to a problem—the next set, which you know will be a killer—and you notice your mind-drift has caused you to miss a turn. You kick harder, pull harder, and return to your breath. There's no space to sort out life's problems or conflicts. To survive you need to maintain the rhythm, and in doing that, you feel your anxiety dissipate.

To this day, I still think of that marlin on the wall in our dining room. Was that mounted fish an eerie prognostication? Perhaps. But my father also had been right on that day at Mt. Lookout when he told Bill Behrens I was tough and could handle anything. Sure, in part I may have hated and feared swimming. I may have looked weak. I may have been anxious half the time. I may have whined and bellyached, stretched my mouth, and slept more than anyone else. But I had grit. In that mile of butterfly, I'd proved it to myself.

CHAPTER 7

With the house came all kinds of unforeseen expenses, and according to Mom, Dad's job at Wamsutta Mills wasn't paying enough. She and Dad would stay up late at night, drinking and brainstorming about how to make more money.

One night I heard them arguing about Dad's parents, whom we called Mom-Mom and Pop-Pop. "What do we have to lose?" Dad said. "We can ask for the money and if they say no, oh well." Pop-Pop, a general practitioner and surgeon, had recently retired and permanently moved with my grandmother to their summer home on Cape Cod.

Mom said, "Dick, don't you think we have enough stress? You remember their last visit?" She was referring to a big fight with my grandmother over her insistence that Pam's hair had been bleached.

"Pammy's hair is naturally blond," Mom had insisted, adamant. "I haven't touched it."

But Mom-Mom wouldn't back down. "That hair is bleached. I know what bleached hair looks like."

The argument was so ridiculous I was relieved the following morning when my grandparents loaded their car and returned home.

"Haven't you forgiven them yet?" Dad nudged Mom. "Family is what this life is about."

I couldn't hear her response, but I imagine she threw up her hands in frustration. Dad won—as he often did—through sheer endurance.

THE DAY BEFORE MY GRANDPARENTS' arrival, Mom lay in bed while Dad gave Ricky and David what he hoped were GI haircuts using the same electric hair trimmer he used for our dog, Mustard. Before our dad got to him, Ricky had an overgrown buzz cut. His hair stuck straight out and needed a little hair gel and a comb. But Dad ran that electric razor along Ricky's head until, without warning, the clip fell off, shaving him to the scalp and leaving a white bald spot. The more Dad kept shaving, the more often the clip fell off, and the more Dad swore as he carved into Ricky's head. But he wouldn't stop. I think some part of him wanted the boys to resemble poor immigrants from Eastern Europe, thinking it would tug on his parents' heartstrings.

Mom-Mom, Pop-Pop, and Aunt Peggy showed up with Peggy's giant dog, Lucky, an energetic slobberer. Between Lucky and the boys' haircuts, hair was floating in the air that day, so it was no wonder that on the first night of their visit, a couple of stray strands showed up in Peggy's bed. Aunt Peggy resembled Lauren Bacall, sultry, with a thick, beautiful head of hair, so maybe she noticed hair more than we did. She told Mom-Mom, "I will not sleep in a dirty bed," and Mom-Mom, not wanting Peggy to get in a fight with Dad, passed the word to Mom.

"I changed those sheets myself," Mom grumbled when she heard the complaint. "They came directly from the dryer."

Mom-Mom, a slight sparrow of a woman, was hard of hearing but too vain to wear hearing aids. She stood with her shoulders stiff, her chin high, reasoning out loud that if the sheets were clean when they came out of the dryer, then Jacquie must've placed the hair there on purpose. She'd already decided that the poster on Jacquie's wall that read, "I'm not hard of hearing. I'm just ignoring you," was placed there as a direct message to her.

Mom said, "I will not change that bed again."

"Don't worry; I will," Jacquie said, already trudging up the stairs.

Wow, I thought, *too bad I have to attend swimming practice and miss all this warm family bonding.*

BY THE SECOND DAY OF THEIR VISIT, it seemed Pop-Pop had reached his limit, too. He retrieved a black briefcase from the guest-room, and when he opened the latches, my eyes widened. The whole thing was packed with money wrapped in paper bands—like you see in the movies, only reeking of mildew.

Dad had been correct that his folks could handle us for only so many hours, and when they left, we had a hard time hiding our relief. Mom hid behind the front door, kissing Dad, as we kids waved good-bye.

"What on earth are we going to do with this cash?" Mom giggled.

"What do you mean, Beej?" Dad squinted at her. "Can't we pay some bills?"

"Are you saying we march into the bank with a grocery bag of stacked twenties? We'll look like criminals, won't we?"

Dad removed his Oxford shirt, frayed at the collar, revealing permanent food stains on his T-shirt above the belt. "We'll figure it out. Let's relax for a while, shall we?" He served up a couple of bourbons for himself and Mom, and Shirley Temples for the rest of us.

MY GRANDPARENTS HAD BARELY ENOUGH time to leave Cincinnati before Dad came up with another wild idea: he wanted Mom to go to work with him at his job at Wamsutta Mills.

This kind of thing embarrassed me; I didn't know why he couldn't manage on his own. Now, I wonder: Was it just that he was lazy and drank too much? Or did he suffer from one of the conditions we knew so little about back then, like dyslexia or ADHD?

Mom didn't think this was such a great idea, but she had been complaining that she wanted different wallpaper in the front hall, more cabinets in the kitchen, and something to be done about the muddy marsh of a backyard. Maybe she thought her help at his office would give Dad more time to help her at home.

To Dad's surprise, his boss didn't think he was getting two for the price of one, and soon after, he fired Dad. Since the money from our grandparents had been used to pay bills already due, in a matter of days Mom was shaking out the last bit of shredded wheat at the breakfast table.

She bit down on her bottom lip. "We can't keep going like this, Dick. You need to find another job."

Dad put his hand on Mom's shoulder. "Beej, we have enough to pay our bills for a while, don't we?"

Mom opened the refrigerator and glanced out the window without answering him.

"Beej?"

"I don't think so, Dick."

"How about if you cut back on getting your hair done? How's Gary, anyway?" He loved to tease Mom that she was having an affair with Gary, her hairdresser.

Mom didn't laugh. She paced in the kitchen, dropping cereal bowls and flatware into the sink with a loud crash. "You are so unaware, Dick."

Dad didn't notice that Mom hadn't been to the salon in weeks. Her 1950s cat-eye frames, meanwhile, were so outdated that on a trip to Chicago, a couple of young women—1970s-style hipsters—she'd shared an elevator with had offered to buy them.

Mom disappeared upstairs and a few minutes later, returned to the kitchen wearing black polyester pants and a white print polyester top as if she were on her way out the door. "Dick, I'm not going to sit around all day and do nothing. What are you doing with those old samples?" She meant the Wamsutta sheets and pillowcases stacked in the corner of the basement, wrapped in cellophane. "Are they going back to the company?"

"I don't care what you do with them," Dad said.

Mom clattered down the stairs to the basement as Dad, in his navy bathrobe and bare feet, swallowed his shame. He'd gained so much weight his robe didn't close, exposing his white T-shirt and jockey underwear.

"Where are you going, Beej?" Dad called down the stairs. When Mom didn't answer, he turned to me. "Get your ass down there and help your mother."

I stretched my mouth behind the dishtowel, opening it as far as I could until I felt the warm blood pouring into my cheeks, and then followed my mother down the stairs.

In the cramped basement room adjacent to the garage, Mom knelt near the ashlar wall, clearing away the loose mortar and gauzy cobwebs covering Dad's samples. She mended the torn wrappers with tape, loaded the teetering piles of samples into the backseat of the Bel Air, climbed into the front seat, jerked the car into reverse, and drove off.

I kept telling Dad not to let Mom get to him—that she was just in a foul mood and would be home soon, and everything would be fine—but I *was* worried. Dad seemed so utterly incapable of supporting us on his own. Mom had been trying hard to build him up emotionally, with little return for her efforts. Within eighteen months, the spacious new house, so promising at first, was beginning to seem like a mistake.

A FEW HOURS LATER, MOM BURST THROUGH the door, weighted with two overstuffed bags of groceries. She set them on the counter playfully, her eyes dancing. "You won't believe this, Dick." She opened her wallet, revealing a huge wad of cash. "A lady in Mt. Lookout Square bought every sample." She let out a breathless laugh, as if she'd robbed the bank and gotten away with it.

Dad reached into one of the bags and pulled out some frozen vegetables. "Where's the booze, Beej?" He bit the side of his cheek, uncharacteristically quiet, as he stared.

I wanted to hug Dad. I could tell Mom's success had hurt his pride.

"You don't sound excited," she said. "I saved us for another week."

He examined every item as he set them on the counter. "This is an act of desperation, Beejay. In one week, the groceries will be gone, and we'll be exactly where we started."

"Oh, Dick." She schlepped a bag of potatoes around him, reached for the phone, and placed a long-distance call to her father in New Jersey, who was semi-retired and sold greeting cards.

Papa had been struggling with Gramma's alcoholism, an uncomfortable subject for the family to discuss. But today Mom seemed galvanized. "The woman told me I was a terrific saleswoman, Daddy," she said. She repeated word for word what she'd told us, and laughed even harder as she hung up.

"Now what?" Dad grimaced.

"Daddy said his job as a sales representative pays 15 percent commission. He encouraged me to contact his companies."

Mom ran around the house, cleaning baseboards and light switches, so animated it was as if she were getting ready for a party. She laughed to herself, stared at us for a moment, then laughed again.

I realize now that this was something she needed badly. To me it seemed she'd sewn up the gaping hole in their financial situation as easily as she took out and resewed the hems of my dresses when I outgrew them.

TWO DAYS LATER, WITH MY GRANDFATHER'S help, Mom was hired by an importer to sell eight-piece placemat sets from Madeira, Portugal. Papa also put her in touch with Philip Stahl, the owner of a greeting card company in New York. Stahl, a well-read and articulate man, had been a disc jockey and drama critic for *The New York Times* prior to starting his card business, and he and Mom hit it off immediately. Within days, samples of greeting cards arrived at the door in oversized cartons.

Mom's success wouldn't help Dad's pride, but I hoped it would give him the kick in the pants he needed. Like Mom, I was getting sick of Dad's lounging around the house, and I was glad to see her doing such an exceptional job of problem-solving. She was brave to go out on her own, and I was realizing she was capable of so much more than having babies and taking care of us, though I had no idea of the larger impact of her success on my father's confidence.

"She hasn't been this excited since David was born," Dad said, marveling at her sudden change in mood. "I guess we'll have to figure something out."

AND AS AWKWARD AND UNCERTAIN AS their financial future seemed, they did eventually come up with a plan. Dad called us to the kitchen, and we gathered on the stairs as if it were Christmas morning.

"We're going into business together." Dad beamed. "We will be 'RC & BJ Peters.'"

My parents, taken around the time they began traveling together.

I guess you could say we let out a collective sigh. We still hadn't painted our rooms or created a playroom upstairs—we were used to Dad's ideas that didn't go anywhere—and by then, we'd lost our enthusiasm for this kind of bulletin.

"What are you going to sell?" we asked. "And how will you find customers?"

They seemed to have it worked out: Dad would do the schmoozing and cold calls to various gift shops; Mom would write the orders. But to me, the idea sounded shortsighted. Was Mom planning to work out of their bedroom office, or ride along with him? How would we get to swimming practice? And who would watch us?

Mom seemed unconcerned. "Look, you can ride most places on your bikes. As for swimming, you can arrange your carpools and we'll drive when we're home. You don't need to worry."

I'm not "worried," I thought. *More like "uneasy."*

Okay, I *was* worried. So many of their actions seemed ill-conceived, and we kids were often the ones forced to repair the damage.

WITHIN DAYS, MOM AND DAD WERE traveling together and Eva, our ironing lady, was spending the night as if she'd been doing so for years. I adored Eva. I loved that she sucked on hard candy, watched TV, and seemed to live her life in slow motion. She made time to talk to us as she watched *General Hospital* and *Days of Our Lives*, and the only time I ever heard her grouse was one summer afternoon when it was so muggy that droplets of sweat dripped onto Dad's shirt as she ironed. When Jacquie and I told her to iron over it, she laughed so hard she had to run to the bathroom.

Eva prepared meals like frozen pot pies and coleslaw or tater tots and fried chicken—the kind of food that Mom didn't fix very often. She had soft brown skin and wore her hair in a loose French twist with bobby pins up the back in a straight line. Eva didn't sweat the details. She had cracked painted fingernails and thick ankles, and wore loose-fitting skirts that she pinned up over her thick waist. She bribed us to stay inside by giving us hard candy, a piece at a time, so she wouldn't have to chase after us.

One of the reasons I loved Eva so much was that she was terrified of our hurting ourselves. She loved to give us hugs and didn't call us "fuss budgets" or expect us to stop whining. She seemed to know when we were hurting.

Eva also gave us choices. She let us go outside or watch TV. If she saw us treating each other unkindly, she threatened no candy and stuck to it. When she was in charge, I had no desire to escape into my room—in fact, I thought I was missing something when I left for the pool. Eva seemed to enjoy my company even when I sat on the couch with a piece of paper and pencil, doodling. I wasn't used to adults wanting us to hang around.

BUT MOM AND DAD'S BUSINESS TOOK a year before it began to pay the bills, and sometimes my mother would ask to delay Eva's paycheck by a week or so. Eva was too nice to tell them she refused to work on an installment plan, but she grew less and less comfortable about spending so much time with our family. Mom and Dad would arrive home from a business trip, Dad would drive Eva home, and Mom would shout for the five of us to help unload the car, organize the samples, and load the car back up again.

"Isn't the business going well?" I asked one day, feeling pretty brave to be confronting Mom.

I wanted her to say, "Well, it was a reasonable idea at first, but we're not making enough money."

Instead, she gave me the hopeful spin: "We have a lot of expenses, Kimmy. It's going to take a while before we start making money."

As with Dad and the swimming, it seemed once Mom made a decision, there was no turning back.

We would sit at the dinner table, our eyes glazing over—did I mention that as the oldest, I had to sit on Dad's right?—and listen to Mom lecturing Dad about money. On one occasion, she was complaining about his latest purchase of a CB radio. "If you want to build this business, Dick, we have to reduce our expenses."

Dad thrust his fork into the fat on the side of my plate. "Why aren't you eating?"

"This?" I made a face. "It's fat. I don't eat fat." Mr. Bergen had been telling us to notice our fat consumption. I was careful not to eat anything I didn't like unless I had to. Plus, I'd gobbled some Hydrox cookies before dinner.

Dad slipped the slab of glistening white beef fat into his mouth and licked the grease off his fingers like it was maraschino cherry juice. I squeezed my eyes shut, pushing away my discomfort. The rest of the family gagged, which egged Dad on.

"Jacquie, Pammy, Ricky, David—pass 'em down," he said.

They handed over their plates and as he slopped the fat into his maw, I watched grease dribble onto the discontinued samples that had become Mom's fancy linen placemats. We gaped from our seats, spellbound, until the ghastly moment when he wiped his face with his greasy napkin, stood up, and pulled his pants up over his massive belly.

"We need a motorhome, Beejay."

Dad did a lot of thinking out loud, especially after a few drinks, and Mom had learned over time that if she didn't react, he would get distracted and go on to another subject. She started to gather the plates.

"You aren't listening, Beej. A motorhome would save us on hotels and restaurants. We need a place for the samples so they don't get moldy in the basement. Hell, we could write the vehicle off on our taxes, and save some money."

Mom turned blotchy red. I knew she was mentally parsing her words. "How on earth do you expect to *pay* for a motorhome, Dick?" She reminded him that we needed a new muffler on our current vehicle, a used Rambler, and our family still hadn't paid the Marlin dues yet, either.

"It doesn't matter, Beej. Once we have the vehicle on the road we'll make so much more money, we won't have to worry. Hell, you've been complaining about the cost of swim meets. You have the state meet coming up, don't you, Butch?" He turned to me and winked. "With a motorhome, we could take the whole family." Dad chewed his thumbnail, spat the piece of nail on the floor, and eyed the rest of the family. "Don't you want vacations at the beach, camping in the mountains, road trips with your friends?"

"Yeeeeeay!" the boys shouted.

Mom spun on her heel, clasping a haphazard pile of dirty dishes and silverware. "Count me out."

In one sense, this was a familiar story: Dad wanted a toy to impress his customers and friends; Mom wanted financial security.

With their new business and spotty income, coupled with Dad's impulsive buying habit, the motorhome made no sense at all, but Dad couldn't stop talking about the positives. "Our expenses will be cut in half, Beejay. We don't have to stay at the Motel 6 anymore."

Mom rubbed her eyes under her glasses. "I don't know, Dick."

IT WAS MAYBE A MONTH LATER WHEN I stepped into the house, ravenous, after practice one night and David said, "They're bringing Kentucky Fried Chicken, we *think*." He verbalized anything that ran through his mind, often sounding a few years older than his age, which was now four. "Maybe they ran out of gas. Or maybe they stopped at the bank." He had his pointer finger on his mouth.

Ricky glowered. "Can't you talk like a normal person? You bug me."

"Shut up, you idiot," David said.

Jacquie shushed them as if she were channeling Mom. She adjusted her glasses, then froze for a moment as what sounded like a huge semi-truck rumbled outside, shaking the house.

David ran to the front window. "Oh, wow," he said, his mouth hanging open.

The four of us watched in amazement over David's shoulder as Dad backed into the driveway in an enormous brown and tan Open

Road motorhome, then swung open the door and stepped out with two buckets of chicken, one on each hip.

Famished and irritable, none of us rushed out to greet him. As Jacquie held the door open and Dad entered with his broad smile, I willed myself to stay positive. Mom was right. This seemed like another ridiculous idea.

We set the table in slow motion and I replayed the motorhome argument in my head. Dad kept interrupting with his pestering—"What do you kids think about the bus? Are you excited?" He combed his fingers through his cowlick, a gesture I'd come to interpret as satisfaction.

I was too tired and hungry to react.

The Open Road was a typical 1970s RV, with a dinette table that converted to a double bed behind two elevated, pickle green captain's chairs. The tiny kitchenette opposite the table had three burners—enough to boil frozen peas or corn, mix simple convenience foods like Rice-A-Roni—and a miniature oven. The best I can say about the bathroom is that there was one. The toilet lid rattled and the faucet knobs occasionally loosened and turned on as we drove down the road. I learned to gravitate toward the back of the vehicle, where I could hide in the corner or sleep soundly on the brown foam cushions without badgering from Dad.

Mom and Dad said that with their unique business model, Dad would still make appointments and Mom would still write the orders, but now they would invite the customers into the motorhome, serve them strong drinks—hopefully write bigger orders—then drive on to their next appointment. Having a vehicle like this would create excitement. It would save them time. No more having to lug those heavy samples from car to gift shop and back again, and overall, they'd make more money. At least, that's what they thought.

And who could blame them for trying new ideas? But for us kids, the decision meant even more work. Cleaning the bus, needless to say, became our job. I anticipated Mom's asking for help and often preempted her with reasons I had to leave the house. Pam and

Jacquie would fight over whose job the shower was—"Have you seen Dad's gross feet? I'm not cleaning that. You clean it"—and Mom would have to jump in and break it up.

Whenever the bus rolled into the driveway, I could count on one hand the number of seconds it took before Mom would shout for us to get out there and help bring in the samples. They expected us to run out, arms extended in welcoming hugs. But we were quick learners. When we heard the bus pull into the driveway, we all took off for the farthest corners of the house. When they left for a trip, it was the same routine: We'd hear the commotion and hide. Then, as soon as they backed out of the driveway, we'd come together to let out a collective sigh of relief.

Though the motorhome meant Mom and Dad would be gone more, the positive was the way it gave our family an aura of celebrity. People would wave from the sidewalk as we drove by, and curious strangers often knocked on the door, asking, "Can we come in and look?"

Dad would beckon with his hand—"Come in, come in. Have a seat. What can we do you for?" he'd ask in his funny way. To Dad, all strangers were potential customers.

Nobody seemed to notice that the bus was thrown together like cardboard or that the whole thing rattled like hell as we rode down the highway. It also smelled to high heaven—like a gas station bathroom or portable toilet—but Dad said that finding an authorized dumping station was tricky. He would wait until one of us had dry heaves before he'd do anything about it.

In 1969, gas was only thirty-five cents a gallon, but the cost of using the generator when there was no electricity was exorbitant. At first, my parents paid for parking like everyone else; then Dad discovered he could pay off an attendant for permission to use an available electrical outlet, and overnight they were breaking even on parking expenses. In Chicago, they parked at McCormick Place and plugged into the outlets used by the boat owners along Lake Michigan. In Columbus, they hooked up to a gas station by Veteran's Memorial Hall.

They tried the same thing with their meals. Before the bus, Mom and Dad chose inexpensive restaurants and ate by themselves when they traveled. Now Mom was preparing Cornish game hens and Dad was inviting customers and fellow salesmen to the bus for dinner.

After one business trip, I heard Mom even before they entered the house: "We have to cut back on the socializing, Dick. We're eating up our profits."

The vehicle added worry, fears, and unnecessary work, but Mom eventually stopped complaining. Perhaps she simply felt powerless to do anything about it. On the other hand, I suspect she grew to enjoy it as an extension of Dad's personality: the motorhome was flamboyant, excessive, and unnecessarily in-your-face—just like eating the fat.

I asked Mom once if she liked having the bus and she seemed surprised. "You talk so much about the cost," I said.

She thought for a moment and as she straightened her navy knit top, for a split second I could tell she felt something. Then she brushed back my hair. "The bus is important to your father," she said, a defeated look in her eyes.

Whatever it took to build Dad's confidence, she knew—and I knew—would be meaningful to the family.

CHAPTER 8

School had closed, I was twelve, and it was early June. By then we had adjusted to their periodic absences, so when Mom and Dad began to prepare for the gift show at Veteran's Memorial Hall in Columbus, it seemed like any other business trip: Mom in a swivet, anxious to get to Columbus to make money; Dad in no hurry; and the five of us kids quietly arguing over whose turn it was to help.

Eva had planned to be with us for two weeks. She sat with perfect posture on the living room couch, her stiff black hair tucked with bobby pins behind her head, her overstuffed purse at her side.

"Dick, will you please put down the damned phone and help with the motorhome?" Mom shouted. "Sorry, Eva," Mom rushed into the living room. "Where's Jacquie? Pammy . . . Dick, can you call your children? Kim, can you please get up and help us? David? Ricky? Did you kids hear me?"

"No." David's puckish smile, which usually charmed her, had no effect on this occasion.

"Get going." Mom frowned. "We need to get out of here."

Columbus was close—only an hour away—but the show had limited hours for setting up booths, and Mom and Dad were running late. Mom, with her usual flair for organization, had created pegboard displays for their gift samples, but she hadn't communicated to us exactly how she wanted the boards packed. "Use your common sense," Dad yelled, swatting Ricky and Pam on the shoulder as Mom ran around the house, a madwoman, grabbing dirty glasses and handing them to anyone close by. I was beginning to hate that damn motorhome.

Mom and Dad's monthly departure usually put me on edge—but at twelve I did love the idea of two weeks of freedom with no haranguing about chores, no nagging about manners, and no direct or cross-examination! I would eat with my fingers or stretch my mouth, go to bed early, and watch *Dark Shadows* or stupid reruns of *Bewitched* or *The Beverly Hillbillies*. These trips were the beginning of my thinking that we were no longer kids.

Mom set a blank check on the counter and reminded Eva of the abundance of food, including some TV dinners for a rainy day. Eva, who loved TV dinners, thought this was funny. She spoke softly to Jacquie, "We'll talk when they're gone."

Jacquie pulled Mom aside to speak to her privately. I stood by for support. "Eva's legs are bad, Mom," she said.

"What's wrong with her legs?"

"She can't walk to the store, and there's nothing decent to eat. We're going to need more than one blank check."

"There are frozen vegetables . . ." Mom said.

"Yuck."

"And pot pies, and . . . look, Eva knows how to cook. She can fix you some nice meals."

Jacquie and I scowled. "Mom, the pot pies are freezer-burned. The American cheese has green mold!"

"Honestly, you two! Scrape it off. You know, that's how they make penicillin."

Mom didn't know that the freezer, overloaded with ice, had caused most of the frozen vegetables and meat to dry out and nothing in there was edible anymore. We liked to eat SpaghettiOs and Jiffy Pop popcorn, foods Mom thought were junky and too expensive.

"Look, you kids can go down on your bikes to buy groceries if you run out." She set a second check on the table. "But use these checks sparingly. If anything comes up and you need to get hold of us, have Eva call. You kids be good," she said as she exited the house. "Try to behave like we're here. No fighting, okay?"

That was a Wednesday.

TWO DAYS LATER, I SAID GOOD-BYE TO EVA and was picked up by Connie's dad and taken to a swim meet. By the time I was dropped back home on Sunday evening, I was bone-tired. Dehydrated. The concrete steps on the front lawn seemed steeper, the distance to the house farther.

When I slipped in the front door, instead of screams and clomping across the floor, there was a dead quiet. The house had that eerie feeling you get when the lights dim on a deserted street in the middle of the night and you're without a cell phone.

Jacquie, Pam, and David were sprawled on the floor, eyes glazed, in front of the television. They turned toward me as a group, their faces ashen. "Where have you been? What took you so long?"

From the dark entrance hall, I spied Ricky on the sofa, his head, torso, and arms wrapped in white bandages. He looked like a mummy with his arms sticking out in front, and his swollen lips—especially on the bottom—were covered in thick black stitches. It looked like his skull had been cracked open, and the sliver of his face that I could see was puffy and bruised and stained with dried, black blood.

"Oh, my God! What happened? Where's Eva?"

"Gone!" Jacquie, Pam, and David shouted in unison.

Jacquie passed me Eva's scratchy note. "Can you read it? Did her mother die? Or her daughter? We tried calling, but her phone rang off the hook."

The note was illegible. I set it on the table and bent over to inspect Ricky, who was moaning, his pained eyes drooping within a mass of bandages. "How did you get him to the hospital, Jacquie?"

"Dr. Engel."

"Dr. Engel? We don't even go to him anymore, do we?" Some part of me was irritated that she'd managed to handle everything by herself.

Jacquie glanced at me blankly. "You act like I did something wrong."

I shook my head in frustration. What I gathered was that Ricky had hit a rock racing downhill on the new Cheater Slick bike with the banana seat that Mom and Dad had gotten him for his birthday. He'd catapulted over the handlebars and onto the pavement, and when he'd screamed in pain, a man driving up the hill who'd seen the whole thing had helped him into his car and driven him home. Jacquie had phoned our old neighbor, Dr. Engel, who'd rushed over—it was Friday, so he had probably been at work—and driven Ricky and Jacquie to the hospital.

Jacquie said they'd pushed Ricky around on a gurney while Dr. Engel tried to call Mom and Dad from a pay phone in the waiting room. "Nurses kept asking me questions. They wanted to know Dad's birthdate and where he worked. They were saying something about insurance. I told them I'm only ten, I don't even know what insurance is!"

"What about Ricky?"

"He's not allowed to eat anything."

At this, Ricky whined.

According to Jacquie, while she was at the hospital, Pam, who was only eight, and David, four, had ridden down on the tandem to Sunshine Market, an independent liquor store in East Hyde Park. "Dr. Engel dropped me off," Jacquie said, "and those two were asleep in front of the TV with a pile of crumpled candy wrappers!" She glared at Pam and David, her tone like Mom's.

"We had to eat *some*thing," Pam said, grinning through her unbrushed blond hair.

"What about the blank checks?"

"There aren't any," Jacquie said. "Eva must've taken them."

"We'll just have to call and call and keep calling until we get hold of them," I said. I picked up the phone and dialed zero. Jacquie spouted the exhaustive list of numbers she'd already tried. But there were no listings for the Columbus Veteran's Hall, Columbus Gift Show, or Columbus Convention Center, where we'd been told Mom and Dad could be located.

"I'm sorry," the operator said.

I was afraid something terrible had happened. Maybe they were in an accident—in the hospital themselves—or caught in the middle of nowhere with something wrong with the motorhome. *Why haven't they called by now?* I was keenly aware of how inept I might have been if I'd been in charge and not away at a swim meet. I couldn't even reach our parents by phone. *How would I have handled getting Ricky to the hospital and home again?* If anything, our futility in trying to reach them gave me a sense of relief that I hadn't been the one who'd had to step in.

A moment later, the phone rang. Pam answered. "No, they aren't here . . . I'm eight . . . Yes . . . Observatory Avenue . . . Yes."

"Who is it, Pam?" Jacquie shouted from the living room.

Pam held her hand over the receiver and yelled back. "What's our street number?"

"First tell me who it is."

"It's a man."

Jacquie reached for the phone. "Hang up."

"What?"

"Hang up the phone right now!" Pam, confused, placed the phone on the jack.

It's possible the hospital was calling—one of the doctors following up on Ricky's condition—or someone was following up on a report of abandoned children, but these ideas didn't occur to us. Jacquie and I were convinced the caller was someone who wanted to hurt us. "Let me answer the phone from now on," Jacquie ordered.

Pam looked more frightened than I'd ever seen her. "I told him we live on Observatory. Do you think he'll come and kill us?"

"No," I said, trying my best to reassure her. "Observatory is a huge street with hundreds of homes. There's no way he'll find us." Still, I trembled as I said it. By then I was trusting Jacquie's gut more than my own. I glanced at Jacquie. "Are we still supposed to go to swimming practice?" I was thinking of the trouble I'd be in with Mr. Bergen if I missed a single workout. "What about the younger kids? Who will watch them?"

"Nobody. They'll be safe for short periods . . . and if they aren't, we'll call the police."

It pained me as a twelve-year-old to feel like I had to be the responsible one because I was the oldest. *How am I supposed to know what to do in an emergency?* Luckily, I felt safe on our street. This was a neighborhood where people left their cars and homes unlocked. It also helped that Jacquie, like Mom, had a can-do attitude.

"They won't call," she said again. "They think we're with Eva, which means we're fine."

I didn't believe it, but she was right. Three days passed and we received a couple of phone calls from random customers wanting to place orders, but no contact from Mom and Dad.

We anticipated their eventual call like the end of a bad movie. We knew it was coming and it wouldn't be satisfying.

ONE WEEK FROM THE DAY THEY LEFT and four days after Ricky's accident, the phone rang. Pam, David, and I hovered around Jacquie as she held the phone to her ear. "Where are you? We've been taking care of ourselves for five days . . . *Why* did Eva leave? I don't know. You aren't listening, Dad. Ricky crashed his bike, busted his head open. He must have fifty stitches. Dr. Engel had to come. Pam had to watch David. I had to go to the hospital with Ricky. We don't have any money, we don't have food, and you haven't called for a whole week! Where are you?"

Jacquie paused for a moment, and I heard Dad through the receiver—"Dammit, you kids are incredible. How did you know to call Dr. Engel?"

"We didn't," Jacquie shrieked. "I called the Engels because we *didn't* know what to do."

"That was the right thing *to* do, and I'm proud of you," Dad said.

Our heads swiveled simultaneously as we looked around at each other, baffled.

"I mean it. Here, talk to your mother."

There was a rattle and then Mom's soft voice came through the receiver. "Hi, honey. Are you kids all right?"

"Are you kidding?" Jacquie shouted. "No! Ricky has fifty stitches in his head and lip. I've been fixing meals and taking care of him." She broke into a full-blown rant, and she was damn good. She tilted the phone so we could hear Mom chuckle.

"You're talking so fast, honey, I can hardly understand you. Maybe I should talk to Eva."

Jacquie held the phone close to her ear and began to cry. "There *is* no Eva. She left us on Friday. Her mother died . . . or her daughter. We can't even read her note." Jacquie shifted her weight from one foot to another. "You don't understand, Mom. You have to come home. Ricky has a bloody bandage around his whole chest. His lip is gigantic. All he can do is lie on the couch."

Jacquie listened to Mom, and as the rest of us squeezed closer to hear, something shifted in me. *Why is Mom hesitating? Does she not understand how serious this is?* Most parents would race home in this situation—hell, this was a damn emergency. Either they didn't understand the gravity of the situation, or they didn't care. But that didn't make sense. Of course they cared. They gave us too much praise and encouragement not to care.

I reached out my arm but Jacquie swatted me away, then stuck her finger in her ear. "I guess so," she said.

I grabbed for the phone—"Let me talk to her!"—but Jacquie held me back.

She slammed down the phone and stared straight ahead. "They're not coming."

"What?"

"They're not coming for two more weeks. They have appointments lined up, and if they don't write some orders, we won't have food." Jacquie's cheeks were red and her breathing was shallow. I could see the disappointment in her downturned eyes. "They're not going to be here for my birthday."

"You should've told them Ricky was *dying*."

"Why didn't *you* talk to them then?"

"You wouldn't let me!" I shouted.

Jacquie pushed up the bridge of her glasses and stomped into the living room.

David, Pam, and I stood by ourselves for a moment—in shock, I suppose—as Jacquie switched into problem-solving mode. "Let's make some brownies," she said.

Jacquie and Pam grabbed two remaining bills and some change tucked into the kitchen corner cabinet and took off on their bikes to buy Baker's unsweetened chocolate. I lay flat on the floor in front of the TV with David—Ricky behind us on the couch—and stretched my mouth wide open. I held it there in protest.

Some part of me might've realized Mom and Dad were knowingly neglecting us, but it was a gulley too dark and dangerous to traverse. Instead, I rehearsed the phone call from Dad in my head. "Dammit, you kids are incredible," he'd said. I didn't think he realized how bad it was, but he was right. We *were* damn incredible. And we were handling it.

No, I guess *we* weren't really handling it. *Jacquie* was handling it. *I should be riding to the store,* I thought. *I'm the oldest. Why am I letting Jacquie decide everything?* I told myself I already had parents, and they were the ones who needed to do their jobs. But their sense of calm and lack of concern stretched credulity. It pulled at the fabric of our family, loosening the threads of trust that made me feel secure. "It must be the alcohol," I insisted when Jacquie returned with the chocolate. "They don't realize how bad Ricky is."

"They realize it," she said. "I'm sure of it."

Two hours later, the five of us polished off a whole pan of Jacquie's brownies.

A FEW DAYS PASSED, AND I GUESS you could say we were adapting to our new routine. We straightened our rooms, arranged our rides to and from practice, and spent multiple hours in front of the TV—whatever comforted us.

Mom and Dad called Jacquie every other day from a phone booth, asking, "How's Ricky?" I would've preferred they come home and deal with Ricky in person, but at least it was a step in the right direction.

On Sunday we dressed in our usual church clothes—for the three of us girls, that usually meant dresses—left Ricky moaning on the couch, and rode, standing up on our bikes, the one mile to St. Mary's, with David on the back of the tandem. Our next-door neighbors, also Catholic, waved from their car, as if seeing us attending church this way was perfectly natural.

On my way to practice or on the way home, I thought of my mother's words when we swam at Mt. Lookout. "Just behave," she'd said, "and nobody will notice you're there by yourselves."

We kept Ricky company by feasting from metal trays in front of the TV. He would lie on the living room couch, groaning automatically like a wireless security device whenever anyone entered the room. There were no drugs, and we must've been too childish to think of ways to help other than bringing him milkshakes. He was on his own to get in and out of the bathroom, and I, for one, thought nothing of it.

We managed to pull together the little we had in the freezer. Some nights, Jacquie fixed grilled hot dogs slit down the middle with a tiny piece of American cheese; on other nights, she grilled tomato and cheese on toast. She taught Pam how to make Kraft macaroni and cheese, and the three of us girls took turns fixing Rice-a-Roni and fish sticks. We made our own peanut butter and jelly sandwiches and filled up on potato chips from a giant can in the closet. At night, after dinner, we did the dishes and swept the floor.

The lights in the house told the neighbors or random passersby that we were not alone, that an adult watched over us. But we were hiding. What was happening was not the way it was supposed to be, and we accepted that nobody needed to know. The reality would only cast a dark light on my parents, who were doing the best they could for the family.

Shortly before they were supposed to arrive home, Jacquie snapped again into problem-solving mode. "David and Pam, go clean your rooms. Pam, you clean the kitty litter."

I straightened my room with a chip on my shoulder. To me, making the house appear so flawless was letting Mom and Dad off the hook for not racing home immediately. I hated the way they would *ooh* and *aah* about their great kids without seeing how vulnerable we were. But on some level, I knew they felt proud. And I knew Dad. If we did nothing, he would go ballistic about the mess—or, worse, start swinging. I ached from the resentment, but it was easier to just clean everything up.

I washed and dried the clothes. Jacquie ironed. Pam cleaned the cat box and took out the garbage. David picked the toys up off the floor in the front hall. Together, we washed and dried the mountain of dirty dishes and even dusted and vacuumed around Ricky in the living room, all the while singing tunes from *The Sound of Music*.

It seemed anxiety had wrapped its arms around me. I had a jittery feeling in my stomach, a deep crevice between my eyebrows. I worried relentlessly.

Around this time, I began to think of my swimming as a job, as my way of saving the family. Watching Jacquie lead us through this crisis had made it clear that even though I was the oldest, I wouldn't be the one to fill Mom's shoes in her absences. Jacquie was a better babysitter, but I was a better swimmer. As such, I could be the hero, proving that ours was a hard-working family with talent.

The hours before Mom and Dad's arrival seemed amplified. I shivered at the click of Cheerios being sucked into the vacuum, startled at the *bzzsssst* of the washing machine cycle, and nearly retched from the acrid smell of disinfectant in the hall. After a full day of work, the house looked terrific and I was more alert than ever.

When Dad walked into the house, carrying a cardboard box of loose samples, he sped straight over to see Ricky. "What in the hell happened?"

Ricky's eyes filled with tears. "I fell off my bike."

"You need more practice, that's all."

Practice. It's what we were doing. Practicing at home. Practicing at school. Practicing at the pool. We were primed for practice. For performing. At least at the pool I was being watched by responsible adults.

I looked over and saw Mom piling boxes on the front porch, her color drained. It seemed all she could do to drag herself into the house. A moment later, she called from the yard, "Come on, kids, you need to help us unload so we can have dinner. Your father is hungry."

CHAPTER 9

Despite the deteriorating situation at home—or maybe because of it—swimming was opening my eyes to the bigger world. I'd been to Lakeside, a meet held in an actual lake with lanes cordoned off between a wall and bulkhead with slimy water that was cold enough to harden your eyelids. I'd been to Plantation Country Club in Louisville and stayed at the Continental Inn, with its palm trees and exotic tropical plants. Pittsburgh, Cleveland, Louisville, Lexington—wherever we traveled, we were broadening our vision of what was possible.

I think most of us thought of ourselves as Cincinnati ambassadors, learning how to compete with dignity—how to be graceful winners or losers—within a program more intense than any other in the region. And it showed. His first year, Mr. Bergen took eight swimmers to the short course nationals in Long Beach, California. By 1969, we were hosting our first national invitational in the Lawrence Hall Pool at the University of Cincinnati. And when word spread from coast to coast of the Marlins' success, swimmers began traveling from halfway across the continent for an opportunity to compete against us.

At Lakeside swim meet, Louisville, Kentucky c. 1969.

When our team membership swelled to more than two hundred swimmers, a group of Marlin bigwigs, led by Bill and Charles Keating, hatched a plan to build a state-of-the-art swimming facility. The pool hours available to us at Aiken and Courter Tech High Schools were limited, and they envisioned a beautiful, fifty-meter pool, eight lanes wide, with a removable metal "flow-through" bulkhead across the middle so we could easily switch from fifty meters to two twenty-five-yard pools, depending on the season. It would have an underwater observation window, deep gutters to reduce waves, sloping starting blocks, waveless lane lines, digital touch pads, and modern locker rooms with wall-mounted hair dryers. By the middle of March, they'd chosen its location—the sixty-acre campus of St. Xavier High School—and even held a groundbreaking ceremony, naming it Keating Natatorium.

During construction, when the pool was finished but the building wasn't, we practiced in the open air, under the building frame's huge metal beams. This was the first time I'd ever practiced outdoors in a fifty-meter pool, and for a while the novelty took the edge off the stress of swimming. I loved going from the cool dew on the grass to the perfectly clear 79-degree water (ideal for swim training), with the warm sun on my back and the occasional wind. I loved the extended length, which meant fewer flip turns. I loved getting a tan. Feeling healthy. Having more distance to get into a rhythm. Swimming was no longer a monotonous repetition of musical scales but a whole symphony of sensory experiences—a sunny melody, rainy interval, windy vibrato—that varied from day to day.

"This will be one of the fastest pools in the country," Mr. Bergen said, "and it's your job as swimmers to make the Marlins one of the greatest teams. I want to see every one of you supporting each other." According to Mr. Bergen, this was one of the keys to our success.

For a brief period, we heard encouraging words from our teammates every day at practice. Before each set someone—usually Deena, one of our team's strongest swimmers—would meekly call out, "Go, you guys," which I assumed was for Mr. Bergen's benefit. By then, most of us had developed a third eye focused on Mr. Bergen. I know I had. I built a mental blueprint of the pool, and was aware of his location at every moment. My internal warning system told me which swimmer(s) he had just excoriated for not being a team player, and when he got within earshot, I quickly joined in with everyone else, chanting, "Go, Marlins! You can do it!"

One day we swam in a fierce thunderstorm, with the snap of lightning and hiss of rain coming down in sheets. The dark clouds overhead moved so fast and furiously, it seemed Mr. Bergen and God himself were conspiring to electrocute us. As parents arrived in droves to pick us up, Mr. Bergen was dripping from the chin and pumped up like Captain Ahab fighting Moby Dick. "Stay or you're off the team," he bellowed.

My heart raced; my nerve endings tingled. It was so much, so fast, I could hardly process what was happening. But I didn't get out. Nobody did. Parents rushed down to the edge of the pool, clutching their umbrellas, hoping to convey a sense of urgency, and Mr. Bergen ignored them. Maybe it was all the gold medals and blue ribbons, but as far as I know, nobody, not even the parents, had the sense or courage to demand we get out until Mr. Bergen gave the word.

WITHIN THE NEXT YEAR, I WAS MOVED INTO "Pressure 2," the second-highest swimming group within the Marlins, whose name was chosen, of course, to remind us of the obvious. Though we weren't as fast as the swimmers in Pressure 1, our practices were nearly identical and significantly more exhausting than my previous Marlin swimming group's had been.

Sitting on the cold concrete deck, glancing at a handful of fellow teammates before practice one night, I noticed that they looked as tired and lethargic as I felt. Connie was usually one of the bubbliest. "I don't know what he expects," she said in the locker room a few minutes later, grimacing in response to Mr. Bergen's statement that we would have to psych up for the night's practice.

"He expects to kill us," Denise joked.

I snickered, knowing her sense of humor. Denise was a year older, a fellow backstroker, who had the guts to speak her mind. "He's a sadist," she added, and we all—Kim, Susie, Kristie, Nancy, all of us with our broad, muscled shoulders and flat stomachs in our nylon swimsuits—shook with laughter.

Connie yanked the T-shirt off her sculpted figure and tucked it on a hook in her locker, then handed me a shoelace as she fit her massive dark pigtails into her cap. "You mind?"

"Not at all." I threaded the shoelace through her back straps, and as I tied a tight bow I peered down at my shapeless figure. Geez! When would I ever develop? At twelve, I was at least two inches taller than Connie, but with my prepubescent flat chest and long, skinny legs, I felt like such a little girl. Thoughts about puberty or periods or boyfriends were the furthest from my mind—I looked like a larger version of my six-year-old self—but it wasn't that way for everyone. Some of the other girls were developing breasts and pubic hair and talking more about boys than ever before.

"We should do something fun," Connie said.

"Like what?"

"Well, Mr. Bergen says we don't act like a team. Maybe we could do something to show him our team spirit. You know, like make T-shirts or something."

I wasn't sure I had time for anything so frivolous, but when Connie offered her house for the weekend and I told Jacquie a white lie about the necessity of my attending—Mom and Dad were gone again—she didn't complain.

Together, we P2 girls cut white medical tape, tied off whole packs of men's white T-shirts, and worked elbow deep in blue Rit dye. Afterward, Connie's parents' basement looked like a hippy co-op, with our matching blue tie-dyed shirts dripping from a saggy clothesline near the ceiling.

"Oh, God, I can't wait to see the look on Mr. Bergen's face," one of the girls said as we left the shirts to dry and trotted off to see *Love*

Story at the local theater. It was such a rare moment, one of the only times I can remember when we played together, laughed together, had fun together.

The thing about swimming is it's such a deadly serious and grueling sport. It seeps into every pore. Most nights we rode to and from practice in silence, too fatigued to talk. Though we swam in the same lanes every day, we rarely exchanged full sentences with one another. At school, I was still a strong student, but the all-consuming nature of swimming had caused me to lose many of my friends. How was I to get to know anyone when I had practice five nights and six mornings of the week? That's not including meets, which lasted all weekend long. And with Mom and Dad now gone a week or two every month, I felt alone at home too. Creating the T-shirts was an isolated opportunity for collaboration.

But as much as I wanted to believe I was like these other girls, in my heart I knew I wasn't. Connie had two parents at home—her father politely greeting us, her mother baking cookies. It was hard not to wonder what my teammates would think if they had any idea what it was like at *my* house. With Mom and Dad on the road and Jacquie running the show, being at Connie's house made me feel like an irresponsible parent who'd abandoned her kids.

MOST OF US COULDN'T WAIT TO STROLL OUT on deck in our artistic creations and see the pride on Mr. Bergen's face. Unfortunately, we had to look fast. As we paraded out of the locker room he said, in a voice only a few of us could hear, "The way you show team spirit is in the water."

I was so ashamed, I wanted to flip the shirt up over my head.

We gathered with the rest of the team in the bleachers, dejected, still waiting for a positive word—I was so sure it was coming—but Mr. Bergen said nothing more about the shirts. He stood beside Darryl, waiting for our undivided attention, and I began to feel silly.

The fact that we had gone to so much trouble with the shirts now seemed pointless and embarrassing.

When it was time to swim, I returned the shirt to my locker and headed for my lane. *What is wrong with him?* I wondered. *Isn't this what he wanted?*

But as I swam the warm-up and released the irritation, it gradually struck me that Mr. Bergen was right. As much as he had insisted otherwise, swimming was an individual sport. The work needed to be done in the pool. Not in someone's basement.

I felt a wee bit more mature that day, convinced that Mr. Bergen was drawing out the better part of us—the tough, aggressive, hard-working part of us. There was no room for fun if we wanted to be great swimmers. Fun was wasting time. Fun was a detour. As I swam on my back, staring up at the beams and ceiling of the newly constructed natatorium that night, I at first regretted the loss of natural light. But sometime in the middle of practice, it was as if a light kicked on in me for the first time. I understood what Mr. Bergen wanted. He wanted us directed, focused, and unrelenting in our concentration on swimming. He wanted it at home and also at the pool: the hand entry, the shoulder roll, the elbows up, the follow through, the backstroke flags, the breath, the turns, the touch. He wanted our focus on every detail.

Without any particular short- or long-term goal in mind, I resolved to prove to him that I could be—*would* be—just that sort of backstroker.

ONE THING ABOUT BEING MOVED UP to P2 was that it meant in addition to three hours of practice every night, we now also had two hours every morning six days a week, not including the half-hour drive each way. I was swimming eleven workouts a week, which was more than twice as much as Jacquie and Pam. I was so exhausted I didn't know the day, week, or month. I didn't know that the Jackson 5 had appeared on the *Ed Sullivan Show*, the Mayo Clinic had performed the first hip replacement, or anything about Apollo 12 landing safely in the Pacific Ocean. My arms were limp, my legs weak. Like a marionette hanging from strings, I'd been following Mr. Bergen's direction, religiously, at the pool and doing the absolute minimum in every other area of my life.

One night, Mr. Bergen pulled me aside. It was seconds before the start of practice, and I was psyching up to hit that cold water.

"You're not improving enough in the backstroke, Peters." His eyes were intense and he stood so close I could see into his pores. He asked why I looked worried, then said, "I'd like to see you in the distance lane."

Focused on the "worried" comment, I didn't quite hear him.

"You mean you're asking if I want to switch to become a freestyler?"

Mr. Bergen let out a rare chuckle. "This isn't a choice. Get in the distance lane. You're starting tonight."

As he spun around and marched the other way, kids dropped like bombs from the blocks, water splashing in every direction— warm-up had begun. I felt my muscles contract. He'd only hit one or two of the older boys with a kickboard, but now I felt as if he'd hit me with one. I stood at the end of lane seven looking toward lane one, not able to think. Where was the distance lane, anyway? I wandered away from him, dizzy, sick to my stomach, wanting to scream.

He turned again. "Oh, and get rid of that worried look while you're at it, will you, Peters?"

It seemed I was being punished, but I didn't dare ask why. Billy Keating, who often drove me to practice, had told me once about Mr. Bergen's "rat theory"—that if you put the sixth-fastest rat in with the slowest rats, when it wins every time, it learns how to win. And yet these were six *faster* rats. Was he teaching me how to *lose*? The kids in the distance lane swam somewhere in the neighborhood of eleven to thirteen miles a day to prepare for the longest event, the mile. I was a middle-distance swimmer—and barely handling the middle-distance load as it was.

I dropped into the lane, and as soon as Mr. Bergen announced the workout—fifteen five-hundreds on the six-thirty interval—my heart shot into my throat. This was outrageous! Why was he doing this? I was swimming all the freestyle events anyway. It wouldn't change a thing about what events I competed in at meets. It seemed so unfair; I'd been following the rules and doing what I was told. Wasn't that enough?

I decided to prove to him how wrong he was to punish me. I pushed off, my arms and legs leaden, and swam the five miles straight, more than an hour and a half of hard swimming without a break. When I pushed myself up on the deck and dragged myself toward the locker room door, my face was so hot and numb, I felt like I was drooling.

Mr. Bergen stood behind the middle lane. "Good job, Peters," he said, as I squeezed the water out of my pigtails.

I had no feeling of accomplishment; on the contrary, I was filled with dread. This was the equivalent of a mile of butterfly *every day*. Overnight, the future seemed terrifying.

CHAPTER 10

Ricky hadn't fully recovered from his accident, but Mom and Dad were anxious to get back on the road. Mom phoned everyone she knew within twenty miles, and discovered nobody wanted to babysit five kids. In desperation, she called Eva, listened to her plea for help—to pay for her pregnant daughter's nursery furniture—and decided not to hire her after all.

Jacquie and I both tried to get her to reconsider, but she wouldn't back down.

"Eva's not trustworthy, honey," she said. "We can't have someone who is that irresponsible watching you kids."

"What if the two of you"—Dad nodded at Jacquie and me—"were to keep an eye on Pam and the boys so we can travel over the upcoming month? Could you handle that?" He made it sound like this was an idea that had only just occurred to him.

We glanced at each other, feigning surprise, though we'd been privately discussing the possibility for days, even reminding each other to ask for more blank checks so we could buy the foods we wanted. Of course we could keep an eye on the kids, but we'd already proved this could be dangerous. And how did they expect us to swim?

I elbowed Jacquie. "Say something."

"What do you want me to say?"

"What about meals?" My head lunged toward Mom.

"You kids can feed yourselves," Mom said. "Eva didn't cook for you anyway, did she?"

I caught a momentary glimpse of despair in Jacquie's eyes. "How will we get to practice?" she asked. She was becoming tougher, developing a thicker skin, trying to hide her fear and act competent as a coping strategy.

"Arrange your rides, and we'll take our turn when we get home," Dad said. "You've been doing that already."

Later that day, in the kitchen, I found Mom bent over the burners, scraping grease, scavenging the underside for any burned morsel or crumb. Under stress, she liked to straighten and organize. "Mom, you know, if you go with Dad, that's a lot for us to handle." I tried to make eye contact, but she wouldn't look up. I could feel myself getting irritated.

"We're trying to stay afloat, Kimmy. We have no choice."

"Of course you have a choice. Dad can go by himself. Why do you have to go *with* him?" I wanted her to feel guilty.

Mom rinsed the greasy cloth in the sink, not looking at me. "We only have one more important trip this fall. In two weeks, it'll be too late for most customers to buy in time for Christmas, and we'll be home for a while. But for now, your father needs my help."

I stood there stretching my mouth. "So do we!"

"I'm sorry, honey. Your father can't handle the business by himself."

I thrust my face in front of her to get her attention. "And why can't he handle the business by himself? Because he can't do the paperwork? Do it for him when he gets back."

Mom let out a deep, melancholy sigh. "That won't work."

"I know what this is about," I finally told her. "You're afraid he's going to go off with another woman, aren't you?"

Mom didn't say anything. I knew she was wishing Dad had kept his mouth shut about Anne Boyle.

"Look, Mom," I said, finally getting her attention. "Bad things can happen." I reminded her of the chilling murder in the neighborhood that everyone was talking about. We didn't know the Dumlers, but we had heard that they were a friendly couple with young children—and they had recently been tied up and shot execution-style in their bedroom. Dad had said they must've owed somebody money; that didn't exactly ease my mind. Mom and Dad owed plenty of people money.

"I'm sorry, honey," Mom said. "You'll have to do the best you can while we're gone. Someday you'll understand."

Mom was making a tough decision; I could see the guilt in her posture. At the same time, by mentioning the affair, I had dug into an emotional wound that hadn't quite healed. I was hoping to give her a little time to mull it over when I spied Jacquie in the breakfast nook, one ear on our conversation.

"I guess we can do it," Jacquie grumbled to Mom.

"Speak for yourself," I shot back, my stomach doing flip-flops. She made me sick the way she modeled Mom's behavior, agreeing to do too much. *I* still needed a parent around. It was as if Mom had led the five of us up the side of a steep mountain and then—surprise!—had taken the last helicopter down without us.

My disappointment in Mom had accumulated gradually. I didn't blame Dad entirely. He was doing what dads in the '60s and '70s did: they worked away from home while the moms took care of the kids. And Dad was such an extrovert he had to be out on the road. But Mom? She could do *something* to help us. Couldn't she have at least tried a little harder to find a babysitter? I kept imagining a moment when she'd wake up one day and think, *Dick, you're fine. I don't need to mother you anymore. I need to be there for our kids.*

One of the things that bugged me was having to call the older swimmers and beg for rides. They charged me twenty-five cents a ride, or a dollar a day, which wasn't much, but since we scarcely were aware from one minute to the next if Mom and Dad would arrive home, there were times when I had to apologize and felt like my father—"I'm sorry I can't pay you today, but tomorrow I'll have the money. I promise." Then I'd slink down in the backseat and say nothing on the way to practice, too ashamed to make eye contact.

From the time of Ricky's accident, we never had a babysitter again. Jacquie became our parent, which I resented because I had to keep proving to everyone that I wasn't selfish. And there were nights when the Dumlers crossed my mind, and I'd jump at the sound of a squeaky door or tree branch scraping the window as I lay in bed. We kids were divided on whether or not Mom and Dad should divorce. I speculated that we'd be better off. Mom would make more money on her own and Dad had enough charm that he might find somebody else to take care of him. But it was too late to broach the subject. We had done such a great job of convincing them we were handling everything that they didn't seem to question their decision. At twelve, I had lost my hope and trust in Mom.

ONE FRIDAY NIGHT DURING THE FALL of 1969—right before my parents returned from their last business trip of the season, when the days were dark and the absence of light cast a weight on my shoulders I can only equate now with their being gone—I heard young, gleeful voices coming from the backyard as I trudged up the steep front steps to the house.

Through the kitchen window, I spotted a makeshift fort cobbled together from rotted doors and a couple of blankets. I heard faint giggling and saw shining flashlights under the blankets as leaves swirled through the yard and the back door squealed under the wind's pressure. I grabbed some stale cookies and tiptoed up to Jacquie's room.

She was lying on her bed in the corner of the room, a book propped on her knees.

"You think it's okay for the kids"—we called them kids even

though we were kids ourselves—"to be out there by themselves? I mean, what if some animal gets them?"

She lifted her eyebrows. "What kind of animal are you talking about?"

"Oh, I don't know. Like a wolf or something. Can't they get attacked by a wolf?"

"A wolf in Cincinnati?" Jacquie laughed.

I hated that she appeared older, wearier, and more studious than I felt, as if she'd settled into her job as a replacement mom.

"Well, I don't know. The backyard is dangerous, isn't it?"

"Not to me."

Even from Jacquie's room, I could hear the happy whispers. What bothered me about the scene wasn't really the prospect of wolves or bad weather or even some weirdo wandering away from the Observatory grounds and into our backyard to molest Pam, Ricky, or David—though those scenarios were easy to imagine with the Dumler murder still floating around like a bad weather pattern in my head. What bothered me most was that I was only in seventh grade, yet I was too tired from swimming to go out and join them. My parched skin was sore where my bathing suit had rubbed, my eyes burned, my arms and legs ached. I didn't mind Jacquie as a mom, but I wanted to be out there in the yard myself: building the fort, playing Parcheesi, and telling ghost stories.

Where was the fun in swimming? I liked the feel of the water. I was healthy—that was positive—and stronger than most kids my age. But where was the playfulness of childhood? After the tie-dye shirts, I had resolved to become the kind of swimmer Mr. Bergen would notice, but achieving that goal was proving to be a slog, and I sometimes doubted whether swimming was worth it.

SOON AFTER MOM AND DAD RETURNED from their business trip, Mom received an upsetting phone call from one of our neighbors. As I entered the kitchen, Dad began firing questions at me about the fort in the backyard, which had by then been cleaned up. He said our neighbor, Mrs. Habel, whose husband was an architect, had called to complain about the eyesore. I was slightly outraged and trying to be funny, so I suggested Dad have Mrs. Habel talk to Pam.

The backyard was a touchy subject for Mom. The previous summer, while watching TV on a Saturday, Dad had come across what he thought was a fantastic deal for a patio on the WCET Action Auction. Before Mom had even finished the breakfast dishes, three men in worn work clothes had unloaded several enormous pallets of concrete block from a flatbed truck and lined them up along the side of our sloping driveway.

"I feel like I can't leave you alone for one second, Dick," Mom said. "What on earth were you thinking?"

Dad leaned back and pulled his belt up over his swollen belly. "Oh, Beejay, it was an auction. Haven't you ever been to an auction? Things happen quickly."

And for the entire day, it seemed, the five of us kids took turns lugging concrete blocks up the front hill and around to the backyard, where Dad set them in the ground with as much precision as he used in telling stories after an evening of hard drinking.

Our makeshift patio was approximately fifteen by fifteen feet and looked okay, at first. But just a week later, a hard rain fell and mud squirted up between the blocks, making it look more like a fitness-training site for the US Marines.

For months, Mom vented about the backyard whenever she looked through the window. Water poured in from the neighbors' driveway and trees blocked the sun, so there was no way to grow grass. What we needed was to trim back some tree limbs to allow light into the yard, but Dad thought that would cost too much money. So when Mom heard that Pam, Ricky, and David had built a fort with old doors and rusty metal chairs back there, the news was a little much for her sense of order.

As she dropped hamburger sauce into a tangle of spaghetti noodles, Dad stopped Pam on her way upstairs.

"You have something you want to tell me?"

Dad thought she would mention the fort. Instead, she said someone at school had called her a bastard.

Dad turned abruptly. "A bastard? None of you kids has to worry about being a mistake," he said, grinning. "You kids were all mistakes."

"Oh, honestly, Dick." Mom grinned too. Dad could snap her out of a bad mood with one joke.

Pam twisted sideways to get my reaction. At eight, she'd already suffered three years of our teasing after dropping hot dog buns in a pot of boiling water in her attempt to help with dinner.

"Were you kids out of control while we were gone?"

"We were fine," Pam said, her head cocked toward Mom, her lean arm muscles tight at her side.

"Well, the neighbors didn't think so. Mrs. Habel called and complained that you and Ricky were fighting."

"No, we weren't." For a moment Pam's eyes flashed defiance.

"If I talk to Ricky, will he say the same thing?"

She nodded emphatically. "Yep."

Dad opened the door to the stairs and shouted at the top of his lungs, "Rick-eeey, get down here." Ricky barreled down the stairs, his shirt dirty and wrinkled, one shoelace untied. "Hey, Slugger, were you and Pammy fighting while we were gone?"

"No."

"What's the story with the fort?"

"What do you mean?" Ricky's eyes were on Pam as if they'd made a pact.

"Mrs. Habel says she doesn't like looking in our backyard."

"Too bad," Pam said with a striking air of confidence. "It's *our* yard."

Dad winked. "Okay, get outta here."

That night Dad changed his whole attitude about Pam. "You know, Beej, of the five kids, I was the most concerned about leaving Pammybuster. I don't think we have to worry about her, after all.

If she doesn't like something, she'll let you know. And if she wants something badly enough," he said, "she knows how to get it." With that, he looked me over, meaningfully.

"What?" I knew he wanted me to be more like Pam, whom he now considered gutsy because she knew how to speak her mind. He was still amused that she had rejected seven stores before she was able to settle on the perfect pair of white go-go boots for her birthday.

He'd been asking me a lot about why Mr. Bergen would pick Super Bowl weekend to schedule the Thoroughbred Invitational in Kentucky. He hated having to decide between football and swimming, and it seemed he wanted me to raise the question with Mr. Bergen.

"You should give him a call," I said.

Dad stared at me, his eyes squinting.

"What, Dad? You look like you want to say something."

"Just thinking about the traits that run in the family," he said. "That's all."

CHAPTER 11

Mr. Bergen scanned our faces with steely, tense judgment. Someone had mentioned he was angry when he found out Linda Corbin, one of the Marlins' strongest senior swimmers, had quit. But a few swimmers quit every few months, and others always joined the team to take their place. It didn't make sense that he would be so upset about one swimmer.

He was wearing only his horn-rimmed glasses and an oversize old man's bikini Speedo, red with a wide side stripe—not a good look for anyone approaching thirty, but especially for someone with a short body and a curly black carpet of hair on his legs. He propped his left foot over his right, his hand on his clipboard digging into his hip, as he waited for our complete attention.

"Excuse me, Pahner. Was there something you wanted to say?" He spoke in a low voice.

"No," she said, grinning. Then she straightened.

Mr. Bergen launched into a team lecture, though it was obvious he meant it mostly for the girls. "We're starting a new program," he said. "I will come up with an ideal weight for each of you based on a national formula, minus a few pounds. I want you to weigh in every night before practice and show progress."

All I could think was, *Wait, what?*

One of the girls raised her hand. "How many calories should we eat every day?"

"If you eat a thousand," Mr. Bergen said, "I guarantee you'll lose weight."

I was tall and thin, compared to most of my teammates, and we had become used to exposing our bodies every day at the pool long before our bodies began to develop. Despite this, I hated that our very weight was now made public, that from that day on Mr. Bergen stood beside the scale on the balcony, within eyeshot of the parents, weighing us like a herd of the best Angus beef cattle.

At school we were reading about Betty Freidan and Gloria Steinem, learning about the harmful standards of beauty that society perpetrated on women's bodies. Across the country, women were tossing their high-heeled shoes, girdles, and false eyelashes into the trash to protest the Miss America Pageant, and particularly its swimsuit competition. Wasn't this kind of like that? I resented the idea of being weighed daily. On the other hand, I also hated the yelling and screaming, and yet all that fear *had* improved my times. I told myself that maybe weighing in was necessary for *some* of the girls, that maybe I was one of the lucky ones.

I was supposed to lose two pounds. My teammates, many of them, had a lot more to lose. The rationale for losing weight didn't make sense to me: *Doesn't a fatter body float higher in the water?* Or did fat create more drag? I wasn't a scientist.

"Next," he said, "I want to talk about the Thoroughbred Invitational."

We were supposed to swim a Marlin Invitational in mid-December, a Pittsburgh meet two days after Christmas, and this one would be in early January, on Super Bowl weekend—not likely to attract a ton of swimmers. I didn't understand why this meet was so important, but it must've been the national exposure he wanted. There weren't many meets in short course meters pools. With less competition, maybe he thought this was a rare opportunity to set national records.

"We will not be tapering"—meaning cutting back on the practice intensity—"through the Lexington meet," he said, "but I still expect every one of you to finish with your best times. I want to see performance. And for that to happen, you will need to be just as disciplined when you sit at the dinner table as you are at the pool."

LOSING WEIGHT TURNED OUT TO BE NEARLY impossible. At five foot seven and 129 pounds, I couldn't find a huge handful of flesh anywhere on my body. Where was this fat supposed to come from? I decided to reduce my water intake, which seemed to work. Then one day I ate a couple of cookies in addition to my usual lunch and all afternoon I was on pins and needles, sure I would be overweight.

That night I stepped on the scale, and as Mr. Bergen slid the weight along the fractional bar, I watched the pointer wobble. Instead of losing two pounds, I'd jumped to 130.

"What's the matter, Peters?" Mr. Bergen narrowed his eyes at me. "You need to cut out the doughnuts."

I awkwardly leaned away from him, putting weight on my right foot, which wobbled the pointer again. He readjusted the weight. One twenty-eight.

"That's better."

THAT NIGHT MR. BERGEN WAS IN RARE FORM, marching along the pool's edge, shouting and name-calling, saying some kids weren't working hard enough, though we had to guess who he was talking about.

After practice, in the car with the older girls, there was even more grumbling than normal. Alice and Heidi sat in front. MaryAnn didn't drive, so she sat in the backseat with me. There was a four- to six-year difference in our ages, so on most days the four of us hardly said a word. But the focus on weight broke through the age barrier.

MaryAnn was beside herself. Extremely skinny, she wore her thin blond hair in two severe knots and was rarely one to let a single strand fly loose around her face. She tucked her shirt into her skirt, covered her textbooks with brown paper to keep them clean, never had a missing button, an untied shoelace, a wrinkle, or a stain. I had been sure that she, of all people, would escape scrutiny.

But Mr. Bergen had been harsh with her. "What's wrong?" he asked her. "Doesn't your mother feed you?" It seemed none of us weighed the amount he wanted.

We gazed with fixed stares out the car windows. Alice and Heidi weren't talkative, but MaryAnn was seething. "What is he trying to do?" she said. "Make us feel bad about ourselves?"

I rifled through Mom's cookbook for a calories chart. Oatmeal, no sugar; sandwich, no mayo; meatloaf, milk, green beans, potato. I could easily rack up a thousand calories with no room for chocolate chip ice cream. I made my calculations. If I were to eat a normal meal and replace two scoops of ice cream with a single Oreo cookie, I could stay at a thousand calories for the day. I imagined that as long as I followed the rules, Mr. Bergen would leave me alone.

AND FOR A WHILE, HE DID. THE FOLLOWING day, I climbed the stairs to the balcony, which sat at the starting end of the pool, above the locker rooms. I proceeded straight to the scale, stepped off the cold concrete onto the scale's rectangular pad, and stood straight up, my weight on my right foot, and—bingo! Two pounds lighter again.

I scrambled down the stairs to the locker room and passed the word around. "If you put your weight on your right foot, you can drop two pounds."

"No way." Connie grabbed her cap, then her goggles (by 1969, we were wearing them regularly).

"I swear to God," I said. "Lean to your right."

That night, most of the girls were under weight. But as we marched down for weightlifting afterward, I heard a group of girls whispering near the entrance to the locker room. "He didn't have to bite your head off," one said, followed by grumbling.

Great, I thought. *So we've cut weight and we're* still *in trouble?* I'd cut back so much on my calories I felt nauseated. Lockers banged and vibrated. My head throbbed. I made my way to the bathroom and glimpsed Deena snarling, her locker ajar, flicking her T-shirt off the nearest hook.

"Who didn't make weight?"

"Does it matter?" she snapped, donning her shirt. *Why is she so touchy?* I thought for a second—but I knew why. As one of Mr. Bergen's favorites, Deena was also the recipient of much of his wrath. It seemed so unfair. At the same time, I didn't appreciate her taking her frustration out on me.

It seemed Mr. Bergen always needed to be angry at someone. And when you're starving, any exercise is hell. Watching the top group of swimmers (Pressure 1) practice before us was like knowing about a murder in the beginning of a novel. At one point, David Cain, one of the few older guys capable of standing up to Mr. Bergen, said a few curse words under his breath and Mr. Bergen hurled a kickboard like a high-speed projectile, just missing his head.

As I waited to begin practice with a couple of friends from the P2 group, watching the scene unfold, the story we got was that two girls from P1—Alice and Debbie, both potential Olympians—hadn't made weight that day, which had infuriated Mr. Bergen. Now he shouted commands for a long, painful freestyle set on a short interval, calling out times for many of the older swimmers, indicating they were slow even from the start.

When P1 was over, we in P2 did our kicking set while Mr. Bergen lectured P1 about the Thoroughbred Invitational—how important it was, and how they weren't working hard enough. Coming into the wall, we could hear him berating some of the swimmers. "Some of you aren't dedicated. You aren't going to make it." These were the best swimmers on the team, with red faces, an unfocused gaze, most of them hugging their knees to their chests, trying to keep their bodies warm, as water dripped from their slumped torsos.

Several mothers knitted at the edge of the balcony, monitoring practice, fully aware of what was going on. Some had the guts to complain to Paul Bergen about his bullying and obsessive focus on our weight, but most seemed reticent. "If you don't approve of my coaching style," he said, "quit!" There was no negotiation, no compromise. Even the Keating girls, whose father had contributed the most financially to the Marlins, were made the objects of his seething temper. Decades later I would come to realize that his brand of equal-opportunity abuse was dangerous, and would scar many of us for life. But at the time it didn't seem personal, and for that reason somehow more tolerable.

As to the parents, I imagine it was difficult to criticize too much when we were breaking more records and swimming faster than we'd ever imagined possible. And by then, we were the only show in town. The other Cincinnati teams had dwindled to a handful of swimmers, all of them mediocre at best.

MR. BERGEN'S MOODS HAD ALWAYS BLOWN hot and cold, but they were increasingly more on the hot side, and there was a heaviness in the air. Every day presented a new spate of conflicts. Were we showing team spirit? Aware of our weight? Eating right? Working hard in practice? It didn't matter what we did—a sharp, unrelenting tension swirled around the pool, and Mr. Bergen's fervor seemed to have ratcheted up a notch. He had always been intense, but now something about him was noticeably off kilter.

Many of the older girls were going to increasing extremes to lose weight. Debbie, embarrassed when Mr. Bergen singled her out, arrived at the pool one day wearing a plastic suit and then stood under one of the hairdryers, hoping to sweat off a few pounds before practice. I'd cut back so much on my calories I couldn't stay warm.

I remember wondering to myself about Mr. Bergen's wife. She had been a familiar presence for a while—volunteering at meets, creating a newsletter. She was cheerful and attractive and apparently a good mother to her three well-behaved children, ages four to seven, but I hadn't really ever thought deeply about her. Now I began to wonder how she could stand to live with a person like him. On the other hand, her existence normalized him in a way. I assumed she balanced his harshness in the same way Mom's consistency and loyalty balanced Dad's impulsiveness and lack of discipline. I pictured Mr. Bergen arriving home at night after practice, removing his severity like a coat he placed in the closet, and melting into his wife's arms the way Dad melted into Mom's as soon as they sipped their first drink.

ONE NIGHT AFTER PRACTICE, MR. BERGEN had us line up so he could dispense a single jelly bean into each of our outstretched palms. This would eventually become one of his rituals. I suppose he was trying to instill some fun, though it felt like a strange Halloween trick.

I'd developed oozing sores that looked like rug burns from where my nylon suit rubbed my neck and underarms, and when I leaned against the wall of the shower, I could hardly move.

At home each night, I slathered on petroleum jelly and stared at my dry, red face and sloping eyebrows in the bathroom mirror.

I tiptoed in to dinner after practice that evening to find the whole family waiting, tight-lipped and ravenous. Dad put his hand on my arm as I pulled out the chair nearest him. "Are you ready for the Thoroughbred Invitational, Butch?"

I burst into tears.

CHAPTER 12

The day of the Thoroughbred Invitational, the air outside was blistering cold. I felt feeble, exhausted, and sick to my stomach. Mom had said she would swing by to pick me up at school and drive me home, and then Jacquie would watch the younger kids while Mom and Dad drove me to the meet in the motorhome. Mom was often late, so when I excused myself from English early and she still hadn't arrived, I ducked into the 1920s tiled bathroom to save time. I glanced at my watch. Two minutes to spare; the worrisome thoughts began flooding in. *Will we make it to Lexington in time?* I pushed open the bathroom stall and quickly unbuttoned. "Oh, no," I said out loud. *Are you kidding me? Who gets their first period on a Friday just before an important swim meet?*

I wadded up a handful of tissue and stuffed it in place, then staggered out to the back circle behind the building. That was it. There was no way I could go to the meet. There would be no time to get tampons, figure out how to use them, and get all the way to Lexington in time for the warm-up. I'd have to tell Mom; she'd tell Dad . . . Jesus. I felt the air crackle just thinking of Dad. I knew he'd want to know all about it.

The wide swath of sidewalk that bordered the back circle was covered with slush and small piles of blackened snow. I tiptoed across it, dodging ice, sure that if I fell, I'd have an even bigger mess to deal with.

Walnut Hills High School was a stately structure, modeled after Thomas Jefferson's Monticello. Students were still in class but the buses were already beginning to line up for the end of the day, splashing slop along the curb. I stood back with my arms and legs crossed. *Where is Mom? She has to hurry.*

Out of the corner of my eye, I spotted her in the old sedan. She swerved around the pick-up circle and stopped briefly for me to climb in.

"Sorry I'm late," she said. "Are you okay? You look peaked."

"I started my period."

Mom took a quick check of the rearview mirror and pulled away from the curb, reacting slowly, apparently not surprised at all. "We'll stop and you can run in and get something."

I suppose I expected a smile, a nurturing word, some anecdote she recalled from *her* mother, but Mom seemed barely to register what I'd just said.

"Mom, I'm twelve. I can't *get* anything." I didn't have the slightest clue what to do.

She told me her mind was on the business and whether or not we could unload the motorhome and still get to the meet on time. We sailed home in the car, hardly speaking to each other. Once in our driveway, she patted me on my thigh. "There's not much time, honey, so hurry."

I hesitated as I opened the car door, imagining Dad's reaction. "Mom, you don't expect me to go into the drugstore, do you?"

"Well, I don't know what you need, sweetie."

"Tampons. Can't you get me tampons?"

Mom unbuckled her seatbelt and turned to me, embarrassed. "Honey, I don't use those things."

I sat for a moment, my head back, staring at the dashboard. This seemed like a major life experience—not something we talked about at the pool—and here Mom was, digging in her purse for her lipstick.

"Mom, promise me you won't tell Dad about this. You know how he is."

"I won't tell him, honey. But run in and get your suit or we'll be late. We'll figure it out on the way."

Mom followed me into the house. I raced up the stairs, gathered a towel, swimsuit, hairbrush, and warm-up jacket. When I tumbled down to the front hall, Dad was standing there, holding the door open, with Mom looking over his shoulder. I was wondering how I was going to get away with his not knowing about this when, all at once, I noticed his silly smile and he broke into song like Frank Sinatra: "Women in the Night . . ."

I jerked my head toward Mom. "How could you?"

Mom gave him a shove. "What's wrong with you, Dick?"

I hurried straight to the back of the motorhome, as far away from Dad as possible, and slumped on the stiff double cushion with a towel over my head. I told myself I'd had enough of both of them. I was determined never to confide in Mom again. Ever.

"Are you psyched up for the meet tonight?" Dad called from the driver's seat. "Butch, did you hear me?"

I didn't answer.

"Butch? Butch?"

"Yes, Dad."

"Are you psyched up?"

Define psyched up, I thought. *You mean, like, ready to strangle my father? Yeah, sure. I'm psyched up.* "Yes."

Dad drove off to Walgreens, where Mom went in without me. A short time later, she appeared in the back of the motorhome with a brown paper sack.

"Here. Experiment." She dropped the bag with a straight arm, away from her body, like she was holding a treatment for head lice and afraid she might catch something.

I shook out three boxes, each a different style.

Dad revved the engine as I whispered to Mom, "I have no idea what I'm doing."

"Read the directions. You'll figure it out." She reached across the cushion in the back of the motorhome and helped me close the curtains before shutting me in behind the accordion door.

The motorhome rumbled down the icy road at top speed, curtains swinging. I lay on the cushions as if I were hiding in a dark closet, jostling from side to side, hoping there wouldn't be any sharp turns. The tampons came in hard-edged, cylindrical cardboard tubes and it hurt like hell when I tried to insert them. I could hear Mom and Dad in the front; they were talking business, but every ten minutes or so Mom would call back to ask if I was okay and I would say, "No."

An hour later, she reached around the door with a compact mirror she thought might be helpful.

Another half hour passed.

"Beejay, you need to help your daughter. We're ten miles away." Dad's PA-system voice reverberated through the vehicle. Mom told him she wasn't going to pester me, that I needed to handle this myself. A few minutes later, she was at the accordion door. "Honey, we'll be there shortly. How are you doing?"

"I'm not doing well at all," I told her, crying. "I can't do this."

"Did you read the instructions?"

"Of course."

"Well, keep trying. I'll yell to you as we get closer to the pool."

Mom looked sad as I massaged my chlorine-fried cheeks. "I can't, Mom. I don't want to swim."

"Honey, we've come all this way. You have to swim. Please keep trying." No matter how bad an idea was to begin with, my mother always had to finish anything she started.

I knew I couldn't say I was sick. Mr. Bergen would insist on teasing out all the terrible details. He seemed temperamentally incapable of mercy. If I refused to explain, I would face unimaginable consequences. He'd either drop me to a lower relay or embarrass me in front of the whole team. And the longer I struggled with the tampons, the more swollen and sore I became.

As for my parents, I tried every excuse in the book, but I couldn't convince them to turn around and go home. Meets were an opportunity for them to relax and socialize. They'd been driving all week, were anxious to sit down, and were mostly unaware of the impact of Mr. Bergen's increasingly erratic behavior. This was their chance to catch up on what I was doing.

A few minutes later, I called Mom to the back of the motorhome and implored her to help. I had open tampons spread across the bed like bad Halloween candy. She looked uncomfortable, but she read the instructions, took one out of the box, and tore open the wrapper, holding the tampon like a doctor about to give me a shot. I closed my eyes as she put her hand on my knee.

"Hold still."

"You're hurting me."

"Sweetie, calm down. You're so upset you're making this impossible. You have to relax."

"I can't relax!" I bawled as the bus lurched forward.

"Be-eej, we're here. You need to wrap this up!" my father shouted from the front of the motorhome.

Mom inspected me closely, touching with her finger like she was testing a cake for firmness. "Everything looks good."

"But I can feel it. You're not supposed to feel it, are you?"

"Honey, I don't know." It seemed she was trying her hardest.

I marshalled my strength, along with my towel and bathing suit, and made my way awkwardly to the front of the motorhome.

"Good luck, Butch," Dad said, as if it were any other day.

I dropped sideways onto the slippery metal step—it was less painful—and hurried through the muck to the natatorium.

In the locker room, I slipped into my suit and glanced in a full mirror to see if I could see anything unusual. My face was as white as my warm-up jacket. I straggled stiffly into the steamy natatorium.

Spectators filled the stands and moisture dripped from the ceiling as the last swimmers clambered out of the pool and began to mill around.

As the announcer called the first event, Mr. Bergen walked toward me. He pulled a rolled heat sheet from his front pants pocket and swatted his thigh. "You missed warm-up, Peters."

"I know." I wrapped my towel around my waist and ambled inelegantly toward a bunch of teammates, towels draped over their slumpy shoulders, singing,

> "We are the Marlins, mighty, mighty, Marlins;
> Everywhere we go-oh, people ought to know-oh,
> Who we ah-are, so we tell them . . . "

The cheer kept repeating, like a series of short sprints. I entered the waiting area—the Clerk of Course—where swimmers in the first three heats sat in rows, waiting to be led to the blocks. "Kim Peters?"

"Yes." An older official handed me a lane card and I tried to straighten up. The pool deck swarmed with officials wearing white and standing shoulder to shoulder with stopwatches and clipboards. I limped in single file with my heat, removed my warm-up jacket and towel, and, when my heat was called, clumsily stepped up to the block. *Every girl has to deal with this*, I told myself. *I'm not the first. Stop being such a baby.*

The announcer adjusted his gun. "This is the first heat of the women's four-hundred-meter freestyle. Swimmers take your mark..."

I bent over, my hands at my feet, and I was sure the officials behind me were wondering if I had male anatomy.

I shot off the block to the first wall. Then, carefully, I flipped. Whew, it was still there. I swam another lap; whew. Still there again.

For sixteen laps, all I could think was flip-whew, flip-whew. The race was a blur.

At the finish, I carefully climbed out and wrapped my towel around my waist, feeling like a soaked sponge. Cheers rippled across the bleachers. Not one or two, as usual, but the whole block of parents seemed focused on me. Some, with eyes twinkling, hid laughter. "Good job, Kim," they yelled.

I tried to return a grateful smile, then dropped into the front row of the bleachers with my back to the crowd. Parents were patting my shoulder, which was odd for such a mediocre swim. I caught my breath, swiveled in my seat, and spotted Dad—leaning back, his arm resting on the bleacher, his chest puffed out, a distant, unfocused smile on his face.

I knew what he had done. All I could do was grimace.

He raised his open palms. "What?" he mouthed. "What did I do?"

For the rest of the meet, he and I didn't talk.

THE MARLINS SLAUGHTERED THE OTHER teams, with 903 ½ points. Greater Lexington Swim Association, the runner-up, tallied 494. Deena set a national record in the 11&12 girls 100-meter butterfly. Yet Mr. Bergen seemed indifferent, which was strange. I couldn't figure out what was going on with him. The Marlins smashed Ohio state records in just about every event, and our coach just stood at the edge of the pool, disapproval etched in his face. He chewed out one of the girls for bringing a giant container of malted milk balls, and was angry with all of us for not cheering loudly enough.

Mom and Dad drove me back and forth the next two days. I personally didn't swim well, but was relieved that Mr. Bergen's clenched jaw had nothing to do with me. By most accounts, we'd cleaned up as a team. And yet he still wasn't satisfied. He'd wanted the relays to finish first, second, and third, and they ended up finishing first, third, and fourth, which made him furious. Not at himself. At us.

Due to icy roads, the meet organizers canceled the finals, so Dad got to see the Super Bowl after all. As we climbed into the bus for our return trip home, he cranked up the pre-game commentary, thankfully too absorbed to want to rehash the meet with me. I barely acknowledged him. As we careened down slippery, unforgiving rural roads with the radio blaring, I curled up in back, my damp towel under my head, thanking God for football.

CHAPTER 13

In the spring of 1970, just as the frost on the natatorium doors was beginning to melt, I wandered into the locker room belting out "Piece of My Heart" in my best rock-star voice when I bumped into Deena.

She spun around. "Who do you think you are? Janis Joplin?"

As a reflex I answered, "Who's Janis Joplin?"

When I saw Deena's expression, I sank a few inches. Clearly, *everyone* had heard of Janis Joplin.

Living a half-hour from the pool meant my ears got at least eleven hours of commuter rock music every week. Forty-four hours a month—four hundred and forty hours a year—of rock lyrics that stuck in my head. So *what* if I didn't know the singers' names? This was one of those moments when I was reminded that, despite being the oldest child in my family, I was incapable of leadership. I wanted someone to rescue me from that role.

Around this time, there was a guy's St. X High School Swim Team state meet party planned at Dick McCarthy's house in Montgomery, a city northeast of Cincinnati, and some part of me thought this might be a chance to learn a bit about popular culture, to play catch-up in an area of my life that was so sadly lacking. So, despite Mr. Bergen's insistence that we all get to bed early and keep a laser focus on swimming, I decided to go.

Dad immediately wanted to hear who would be attending. He stood in front of the TV in his undershirt, one eye on Walter Cronkite.

"I don't know, Dad. Mostly older kids." I envisioned a mass of girls and guys in bell-bottoms and tie-dyed T-shirts, drinking Pepsi, eating potato chips, and cavorting to Beatles music in the dark.

Dad was more excited than I was, and he insisted that Mom and he come up with a curfew.

"This is a swimming party," I reminded him. "Swimmers don't have energy to stay up late." At least *I* didn't. "Besides, Mr. Bergen will probably be there."

"I don't give a damn. Are you telling me the party's over at ten?"

"No."

"Then you need a curfew. How about eleven? Can you be home by eleven?"

I beamed. One of the worst things in the world was jumping into a cold pool at six o'clock in the morning. But even worse was jumping into a cold pool fatigued. Eleven would be just fine.

"All right, then. Eleven o'clock," he said. "You make sure you stick to it."

THE GUYS' STATE MEET WAS IN UPPER Arlington, a Columbus suburb, and I rode with some of the older girls. We cheered as St. X smashed state records and fought neck-and-neck with Upper Arlington, then won by a few points by getting first place in the last event, the 400 freestyle relay.

I hitched a ride to Dick McCarthy's house with several teammates, and when we arrived at ten thirty, the place was a mob scene. We had to squeeze through a raucous sea of guys, pumped up after their win, laughing, telling loud stories, calling each other wusses, and punching each other in the chest. I had never experienced so much testosterone. Mrs. McCarthy had filled the kitchen counter with baked goods and kids were in the front and backyard—some smoking and drinking, though I didn't know it at the time.

I must've been the youngest one there—my straight hair behind my ears, wearing culottes, knee socks, and loafers, a little twelve-year-old at a teenage party. Since I would have had to leave immediately to arrive home in time for my curfew, I proceeded to the telephone to warn Dad I would be late. At first, he was his usual jovial, inebriated self. I could hear the television in the background and he sounded distracted.

"You and I agreed on a time, Butch."

"But the party just started."

"I don't give a damn," he said, his tone hardening. "You get your ass home."

I gazed at my Timex. Who could I ask to drive me home so early? I gobbled a few of Mrs. McCarthy's chocolate chip cookies, watching the combat from behind the kitchen counter as I scanned the party for a familiar face.

At eleven o'clock, I called Dad again. This time Mom had gone to bed.

"Can you come get me?" I was thirty minutes away.

"Hell, no. You get a ride. That was our deal."

I gathered my courage to interrupt Billy Keating, who was telling a funny story to someone I didn't know. "Is there any way you could take me home? My father will kill me."

Billy was four years older, had driven me to practice on occasion, and had a habit of talking to girls like he was whispering. I couldn't understand what he said at first so I tried again: "My father will *kill me*."

"Oh, yeah? Well, *you're* killing *me*," he joked. "Ask Ned Wenstrup. Maybe he'll take you."

Ned didn't say much as we walked across the lawn toward his car. He'd rarely uttered two words to me, so I didn't think anything of his silence. Like most Marlin guys, Ned was long-limbed, well-built, and good-looking, but he wore thick, black-framed glasses that were, at the moment, slightly off-center.

As he fumbled for his keys, he tripped.

"You okay?" I asked. He seemed lost and somewhat dazed. "What color is the car?"

Directly in front of the house was a dark Chevy Impala with steamy windows. Ned unlocked the front passenger side, and as naive and absurd as it may sound, when I spotted two kids from our team—Val and Grimmer, both maybe fourteen—snuggling in the back seat, I figured Ned must be taking them home too. They smiled tentatively at me as I got in.

Before I knew what was happening, Ned slid in behind me on the passenger side, pulled me close, and stuck his tongue in my mouth. At twelve, I hadn't seen or imagined anything like a French kiss, but instantly I registered why Ned had been fumbling. His mouth tingled with the sweet taste of alcohol and made me feel like I was mature for a second.

"No, Ned, no." I pushed his hand away.

The two in the backseat fidgeted. "No, Ned, no," they tittered. For a few minutes, I half resisted, half enjoyed his fumbling kisses. The whole scene felt unreal. Ned caressed my hair with one hand and my back with the other. Then he started to unbutton my shirt.

"No, Ned, no!" I squeezed hard on his hand.

"No, Ned, no," Val and Grimmer echoed.

I pushed his hand away again, but he kept wrestling with the buttons. As he kissed my neck, I held his hand tightly, hoping to discourage him. But I couldn't stop him. Finally, clutching at the buttons of my half-opened blouse, I leapt out on the driver's side and stumbled toward the house.

Inside was a strange group of guys I didn't recognize. Billy, seated with others in a semi-circle, was still telling stories, and this time Denny White, the St. X coach, was a part of his audience. I stomped straight over and asked Denny for a ride. He smiled in a strange way, reminiscent of my father.

"Is something wrong?" I asked. I placed a clump of hair behind my ear.

"I'm going to call you 'Sneaky Pete,'" he said.

Pete because my name's Peters, but why "sneaky"? I was a sixth grader. Did he seriously think I'd stepped out to the car for some action?

Denny drove me home and the whole way I slunk down in the backseat like a little kid, watching the streetlights pass in the dark neighborhoods, as Denny chatted with Terry, a guy five years older who attended Walnut Hills and sometimes drove me to practice. *Ned*, I thought. *Kissing me like that.* I felt surprisingly excited. I hardly even knew this guy and he had kissed me like I was Scarlett O'Hara. The exhilaration reminded me of the first drop on the Shooting Star at Old Coney, the local amusement park.

Would Ned remember any of this? He and Billy lived in the same neighborhood. Would he tell Billy and the other guys what happened? Or would Grimmer say something? Oh, God. Nobody was going to hear about this, I decided. Nobody. In the space of ten minutes, the cavernous expanse at my core was filled by a queasy dread. Grimmer was not one to forget something like this.

Sufficiently sloshed but not incoherent when I arrived, Dad met me at the door in his navy-blue bathrobe. He'd been watching the last of Johnny Carson. When he ushered me to my room, I said good night and closed the door until it latched—something I rarely did.

"We'll talk in the morning, Butch," he said through the door.

THE NEXT MORNING AS I CLEARED MY dishes from breakfast, Dad snagged my arm. "Hey, how was the party?"

"Fine."

"Fine, huh. Why were you so late?"

"I don't know, Dad," I said, shrugging. "The party started late." I focused on the plates, knowing Dad would pick up on any discomfort and go right to it like a fly on raw meat.

"You aren't giving me much information, Butch." He set his dish in the sink and poked his head around the corner and into the dining room. "Beejay, will you come here for a minute?" I could tell by her disappearance that they'd already discussed the matter and were in disagreement about interrogating me.

Mom entered the room, still in her bathrobe, clearly anxious to get dressed and on with her day. Her attitude bolstered my confidence. "Mom, Dad is trying to get me to say something, but there's nothing to say."

"Dick, wasn't there enough tension for you at breakfast?" Mom said immediately. She was referring to the boys' complaints about Dad's gray eggs mixed with slimy vegetables from the back of the refrigerator.

"Beejay, this is important." He turned to me. "Were any of the kids paired up?"

What does this have to do with anything? I wondered. *And why does Dad care so much?* "I guess so."

"Well?"

"Val was with Grimmer."

"Interesting." Dad's eyes showed the same spark of delight as when Mom pulled a roast from the oven. "So . . ." He paused for a moment. "Were *you* with anyone?"

The gray eggs began to bubble to my throat. I didn't want to tell him but I knew I had to. He would never, ever, *ever* leave me alone. I thought back. *Who else was at the party? Should I make something up?* It was as if he were tiptoeing into my room, trying to catch me with my clothes off. "Why do I have to tell you?"

"Is this a *problem*?"

Think, Kim, think! "I just don't want to talk about it," I said, finally.

"Why not?

"I just don't." My tears began to well up and I wiped them with the heels of hands.

Mom anxiously straightened the plates, setting them in a perfect line in the cabinet. Then she turned abruptly. "She doesn't want to talk, Dick. Why can't you back off?" Mom seemed prepared to get in his face, which settled me for a moment.

"Beej, do you realize how late she arrived home?"

They both looked at me and waited.

"Okay, fine." I hugged my stomach. "It was Ned Wenstrup."

Dad took a deep, satisfied breath. His huge midriff leaned toward me and I stepped back, tightening my bathrobe. I could feel his breath on me. Mom put away the silverware at a snail's pace behind him.

"What did he do? Did he kiss you?"

I gulped and just stared.

"Butch?"

By then, tears were rolling down my face. "Yes, okay?"

"A lot?"

"Yes."

"What else did he do?" Talking with Dad about anything private was like holding back a hungry pit bull with treats in your pocket. He wanted something to chew on. Anything.

"I don't want to talk about it."

"Why not?" He hesitated for a moment. "Did he unbutton your shirt? At least answer that."

"Dick, please!" Mom sounded indignant. "Is this necessary?"

"What's the matter with you, Beejay?" He turned away from her and his head lunged toward me. He couldn't stand the idea of somebody's knowing something salacious that he didn't know. "So he unbuttoned your shirt?"

"Yes."

Dad pulled a glass from the cupboard; his eyes were still on me as he dug into the ice bucket. When Mom ducked into the butler's pantry, Dad called her back. "Beejay, where are you going?"

"I'm putting something away, Dick. Honestly!"

Dad waited for Mom to return. She stood behind him, drying her hands with a towel, compassion in her eyes, as I fell into full blown sobs. I don't know why I didn't just walk upstairs, but I knew

Dad would grab me or follow behind. I felt like I was passing him the fat so he could devour it.

"He unbuttoned your shirt. Okay. Did he do anything else?"

My heart fluttered like I was about to step up to the starting block.

"Dick, why don't you leave her alone?" Mom interjected. "Can't you just leave . . . her . . . alone? If you've got an itch, you've just got to scratch it, don't you?"

He seemed to be taken aback. "Is this too personal?"

"Yes," I sniffed.

"Why are you so upset? We need to know what happened."

I was thinking, what do you *think* happened? I considered telling him that I'd said no, that I'd leapt from the car, but I knew this would have no meaning to him. No didn't *mean* no to my father. It meant, *Okay, just a little bit more.*

His eyes darted to Mom and he stopped in the middle of the kitchen. "Did he unzip your pants?" There was dead silence.

"No."

"No?" Dad sucked in loudly through his teeth, stirred his water with his index finger, then licked it. "Isn't Ned Wenstrup the kid who lives up on Alpine Terrace? The one with twin sisters?"

"Yes." My voice was barely audible.

"Oh, hell, he's from a prominent family. You got nothing to worry about. Now, if he had tried to unzip your pants, I'd worry. But a hand down the shirt? No big deal. No big deal at all. You're going to have a lot of boys who will want to kiss you and put their hands down your shirt. But the Wenstrup kid? Aw, you got nothin' to worry about." Dad stared at me for a moment. "Capeesh?"

I nodded and headed for my room, feeling as if I'd been strip-searched. At the same time, I felt an unexpected sense of relief. Even though Dad was offering me support in a form that was all wrong, I'd wanted to tell *some*body. I didn't understand why Mom was so unwilling to enter the conversation. She must've been curious about what had happened. Or was she thinking about the way Dad had violated *her* privacy by revealing the dirty details related to Anne Boyle?

I lay on my bed, staring at the flies crawling on the dirty glass of my ceiling light and thinking, *What is wrong with Dad? Wouldn't a normal father say, "Aw, that must've been upsetting, honey, but you did the right thing." And what? Rules can be broken if you're from a privileged family?* What was I supposed to learn from *that*?

I didn't tell Dad that Ned had been drinking. For one thing, it wouldn't have mattered to him. But another part of me wanted to keep that detail for myself—for something to be my secret, to feel at least a little bit protected from Dad's relentless invasiveness. My biggest fear was that kids on the team would find out about Ned, and I'd feel even more isolated. I felt stupid for not realizing what I'd walked into, and I dreaded the thought of fellow swimmers making up their own stories about what might've happened.

It was too early for me to realize the widespread loneliness of the sport. With your head in the water, your body performing rote actions, it's you and you alone for long hours every day. Had I tried, I might have discovered a teammate or two who would've been able to offer emotional support, but revealing to any of my peers what had happened never occurred to me. I'd learned from my father and mother to keep shame hidden in a false-bottomed drawer.

ON MONDAY AFTER SCHOOL, I BLAZED into practice with my nerves jangled. Word had gotten around that some of the guys had been smoking at the party and Mr. Bergen had temporarily kicked them off the team. I felt a cold shudder, my shoulders and neck seizing up, when I heard this rumor. But then I saw Val in the locker room and she said hi, and I realized I was worrying way too much.

I quickly undressed, threw on a T-shirt, and stepped out on deck, headed for the weightlifting area. Some of the older guys were gathered in a scrum near the entrance to the guys' locker room. I gave them a weak smile as I approached.

Someone whispered, "No, Ned, no," and they all began to laugh and chant, "No-Ned-no! No-Ned-no!"

I pasted on a smile to show I was unaffected, but when I reached the weights, I couldn't hold back the tears. *That damn Grimmer*, I thought. *He must've told them.*

Mr. Bergen approached me just before the warm-up. "Are you okay, Peters?"

"I'm not feeling well."

"Are you sick?"

I nodded.

"Do the best you can," he said.

I reluctantly slipped into the pool, swam the short warm-up, pushed up to the deck, and, weeping, headed down the back wall toward the locker room as Mr. Bergen eyed me with suspicion.

"I can't practice," I said. "I'm sick."

He patted my back—it was the first time he'd ever touched me—and gave me an understanding nod. "Get dressed, Peters. Tomorrow you'll feel better."

I glanced at him, surprised. Had I underestimated his capacity for empathy?

In the locker room, I tore off my cap, and tossed it onto the locker's top shelf. At that moment, an instinct kicked in—an instinct to question what had just happened. Had he known why I was distraught? He'd seemed genuinely concerned. I'd watched him with some of the better swimmers, seen how he'd placed his arm around them or sat on the bleacher seat with his knees touching theirs. His comforting touch was the silver lining to the cloud of embarrassment I'd experienced with Ned.

Luckily, Mom and Dad were still home, and Dad agreed to come get me.

I waited in the bleachers, listening to the team splashing and the echo of kickboards slamming the deck in front of me. Swimming had been a place where I wasn't made to talk to anyone. Where I could banish the incessant thoughts about what was going on at home. Now, after one teenage party, I felt exposed. The pool was no longer a place where I could feel a cozy sense of invisibility, no matter how much Dad had tried to reassure me in his awkward way that what had happened didn't matter. Like everything related to swimming, the experience with Ned had occurred a few years earlier than my mind or body could handle.

I decided I had only one option if I wanted to feel safe. I needed to tuck the whole event—including my conversation with Dad—into that false-bottomed drawer in my brain and out of harm's way. It's not that I wanted to deny to myself that anything like this had happened, but maybe I wasn't ready to move into a more feminine form because I hadn't had a proper chance to enjoy being a child yet. I wanted to go back to that cozy sense of invisibility just a bit longer.

Of course, I wasn't the first girl in history to use this strategy. You block out the whole event when it's over, and when it happens again, you block it out sooner. Eventually, you're in a car, kissing some guy, and you're up above the car looking down at yourself as if you're in a movie. You're telling yourself that person is somebody else.

You feel for her, but it no longer hurts.

CHAPTER 14

Mom and Dad were spending increasingly more time away from home. I had mixed feelings when they traded in their Open Road for a fancier Winnebago Chieftain, but Jacquie and I were told the motorhome saved the family money. They didn't have to spring for hotel rooms and, since it was a "second home," the mortgage interest could be deducted at tax time. Still, at twelve, even though my knowledge of financial matters was a big zero, I felt a mounting intuition that despite Mom and Dad's rationale, the Winnebago was digging us deeper into debt.

Mom and Dad thought the 1970 Ohio State Championships in Columbus would be a fun trip for the family—in other words, a great way to show off the new vehicle. As Dad plowed his way north on I-75, I bounced around the Formica dining table, trying to annoy Jacquie by tapping my fingers on the table's edge—I knew she reeled from the slightest repetitive noise.

When I broke into cheerful song, that was her cue to go to the bathroom. She disappeared for a moment, then scurried to the front of the bus. "Mom, quick! You have to come!"

"What, Jacquie? What's the emergency?"

"Go see what it is, Beej, will you?" Dad said, detecting a story.

I heard a loud rush of air as the bathroom door beat against the gypsum wall of the compact kitchen. I peered over Mom's shoulder. She lifted the toilet seat, and we watched the wet pavement of Interstate 75 whoosh underneath where there should've been a pan of chemical-laced water.

Mom began to laugh hysterically. She braced herself as the motorhome rocked. "Dick, the holding tank is gone."

"The what?"

"You heard me. The holding tank isn't there."

Dad pulled the motorhome off to the berm and sauntered back to the bathroom to have a look. At first, he didn't say anything, which tickled Mom even more. The harder she laughed, the more she choked. Her hysterics woke Pam and Ricky, who had been fast asleep, and they poked their heads around the drawn curtains in the back. Dad stood and stared down at the toilet, one hand on the bathroom door knob, as if contemplating how he would use the bathroom over the weekend. Then he ambled back to the front of the motorhome, casually settled into his captain's chair, and put the vehicle into gear.

"What are you going to do?" I asked into the dead air.

"Nothing."

"Nothing?"

"That's right. We're going to drive on and pretend nothing happened."

Mom grew serious. "But Dick, there must be a terrible mess out on the highway. Don't you think we should go back and see if we can find it?"

"Come on, Beejay. It's cold and wet out there. If we find it, what will we *do* with it? You going to hold the tank in your lap 'til we get to Columbus?" Dad pulled back onto the highway and we sat there, waiting for him to come up with a plan.

"Well, what will you tell the mechanic?"

"What do you mean, Beejay? I'll tell him the truth."

Mom's eyes glinted with curiosity. "That we left the holding tank out on the highway?"

"Hell, yes. I'm going to say it dropped off as we drove, and that's all there is to it."

Mom closed her eyes and inhaled. "I can't believe it."

"I guess it means we're no longer full of shit, Beejay."

Mom snickered as she glanced out the window. "Well, some of us aren't, Dick, and some of us are."

This was around the time we kids realized we needed to step in and protect ourselves. To this day, I carry around that hypervigilance. I drive to a new place and scan the area. Is there anything that can get me? I hear a rattle. A thump. Is someone breaking into my house? I pay a therapist to remind me to take deep breaths, to recognize the triggers. To help me feel peaceful. To assure me that I am safe.

THE MOST MEMORABLE EVENT OF THE OHIO State Meet of 1970 was our 11&12 girls 200 medley relay. Kristie, Sue, Deena, and I, four little girls who had barely reached puberty, walked over to Mr. Bergen before our race.

"Don't think about the other teams," he said. "Remember KISS: *Keep it simple, stupid*. Just get out there and swim smart."

Deena was our butterflyer—short, muscular, and exceedingly flexible, with double-jointed shoulders. She could lace her fingers together and, with straight arms, rotate them behind her head, hands still clasped, and step through them like a jump rope. Just a few weeks earlier she had placed fifteenth in the 100 fly—as possibly the youngest competitor at Senior Nationals—and blown older, more experienced butterfliers out of the water.

We four said a few encouraging words to each other before our race, and by the time Deena was up, we were several arm strokes ahead of the field. I stepped up to the block for the freestyle finish, my gut tense, my shoulders rounded. I did a right arm circle, left arm circle, then shook out my legs. With toes clutching the edge of the block, my hands dropped slowly, and there she was.

Boom! I was in the water. Stroke, stroke, stroke, hard flip-turn. Kick, pull, stroke, stroke, stroke. As I slammed into the wall a body length ahead of the second-place finisher, I could hear the cheering of fans in the stands.

I gathered my towel and waited as the officials recorded the times from their stopwatches. Just before they handed our card to a runner, one official approached us and bent over to review the final time. "Congratulations, girls," he beamed. "You beat the national record."

We stopped abruptly. *Wait, we did?* A few minutes later, the announcer reported our time—2:00.1—then read out our names, declaring us national record holders.

One of the parents ushered us into a room for photos; as we made our way there, random officials slapped our backs and people cheered and clapped from the bleachers. *Geez*, I thought, *this isn't bad, this record-breaking thing.* I felt love-drunk. Everyone seemed so pleased with us. But when we wandered over to see Mr. Bergen, hoping for some encouraging words, he only said, "Rhodenbaugh, you need to hit the wall harder next time."

We glanced at each other, confused. *Wait. That's it? No other comment?*

He walked away and I followed him. "Did you think we did a good job?" I felt like a fruit fly, buzzing around him too close.

"You did fine, Peters," he said. "Stop worrying."

From left to right: Kristie Rhodenbaugh, Sue Flerlage,
Deena Deardurff, Kim Peters. Photo © Swimming World Magazine.

THAT NIGHT IN THE MOTORHOME, SOME of us gathered to tell jokes and sing along with songs from *The Sound of Music* on Dad's 8-track tape player. Dad was so delighted to have us there that after the last of my teammates left, he got a little carried away with the praise.

"You girls really clobbered that record. You're going to do something big with the swimming, Butch."

I turned away from Dad and stretched my mouth wide open for a few seconds.

He stared at me a moment. "Are you still doing that?"

"What?"

"Stretching your mouth. What's going on with you?"

"I don't know." I *did* know, though. It had something to do with the pressure, since I found myself doing it mostly around Dad.

"You'd better stop or your mouth will be too big for your face," he said.

I didn't react outwardly, but the thought that he might be right only made me more anxious. Whenever Dad tried to encourage me, my first reaction was to explain what he didn't understand about swimming. I told him that Sue, Kristie, and I had been riding along on Deena's wake, that without *her*, there would've been no national record. I wasn't afraid of succeeding. I just thought my father was unrealistic about my ability and I didn't want to disappoint him.

Dad thrust his head five inches from my face. "Are you saying it was a fluke? Were Alice's world records a fluke?" Alice Jones, one of our best senior swimmers, had won the 100 and 200 butterfly at US Nationals the previous summer, setting world records in both.

"Alice has nothing to do with our relay."

"Or that it was only Deena who broke that relay record?" He let out a deep, exhaustive sigh.

"Yes!"

"That's baloney. You contributed. Every one of you contributed. Don't pretend you didn't have something to do with that damn record." He stepped into his captain's chair, his plate in his lap. "You swam your ass off and it showed." He frowned and his eyes blazed as Mom handed him a fork. "We're not quitters in this family," he said. "Quitting is a habit. You continue to swim your ass off and we'll see what happens."

But I didn't *want* to swim my ass off. Now in seventh grade, I enjoyed school. My art teacher, Dorothy Dobbins, had given me so much praise about one contour drawing that I believed I had a future as an artist. But swimming was important to Dad. He told me once that he had been forced to play the piano as a kid. I'd been told he had perfect pitch, that he was a child prodigy. But he never played for us, not even once. My complaints about swimming must have reminded him of the way he quit playing the piano—his inability as a child to follow through in an area where he was truly talented. It seemed Dad was determined not to let the same thing happen to me.

I didn't want the hard work and intensity of swimming, but every time the issue of quitting came up, the endless discussion fatigued me.

WHEN I LOOK NOW AT OUR PICTURE in *Swimming World* magazine, what strikes me most is how little we were. The four of us—Deena, Sue, Kristie, and I— wearing our matching bathing suits, were lined up like cadets, equidistant from each other, with our backs against the wall, our wet hair combed. We stood there with our hands tucked behind our backs, following the rules, doing what we were told.

By the time the magazine had been printed, I was already wondering if it had been worth the hard work.

For one thing, Mom and Dad had been telling us we had to pull together as a family to offset the high cost of repairs to the bus. Giving up swimming, which we were told was expensive, seemed a natural way for me to help. "Wouldn't you and Mom be better off if we go back to being 'normal' kids?" I knew Dad would have some reaction to my bringing up the money.

"You aren't normal. None of you kids is normal." He smiled as he winked at Mom from his captain's chair. "Swimming is what you personally can do for the family," he said. "Kiss me."

I cringed a little as I leaned over so he could kiss me. Then, with his plate in his lap, he twirled the spaghetti on the end of his fork and eased the fork into his mouth.

"You just need to stop worrying," he said.

But I *couldn't* stop worrying. Mom was the one with the handle on the financial situation and by then, I could hear her voice in my head: "Dick, we have to cut back on our expenses."

I made one last half-hearted effort to point out to Dad the financial cost of swimming to our family. "So you're still going to pay for swimming even though we can't afford it?" I waited for him to say something as the seconds ticked by.

He stood up for more spaghetti, his lips tight, an arm wrapped loosely around Mom's shoulder. "Nice dinner, Beej," he said.

CHAPTER 15

Behind the bleachers at the natatorium, a narrow bench sat against the wall, and often I would hunker down on it to wait for Alice after practice. One day, Mike Grimmer, the guy who'd been making out with Val in the backseat of Ned's car, sat down beside me.

Two years older than I was—fifteen to my thirteen—Mike had the physical features I equate now with high testosterone. Think Clint Eastwood meets Jim Carrey, with a strong, defined jawline, wide shoulders, an oversize Adam's apple, and deep voice. He was known for his dirty jokes, which I rarely understood.

"Alice will probably be a while," he said, his eyes glinting. It was too hot to wait in Alice's Galaxy 500, and she'd been up in Mr. Bergen's air-conditioned office for at least an hour. Mr. Bergen was spending more and more time with her before and after practice while MaryAnn, Heidi, and I waited for her to drive us home.

I leaned back against the wall and threw my legs out in front of me. "What's taking her so long?" I glanced at Mike, hoping for insight.

He bent toward me, a little too close. "Maybe they're conducting business."

I was certain he was making a joke, but at thirteen the word "business" took me back to Anne Boyle. "What are you saying?"

"Nothing," he said with a funny grin. He placed his hand on my leg, leaned way over, and kissed me on the lips.

"Whoa." I angled back and saw double. "You shouldn't do that." I inched away.

"Why not?"

I glanced into the dark space behind the full span of the bleachers. "You just shouldn't. Somebody will see us."

"There's nobody here." He bent over and kissed me again, and this time I moved close enough to wrap my arms around him. I knew instantly that my five minutes in the car with Ned the previous month were what had piqued Mike's interest, but I didn't care. I loved that he was kissing me, unclouded by alcohol. And this time, nobody would know.

MIKE MUST'VE CALLED EVERY NIGHT that week. Mom and Dad were home, and Dad enthusiastically suggested I invite Mike to the house, which I did. The night I introduced him, Dad was helping Mom by sipping her drink and tasting the meatloaf. I'd hoped to make the meeting brief, but Dad acted as if he were conducting a job interview.

"What's the story with your father's arm?" Dad looked genuinely concerned.

"He worked at a meat-packing plant and lost it in a slicing machine," Mike said.

"Oh, me." Dad patted his huge midsection as he shook his head in amazement. "How does he deal with, you know, not having a hand?"

I cringed. There was no stopping Dad on a fact-finding mission.

"You don't have to answer," Mom said. "Sometimes he can't help himself."

Dad held up the bottle of bourbon and tipped his head to Mike. "Drinking is a lot better in the privacy of your own home than out on the road where you can hurt someone. Would you like some?"

To my great relief, Mike's eyes narrowed, revealing his bewilderment. "I don't think my parents would appreciate that—or Bergen, for that matter." Clearly, Dad was trying to shock Mike the way he often did with us.

"What do you think about those hippies at Kent State?" For weeks Dad had been glued to the television. The University of Cincinnati had closed down due to an anti–Vietnam War march all the way to Fountain Square. Being a staunch Republican, Dad had thought the kids had acted unruly.

Mike glanced at me uneasily. "Well, four students were killed."

"Do you think they should have the right to throw hand grenades at police officers?"

Mike, with erect posture, towered over Dad, but he drew back, making himself smaller. "They didn't have hand grenades, did they?"

"Oh, Mike, don't even get started," I said.

Years later, in conversation with Pam about our father's often misguided ideas about race, religion, and politics, I asked if she thought Dad was also homophobic. She said, "He's alottaphobic."

In my awkward way, I explained this to Mike as I led him away from the kitchen.

"I'm sorry, Mr. Peters," he called over his shoulder, "can we talk about Kent State another time?"

From the other room, I heard Mom scolding Dad—"Dick, he's here to see Kim. He didn't come over to talk politics."

We ate dinner together, and eventually my parents made their way upstairs, at which point Mike and I wedged ourselves onto the threadbare sofa, where we discussed—of course—Mr. Bergen.

"Have you noticed, when he meets girls in his office, he has the doors shut?" Mike said. "What does that tell you?"

I shrugged. Alice often drove home with tears in her eyes after talking to Mr. Bergen. It didn't seem like private meetings with him could be much fun. Some of the guys had been cracking jokes lately, calling attention to the perspiration on Mr. Bergen's lips or leaping around the pool deck, their arms dangling ape-like, and calling the girls "ogres" or "trolls." I was sure they were jealous of the time Mr. Bergen spent with the best girls on the team.

Mike reached his arm over my shoulder and I devoured the sweet mix of Head & Shoulders shampoo and chlorine as I kissed every inch of his mouth until my lips were raw. "Mmm . . . oh. Mmm . . . oh," he kept saying as he pawed me. It was as if the two of us were swimming eight hundreds on the ten-minute cycle. Overheating. Heavy breathing.

I was outside my body, watching myself hit the wall, until I heard creaking at the top of the stairs and instantly returned to my body, my brain swimming on high alert. "Dad? Are you there?" I sputtered.

Nobody answered, but the creaking continued.

I sprang up. "Mike, he's around the corner. I can hear him."

Perspiration blistered across Mike's face. "I should go."

"No. Don't go. Stay, please?"

He was playing with my hair when I heard another floorboard snap.

"Kimmy, Mike needs to go home," Dad called from upstairs.

I rearranged my training bra and buttoned up my shirt faster than a flip-turn. "Okay, Dad, he's leaving." We continued with our workout. I lay there on the living room sofa, fully clothed, my arms and legs tangled up around Mike, my brain floating off to the second floor, where I imagined Dad standing with his ear pointed in our direction.

My brain was with Mike, then Dad, then Mike, then Dad.

Mike gave me one last kiss. "Good night."

Dad greeted me outside my room, naked except for his white Jockey underwear. "Did you have a nice time?"

"Yes, Dad," I grumbled, shutting the door between us. Case closed for the night. No more F.B.I. cross-examination.

MIKE WAS A DREADFUL TEASE—the type who, had he lived fifty years earlier, would've been dipping my braid in an inkwell. And yet having him as a boyfriend made me feel less alone. He made me feel attractive and feminine in the midst of relentless teasing from the guys about our strength and masculinity. And—I don't know why, maybe because he was my legitimate boyfriend—I wasn't afraid of other swimmers finding out about us.

I could talk to Mike about my love–hate relationship with Mr. Bergen and he seemed to understand. But I didn't tell him how much I missed my parents when they were gone, and I don't know if he even realized my siblings and I were left on our own for a week or two every month.

During our "dates"—on the weekends we didn't have a meet—Mike would tell me what he'd heard in the guys' locker room about girls who were considered "ogres." I appreciated that there appeared to be an unspoken rule that girlfriends were off-limits when it came to this brand of teasing. I'd tell him who on the team were the nice guys and who were the jerks. And sometime during his visit, we'd curl up on the sofa, he'd look me in the eye, and he'd tell me he loved me.

"I love you too," I'd say, and together we'd gradually drift off to sleep.

With Mike, I felt protected in a weird way from Mr. Bergen. Mike was twice his size, with enough strength to hurl him over his shoulder if he needed to. He could think on his feet and had a talent for throwing others off guard with his sarcasm. Maybe that's why Mr. Bergen left him alone.

ONE COOL WINTER EVENING, WITH MY PARENTS out at a dinner-dance they called the Mad Hatters, I had a tedious phone conversation with Mike about who would be going to Pullman Nationals. I didn't see how I could possibly go. I hadn't swum fast enough in any of my individual events and I wasn't in the top four to make a relay either.

I hung up the phone after a couple of I-love-yous and returned to my bed in sheer fatigue, thinking of Pullman Nationals and Mike in that quiet space of drifting sleep. It must've been after midnight—the lights out, the house still—when I heard heavy foot-steps, then my door clicking open, and noticed the bilious smell of liquor. Dad's odor, a combination of stale cigarette smoke, alcohol, and Old Spice, was so rank it could curdle milk. I rolled sideways, wondering if he would make me kiss him.

Instead, he yanked back the covers. I was wearing one of the baby doll nightgowns with a scoop neck Mom had bought me that was two sizes too big so I could wear it forever. Dad grabbed me by one arm, hauled me into a standing position, flung my left arm over his shoulder, and pressed my face into his sour-smelling neck. Then he grabbed my right hand in his left, wrapped his other hand around my waist, and swept me toward the hallway, singing "Unforgettable" like Nat King Cole.

I whined and called to Mom to get him off me but there was no sign of her. In a muddled stutter, Dad said something about how I had to loosen up, that I was as stiff as his last drink. In that instant, Mom's head popped up through the balusters of the stairway.

"Dick, go to bed. Haven't you had enough fun for one evening?"

He thrust me into the wall, banging my head. "Mom, tell him to stop," I wailed. He let go of me and staggered toward their bedroom, shaking his head. I wanted to push him down the stairs, but he was two hundred thirty pounds or more.

I whirled around to face Mom. "Why don't you ever stop him? You're never around!"

Mom's sigh told me everything. "Your father loves you, Kimmy. He was only trying to have some fun."

"You call that *fun*?" I kicked the door closed with my foot, louder than I intended. "It's not fun for me!" I climbed back into bed, my anger leaking tears.

I WAS SICK OF DAD'S BIZARRE VALUE SYSTEM and irrational belief that he could get away with his outrageous behavior because he was somehow of a higher social standing than everybody else. Dad wasn't fooling anyone. The motorhome in the driveway, the house needing attention, all of his bluster . . . I was sick of it.

But within a short time, I was back to making excuses for Dad. He could be entertaining with my friends, often funny, lighthearted, and engaging. For some reason—perhaps the aloneness of swimming—I missed our conversations when he and Mom traveled. And despite the unprecedented horridness of his grabbing me that night after their dinner dance, I still found myself wanting to catch up in between their trips.

We had developed a routine. I would walk in the door at night after swimming and Dad would ask, "How was practice, Butch?"

He'd crowd me and I'd push him away with a straight arm. "You're in my zone, Dad."

He'd make some wisecrack about my having "the biggest damn zone" he'd ever seen, and I'd groan, and then he'd launch into a question about the front-page news, which would evolve into a debate such as whether or not Nixon was a crook. Mom didn't care for this kind of chatter and would stand at the stove, stirring whatever she was making for dinner. There were no chairs in the kitchen, so I would sit on the linoleum floor and lean against one of the cabinets while Jacquie, Pam, Ricky, and David hid in the various nooks and crannies of the house or, in the summer, up at the Observatory somewhere. I wanted to be adaptable and had trouble being direct enough to gracefully end these discussions. And Dad had trouble restraining himself.

One time he and I were in the middle of a deep disagreement about whether or not eighteen-year-olds should vote when Mom said she thought she might've added too many beans to the chili.

"You got a problem with beans?" Dad leaned over her shoulder.

A few minutes later she said, "Maybe it's the vegetables. The chili is too thick."

"What's wrong with thick chili?" Dad asked. "You got a problem with thick chili?"

The conversation rambled on like this, back and forth, as if Dad were trying to start an argument. The more he drank, the more the conversation dwindled.

Finally, I said, "Dad, she's thinking out loud. Why do you have to comment on every single thing she says?"

"It's foreplay," he said, "Catholic foreplay." He looked as if he were about to pinch Mom, which ended the exchange.

Finally a teenager, I could see that our kitchen had become Dad's favorite bar. Mom and I were the guys on the barstool alongside him, with Mom tossing in a comment every so often to keep the conversations going. I needed a place to vent about swimming and felt special that Dad would draw me into debate where I could express my feelings. And the conversations could be amusing. After Dad slugged down several glasses of rum and Tab, however, the arguments would become endless loops that went nowhere and sometimes continued through dinner, with Mom's adding her two cents at the end, hoping to provide a practical spin to wrap up the running commentary.

And no matter how contentious the conversation, it always ended with Dad's asking for a kiss.

ONE NIGHT, CUDDLING ON THE COUCH with Mike, I decided to tell him about the terrible night when Dad yanked me out of bed. I grappled with the words at first. Then I said, "Something happened with Dad a few weeks ago. It made me so angry. I don't know if I should tell you."

"What?" he said, smoothing a clump of hair around my eye. "Of course you can tell me."

I set up the scene. Told him I was half awake, half asleep, and my arm was being jerked out of its socket. I told him I was only wearing my nightgown, that it was too big and "Well, he saw everything."

I wanted to hear, "Oh my God, that's outrageous."

But as Mike listened to every word, a sly smile came over his face. "Your Dad is funny. I like him," he said, which stung. Mike had seen my father only during the cocktail hour.

"You think he's funny when I tell you he dragged me out of bed at two in the morning?" I snapped. "I'll tell you more about 'funny' if it happens again."

That was the emotional end of my relationship with Mike. Something in me had shifted with his reaction. Who could I talk to? Not my parents. Not my coach. Not Jacquie or my other younger siblings. Now I was questioning even Mike. Mr. Bergen had been telling me that if I wanted to make Nationals, I needed to be more aggressive. Ironically, I realized that swimming was giving me the power to stand up to Dad.

I was determined that what had happened the night of the Mad Hatters would never happen again. Ever. Next time, I would hurt him.

CHAPTER 16

The guys wore suit jackets and ties. We girls wore white blouses and blue skirts with belts in red, white, and blue stripes. There were no parents going—many couldn't afford the cost of plane travel—but Darryl was there, wearing a red, white, and blue dress shirt, his chin up as he smiled and reassured parents that he would take care of us.

By all accounts, we looked terrific, and enough alike with our chlorine-bleached hair, lean muscles, and trim appearance that, in my opinion, our clothing didn't need to match. Other travelers on their way through the airport tried to guess who we were and what we were doing there; we were a good-looking bunch—smart, polite, with caring parents—off to light up the swimming world.

I hadn't imagined swimming at the Pullman Nationals, and I didn't feel ready. I'd been zoning out during our nightly talks before practice, staring at the concrete wall, assuming Mr. Bergen's lectures about Nationals didn't apply to me. But when he called my name in the list of swimmers, I snapped to attention. *There will be two 400 freestyle relays? And that is the event I will be swimming? How did that happen?*

From left to right: A Relay: Heidi Lipe, Alice Jones, Jenny Kemp,
Deena Deardurff, and B Relay: Mary Keating, Kim Peters,
Beth Keating, MaryAnn Stevens. Photo by Rob Paris.

He said he wanted to give some of us the experience of national competition. In the locker room I heard whispers about Mr. Keating's twisting Mr. Bergen's arm, since two of the twenty-three swimmers on the extra relay were Mr. Keating's daughters. But so what? I didn't care how I ended up on the roster. I wanted to go.

To raise money for the trip, Mr. Bergen had insisted we run around our neighborhoods, asking people to pledge for the Marlin Swim-a-thon. It seemed a worthy cause, but asking for money made me feel like a clone of my father. Most of my neighbors had no idea how far I could swim. I gave them the example of pledging a modest amount per lap for a total of five dollars—but when I returned to collect, I explained that I'd managed to swim ten times farther so they owed me fifty. One woman took forever to answer the door. She looked over toward her neighbor and said, "Don't you live in that big house with the motorhome in the driveway?" She slammed the door on me as if I were carrying a Bible.

But seeing our group and knowing we were in this together somehow lessened the guilt.

AT THIRTEEN, THIS WOULD BE MY FIRST plane ride. I was so pumped I couldn't stop thinking about it. We flew to Denver, and from there, connected on a bumpy flight to Spokane. I sat near the window, hugging my stomach, as our bags jostled in the overhead shelf in the middle of a lightning storm.

Never in my life had I drowned in such an aromatic perfume of pine, fir, and hemlock as when we exited the Spokane airport and boarded our bus to Pullman. The contrast to the smoggy air of Cincinnati was so powerful, I felt light-headed.

We checked into our dorm at Washington State, a low brick building surrounded by evergreens, and instantly, word got around that Mr. Bergen was furious and wanted to see us in the main lounge.

We congregated in the dark curtained lobby, where he stood picking at his nails, not saying a word, as he waited for complete silence. Then he lapsed into full tyrant mode, the air around him popping with tension. "This is Nationals," he growled, his eyes focused down. "And not one of you thought to cut your hair. Apparently, you don't understand the importance of this meet."

It was clear he was mad at someone. We just didn't know who. I watched his every move as he went on his berserk tear.

"You need to finish hard at the wall; you need to streamline off your turns . . . This is the biggest, most important meet of the year and some of you have the potential to go to the Pan Am Games. I want to see you start caring about that."

I'm sure the rant wasn't about hair. Mike, having asked to be my so-called "friend" and no longer my boyfriend, told me Mr. Bergen had caught some of the older girls hiding candy on the plane. I glanced at Nancy, my roommate, seated on the floor a few feet away; one of the lucky ones, her wavy, dark hair was short enough that Mr. Bergen wouldn't yell at her. Still, she was hardly breathing.

We huddled in our warm-up jackets, sad sacks, letting the criticism float through the college dorm's stale air. The trouble was we weren't acting like a team. The trouble was we weren't focused. The trouble was we weren't taking swimming seriously. The trouble, the trouble, the trouble. Wondering why Mr. Bergen was still in clampdown mode, I zoned out on automatic, my brain drifting farther away with each new attack. It was as if my restless internal voice had slowly dissolved, his voice had receded, and I was filling up with gratification that the hard work of swimming was already paying off. I was two thousand mind-blowing miles away from home, at the US Nationals. The excitement I felt was so palpable, I hardly registered Mr. Bergen's outrage.

"At night you will shave for the following day's events," he said—and I snapped to attention.

The guys didn't register confusion, I assume because they thought he meant their faces. I didn't flinch either. *Shave our legs? What's the big deal?* I shaved my legs regularly by then, at least from the knee down.

"That means the works," Mr. Bergen said. "Even you, Alsfelder." He stabbed the air with his pointer finger.

Bob Alsfelder, one of the oldest on the team, was also one of the hairiest. His smile seemed to reflect admiration, not outrage. "You want us to shave our *legs*?"

"Yes." Mr. Bergen glared.

"Our arms?"

Whimpers of mirth spread through the group as we examined our forearms. *Will the hair grow back thick and coarse like a man's beard?* I wondered. There were a few awkward smirks. When Mr. Bergen looked at me, I averted my eyes.

"This isn't a joke. I want you to shave your arms, legs, backs—everything."

"Not *everything*," one of the girls whispered.

"Everything we can see except your heads. You girls don't need to shave your faces—or necks, either—but if you look closely, you'll see you have hair on your upper arms and back. So, shave them."

THE FIRST DAY OF THE MEET ARRIVED, with hordes of buoyant spectators and a sizable cast of Olympians—Mark Spitz, Gary Hall, and Debbie Meyer, to name just a few—all warming up for their events in front of me. Since I was dressed in street clothes and swimming only on the last day, I sat on the edge of the bleachers with the team. As the cool smell of menthol wafted through the damp air, I tied and retied my pigtails, torn to pieces by the rubber bands and chlorine. I felt like a seat-filler at the Oscars.

Bill Schulte, one of the biggest guys on the team, emerged from the Men's Room with tiny pieces of bloody toilet paper stuck to the cuts on his chest. We girls were used to shaving our legs and underarms and didn't have any trouble, but the guys who followed Bill from the Men's Room, one at a time, all wore the tiny toilet paper swabs as well. Mr. Bergen glowered; his jaw clenched.

Deena and Alice were about to battle it out in the 100 butterfly finals on the first day. Alice was one of the most muscular women on the team. With her broad shoulders and powerful kick, she'd set two world records the previous summer and seemed the natural favorite. But Deena had been beating Alice in practice. Almost six years younger, Deena was shorter—five foot three and only 116 pounds—but she was just as strong, maybe even stronger, and had a faster turnover.

The announcer called the event. Deena and Alice stood behind their lanes, shaking out their arms and legs, not looking at each other. There was a hush over the crowd as the announcer called the swimmers to the blocks. In those days, swimmers started at the edge of the block, their toes tucked. They listened for the start—"Swimmers take your marks"—and . . . Swish! Alice and Deena exploded off the blocks.

I felt a tingling, as if I were there in the water, a current of cortisol shooting through me. The two soared down their lanes, Deena's undulating strokes higher on the surface, Alice power-stroking close by her. The race was neck and neck. As the two battled, the crowd went nuts, standing up, shouting and whistling. The natatorium vibrated with cheers. At the last turn, Deena had a slight lead. She took an extra kick into the wall, and the whole crowd turned toward the digital clock, erupting in applause. She'd touched out Alice by six tenths of a second. A new American record, and an awkward moment for the team: the nineteen-year-old world record holder, beaten by a girl who was only thirteen.

Deena and Alice hoisted themselves out of the pool, and both were crying. Deena, I assumed, wept tears of joy; Alice, disappointment. We shouted a collective "Way to go, Marlins!" and the two wandered over to where Mr. Bergen stood with his clipboard. He put a congratulatory arm around Deena's shoulder first, made some brief comment, then walked away to comfort Alice.

As I look back, much of my swimming under Paul Bergen was similar to dealing with my father. We swimmers had come to the Marlins with our own unique histories—living in different neighborhoods, attending different schools, with varied family situations—and Mr. Bergen had become our fill-in parent, providing direction, imposing rules and consequences, and projecting a sense of order. To the outside world, we looked amazing. Inside, we were doing our best to please him, and yet there was always someone crying, someone in trouble, and the rest of us whispering about what on earth could be getting him this time.

THE MARLIN TEAM HAD A SPOT IN the bleachers adjacent to the Indiana University guys and I couldn't keep my eyes off Mark Spitz, who was a familiar face on TV after having starred in the 1968 Mexico City Olympics. He was swarthy and handsome, with an easy walk, and it seemed all the girls wanted to sit by him. Some of the girls on our team gossiped that MaryAnn had a crush on him. She arrived for the finals wearing her curly blond hair down and full, and Spitz called her "the girl with electric hair," which worked Mr. Bergen into a lather.

As I sat in the bleachers, waiting for the meet to begin, I whispered questions to Mary Keating about why Mr. Bergen seemed so angry. She told me she'd heard that his father had not been much of a part of his life. For me, this explained a lot. Mr. Bergen was short, an introvert, marinating in abandonment from his father and, perhaps, resentment toward his mother. I could identify with not having a parent around. I put my own imagined pieces of his backstory together in my head so I could feel sorry for him. And when he lectured us about paying too much attention to the Indiana swimmers, I chalked it up as his feeling it was a threat to him personally; maybe, like me, he wanted more attention.

MARY, BETH, MARYANN, AND I FINISHED last in our heat and second to last in the entire event. I have a vague memory of receiving the cold shoulder from Mr. Bergen, but it didn't matter. I had spent so much of the meet soaking in the drama and paying attention to the superstars that when I buckled into my seat on the plane—engines rumbling, teammates dozing, watching an immense landscape collage through my tiny window—all I could do was smile. In a short two years, Mr. Bergen had lifted me from mediocre swimmer to National competitor. I was slipping into my bathing suit as into a second skin, watching from the bleachers opposite Olympians, and it felt terrific. The lights—not ordinary houselights but the Hollywood kind, the bright, focused search lights, so stunning they make you sweat—had been blinding.

Maybe it was the realization that we were connected. All these swimmers, working to utter exhaustion for months and then shaving down, psyching up, preparing to compete at the national level. What connected us was the isolation from our families, the reliance on our coaches, the daily exhaustion and painful work that had gotten us there. And maybe an intimacy not of words, but of the body. Where you swim sandwiched five seconds behind your teammates in a lane and you rarely touch each other (and when you *do* touch, you apologize). You share the same water, the same kickboards, the same pull buoys and paddles. You push off the same spot on the wall. Skin your knuckles on the same lane lines. You are guided by the same schedule. Inspired by the same teammates. Harassed by the same coach. You know each other and you don't.

As I soaked in the euphoria, I considered my parents. How proud they must be of me—especially my father. I had been so damned sure that swimming was not my thing, not what I wanted to do with my childhood, and now—overnight, it seemed—I couldn't wait to get home to our house on Observatory, lean against a kitchen cabinet with a handful of Ritz crackers, and wait for Dad to say, "How did you do, Butch?"

I was ready to tell him, "You were right, Dad. You were right when you told me I should swim my ass off and it would eventually pay off." For years, I'd wasted no opportunity to let Dad know that I didn't really like swimming, that I was just doing it for him. But on that airplane, a new feeling took hold. I saw the good in swimming— the connection, and the future it promised—and for maybe the first time, I was genuinely enthusiastic to see where it would take me.

CHAPTER 17

Despite my elation following the trip to Pullman, returning to our swimming regimen played havoc with my health. Still restricting my calories, I shivered constantly, my skin sloughed off from dryness, I had low or no energy, and I was constantly irritable. I figured it was mostly psychological—that I must be depressed—but it was also physical. When you're in the water or lifting weights five or six hours a day, and spend another two hours on the road getting to and from two practices, that's a full eight-hour day. Then you add school—what, another six hours—and an hour for studying hard enough to get A's and B's, and that leaves nine hours for sleep, eating, and everything else. Every day I was climbing a steep cliff, overlooking a dizzying landscape, trying not to look down.

Mom noticed my health deteriorating. "I'm concerned about how much you sleep," she said one night as I headed to bed. "It's just not normal."

Later, from my room, I heard Dad say, "You need to find out what the hell is wrong with her."

And maybe I *did* have something wrong with me. No matter how much I slept, I could rarely get enough, while other swimmers on the team seemed to function just fine.

At Dad's urging, Mom trotted me off to Dr. Wiseman, her gynecologist, who happened to be the father of Wendy, a childhood friend. Dr. Wiseman had ridden on the bus with us on field trips in elementary school. His wife, the office secretary and nurse, had been my Brownie leader. They were both caring professionals, but being asked at thirteen to take off my clothes and then spread my legs in front of them, I felt like an oversize, undressed Thanksgiving turkey. My mother was relieved to hear from Doctor Wiseman that my hymen was still intact—that, contrary to her fears, I hadn't slept with Grimmer after all. But she didn't have to pay for the doctor's appointment. She could've asked.

The positive thing was that within a few weeks, Dr. Wiseman diagnosed my condition as hypothyroidism, which was not a dire condition. The downside: I would have to take medication for the rest of my life. Proloid, a drug developed from hog thyroid, became my Vitamin P, and almost instantly I felt better. I had fewer muscle aches, the cold water became tolerable, and I seemed to have more energy. After several weeks, I lifted more weight, finished sit-ups and push-ups faster, and noticed greater power off my flip-turns. I recovered more quickly from hard workouts. And some days I even moved up in the distance lane so I wasn't dead last.

The downside was that I didn't sleep as soundly, and when I came home in the evening Jacquie would calmly say, "Hi," and I would jump out of my skin. But hyper was better than lethargic (or should I say anxiety was better than depression?). I continued to improve in swimming, and with the added energy, I gained confidence and even began to look forward to practice. It gave me a way to get out of watching the younger kids when my parents traveled.

BUT AS I GREW MORE INVOLVED IN swimming, the rest of the family began to find other interests. Mr. Bergen had introduced water polo as a way of breaking up the monotony of the long winter season. In 1970, there were no high schools or colleges and very few

Coach Bergen with women's water polo team,
c. 1970. Photo by Peter Dernier.

private clubs playing women's water polo, but we were playing it from September to November.

I don't mean to imply that water polo was meant to be fun. Mr. Bergen approached the sport with the same intensity as swimming—hurling water polo balls instead of kickboards when he was angry, and shouting when some of us missed a shot or lost the ball.

One day he announced his new plan to hold water polo scrimmages with both girls and guys playing together. I don't know why—maybe it was my father's behavior that had influenced me—but I imagined some of the more aggressive guys grabbing us inappropriately underwater. That never happened. Instead, it was athletically brutal. Guys who were over six feet tall and forty pounds heavier than most of us were kicking and shoving us, even giving us black eyes.

Being such an extrovert, Jacquie took to water polo right away; she preferred the camaraderie of the team sport and had begun to excel more in water polo than in swimming.

One night when our parents were away, I arrived home from practice to a locked door and my siblings conspiring in a circle in the living room. At first, I suspected they were planning to run away; we had talked about it so many times. But after listening to Jacquie, they were poised for my input. It seemed they didn't want to attend church and were waiting for my reaction.

My eyes lit up. "That's easy. Let's not go."

"You mean it?" Jacquie began arranging the throw pillows, unconsciously straightening the living room as if she were Mom. "Mom and Dad don't have to know, right?"

"Of course not." Even though I appreciated some of the rituals, there was a lot of church that reminded me of swimming: stand up, sit down, kneel, stand up, sit down, kneel. If I could, I would've skipped church every week. There were too many rules and too many inconsistencies, and I had too many questions about what it all meant. To me, accepting the church dogma was like letting a bat in through the chimney. It hides behind a picture on the wall or hangs from the ceiling in some obscure location, so you ignore it—try to forget it's there—but you can't. You live in fear that one day that bat will swoop down and suck the blood out of you.

I HAD NO PROBLEM PRETENDING SUNDAY was Saturday. Eggo waffles bounced out of the toaster. Bacon sizzled in the pan. David carefully carried the milk to the table as I sang "Hosanna" from *Jesus Christ Superstar* as a joke. Pam delighted in seeing me slaphappy. Even Jacquie was high-spirited as she forked the bacon onto a paper towel.

I was about to compliment her on her idea to skip church when Ricky—trying to be helpful—reached for the blistering handle of the cast iron skillet and the pan dropped to the floor with a loud plunk. Bacon and scalding grease splattered onto his chubby legs. His face froze in shock, then he shrieked and pranced around the pan, shaking his hand, his face flushed crimson to match his plaid pajamas.

I grabbed his hand and thrust it under cold water, but he only screamed louder.

"What are you doing?" Jacquie hollered. We clustered around Ricky, trying to console him, but when Jacquie used a towel to lift the pan off the floor, we gasped at the seared black twelve-inch diameter ring in the middle of the linoleum, nearly a complete circle.

We scrubbed and scrubbed—with Comet, SOS, and Palmolive Liquid—but no amount of scraping would erase the stain. It was as if the hand of God had swooped down and slapped us for missing church.

Jacquie tossed the sponge into the sink, staring with a terrible, blank face. "We're in big trouble."

"No!" Pam said, already problem-solving. "Ricky's in trouble." She scratched the spot with her fingernail.

I handed Ricky some butter to rub into his burn as he cried.

"Thanks a lot, Ricky," David said, his lip curling. Ricky didn't react, so David got up in his face. "We're going to get paddled."

Ricky shoved him with his shoulder. There was something about David's voice that grated on Ricky under pressure. "Shut up," Ricky snarled.

David backed away. "No, you shut up." He glanced up at Jacquie, who placed a firm hand on David's back.

"Hush. All of you," she said. "We'll explain it was an accident."

RICKY'S INJURY CLEARED UP IN A DAY or so, and Jacquie was right: Mom and Dad didn't ask about church or if Ricky got hurt. The seared linoleum was another story. As soon as Dad set foot in the kitchen, he roared, "Kimmy, Jacquie, Pammy, Ricky, David, get down here! What in the hell happened to the floor?"

"Well, hello, how was your trip?" I said, trying to be funny.

Dad pointed. "You mind telling me what happened?" He reached into his pocket and pulled out a worn handkerchief to wipe his nose.

"I dropped it," Ricky said, his cheeks red.

"Well, that's a bitch. Why didn't you use a potholder?"

"I don't know."

"You don't *know*? You kids weren't working together." Dad sniffed for a moment, then stuffed his handkerchief back in his pocket. "Why does this house smell like the goddamn kitty litter?" He faced the three of us girls as he slammed a stack of orders and catalogs on the counter. "Dammit. We go away for two weeks and come home to a stinking house and a linoleum floor all burned up. Why can't you behave as you would when we're home?"

I hadn't cared for the hideous linoleum anyway, which was worn to the color and texture of masonry blocks. I viewed the stain as similar to graffiti on a nondescript building: it had finally given our floor some character. But Dad couldn't stand it. The mark had exposed his insecurity like an empty wallet.

I guess I should've felt bad about damaging the floor, but I didn't. I felt good in those days—independent, cheery, strong. Maybe it was the thyroid medication, or maybe it was the decision I'd come to on the flight back from Nationals. I was in a good place with swimming, and nothing else really mattered. Once in the water, my lungs expanded, my blood surged, my body produced endorphins.

Swimming had become an escape, an act of jumping the fence. Instantly the problems at home lessened, and the problems at the pool became Alice's or Deena's or somebody else's. The mental gymnastics were an effort, but I was working on a new plan of action, which was simple: Find a way to make the mental shift automatic. Learn to hop the fence in my head so I would feel stronger and better able to stand up for myself in the moment.

A MONTH PASSED, MOM AND DAD were gone again, and this time we kids were sleeping late, skipping church, and eating brownies like it was a regular part of our routine. One Saturday afternoon, while we were gathered in front of the TV, Jacquie's eyes flickered. "How about if we fix the linoleum? It's so ugly."

I tossed a throw pillow in the air. "The floor was ugly to begin with."

"Oh, come on, Kim. We can use one of the blank checks to buy flooring."

I leaned back in my armchair. "Jacquie, we don't have the skill to lay linoleum." This drove me nuts about Jacquie. She was constantly trying to do projects as a coping strategy to win Mom and Dad's approval. I popped another brownie in my mouth.

"It can't be that hard," she said with Mom's cadence and confidence in her tone.

"Don't . . . even . . . think about it," I grumbled. We couldn't even make sandwiches without slathering jelly all over the counter.

She held her index finger to her pursed lips, and I could tell her brain was doing cartwheels. Mom had left us two blank checks, and we only needed one for groceries. "Come on. They'll be happy."

"How will we get the linoleum up here?" Pam was turning into the practical one, wondering if she could ride her bike up the steep hill loaded with flooring.

"Come on, Kim," Jacquie said, her voice softening. "We have baskets on our bikes. If the flooring is too heavy, we can walk."

"Count me out." Mr. Bergen had offered to some of us—those of us whose parents couldn't afford money for trips—the opportunity to clean the pool on Sundays as a way of paying our way to winter Nationals in Dallas. This was my excuse for not helping.

But I had an ulterior motive.

Tom Olson, one of the most well-built and handsome guys on the Marlins, had recently placed his hand on my thigh. Known as "Quicksilver" for his silver front tooth, as well as his speed and the popular character in Marvel Comics, he wore thick glasses—could hardly see without them—and was as tall, muscular, and broad as a genuine superhero. Word had gotten around that Grimmer and Nonny, a younger teammate, were now an "item," but with Tom on my mind, the news flash had hardly registered on my radar. Cleaning the pool with Tom sounded more interesting than laying linoleum. I was no longer willing to do things to impress Mom and Dad. By now my main "project" was a fifty-meter swimming pool on the west side of Cincinnati.

"You're just like Dad," Jacquie hissed. "You always have something to do when there's work around here."

"Fine, maybe I *don't* do as much, but this isn't real work," I said. "It's invented."

Redoing the floor wasn't that outlandish compared to some of Mom and Dad's ideas—for instance, covering the kitchen wall with brick-style contact paper or the foyer with fake slate. We had learned to speak to creditors and bank managers, buy groceries on credit, and treat most medical emergencies. We could bake anything from scratch, snake out a drain, and wash and starch Dad's shirts. We also could sell anything to anyone. We answered phone calls from customers, wrote and placed orders, and viewed ourselves as associates in the family business. We did what we could to help Mom and Dad. We'd become miniature adults. But it hadn't done anything to keep them at home longer. If anything, it was the opposite.

"Don't you see that we're constantly doing things for them?" I said.

"This is for us," she insisted. "I hate the kitchen. Don't you?"

"No." It wasn't the most attractive room in the house, but I repeated what we both heard often from Mom: "Every room needs something, Jacquie."

Like Mom, once her mind was made up, Jacquie was nearly impossible to convince. "Come on; Mom and Dad don't have the time. They'll be surprised."

That's when I decided I was finished with Jacquie's projects. I'd thought I would have to make a big pronouncement, but it happened organically.

I did agree, however, to wait with Ricky and David at the house while she and Pam rode their bikes to Zayre, a discount store behind our old house on Portsmouth. After scouring the aisles, they stumbled on an ample supply of peel-n-stick, twelve-inch linoleum tiles, which they lugged up the steep part of Herschel View Street, around the corner, and into the house at the exact moment I needed to head for the pool.

I left the house with a sigh of relief. Swimming, and all that went with it, was all I could handle—period.

CLEANING THE POOL STARTED WITH A FEW stolen glances at Tom Olsen and ended abruptly when I slipped on the bulkhead, dropped four feet, and, straddling the metal support, instantly hemorrhaged. I thought I might have to be driven to the hospital, but the bleeding eventually stopped and two hours later I was home again.

I peeked into the kitchen: Jacquie and Pam were on their hands and knees, exhausted, with most of the floor covered. David and Ricky jabbed at the linoleum with paint scrapers, forcing down the corners where they curled. I stood staring for a long while as Jacquie was about to place a tile with too wide a gap next to the wall.

"What do you think?" she said.

I knew she was looking for reassurance but I didn't know what to say.

"Where should we leave the crack? By the wall or between the tiles?" She was dead serious, asking for my artistic opinion.

"Did they come with instructions?"

Jacquie jerked her head toward me. "Do you think we would start this without instructions? Leave us alone," she said, grimacing. "We'll finish without you."

"I fell on the bulkhead," I said coolly. Jacquie looked up, concern written on her face. But our eyes darted instantly to the corner, where Pam was wiping away dead flies with her bare hand.

"Pam, what are you doing?" Jacquie barked. "I told you to clean first."

Pam held her mouth open, pretending to be shocked. "You don't have to yell."

Except for a few rectangles requiring cutting and piecing, Jacquie and Pam finished the floor, and it looked exactly like what it was:

linoleum squares installed by kids. Whole sections of tile were askew, with curled corners and sizeable spaces between them.

Mom called that night to see how we were doing. By then, thoughts of my pool accident had vanished. "We have a surprise," Jacquie said.

Mom said "Oh, dear. I hope you haven't re-roofed the house."

Jacquie sighed. "Well, not exactly."

WE WAITED PATIENTLY AT THE DINING room table for our parents' return. The younger kids played Monopoly, Jacquie read a book, and I worked on my eighth grade rya rug with a thick needle and a ball of green yarn.

When they opened the door, Mom and Dad stopped abruptly at the idyllic scene. Mom set down a couple of boxes and gave us an odd smile. "Something's wrong. Why aren't you up in your rooms?" She stared at us with amusement.

Dad hauled a heavy pile of orders over the dining room table, and as he plopped them down David bubbled over with so much enthusiasm that for a moment I hated that I'd been so argumentative with Jacquie.

"You're going to be surprised," David chirped.

Mom held David's hand as he pulled her toward the kitchen. When she saw the floor, she froze, her eyes wide. Dad peeked over her shoulder.

"What do you think?" Jacquie sounded hesitant, seemingly aware that their job left a little to be desired.

"Sonuvabitch," Dad said. "You kids are amazing."

"Kim didn't do anything," Jacquie grumbled. She stepped forward to point out the flaws.

Dad's exuberance told me he and Mom had guessed the surprise even before they arrived home. "You kids are really something. Let's celebrate," he said, pouring Mom her rum and Tab and rustling up his version of a Shirley Temple with a cherry on top for the rest of us.

Dad handed Jacquie her special drink. "What gave you this idea?"

"It looked so terrible," she said, dropping onto the third step.

I climbed over her, irritated, and made my way upstairs.

Over time, Mom and Dad had convinced me that nothing we did for them could keep them home. I wanted the family around for the little things: for chocolate chip ice cream cones, hunting for school clothes; for playing hearts, or baking bread, or raking leaves in the yard. Was that too much to ask? I wanted them to turn on the Victrola and swirl around the living room as they sang to their favorite musicals. And I wanted their awareness. I wanted them to check in periodically, to ask about my thyroid: Was the medicine helping? Did I notice any change? I wanted to tell them that the hemorrhaging after the fall had frightened me. I guess I could've said something, but I didn't. The linoleum floor was yet another symbol of our separate lives.

A FEW WEEKS PASSED AND I WAS RECOVERING from a grueling Saturday workout—my muscles aching, my body just sinking into sleep—when I heard the front door squeak open. Forgetting Mom and Dad had gone to their last dance of the season, I sat upright, thinking we had a burglar. A few minutes later, I heard Mom and Dad's footsteps headed for the kitchen, followed by the ping of ice cubes and pouring of liquid in a glass. One last drink for the evening, I figured, and threw my head back on the pillow. I could hear Mom giggling.

Soon the loud chatter turned to argument and then Dad's heavy stomp up the stairs. It hit me that Pam and her friend Mary were sleeping in the room adjacent to mine, Jacquie having given them her room for the night. The thought raced through my head that Dad would wake them and embarrass Pam.

I clutched the blanket under my chin as my door swung open. With my eyes closed, I detected the light from the hall and braced for the moment, adrenaline surging. Dad tiptoed to the side of my bed and clutched my arm. Instantly, I swiped, striking at his mouth. He recoiled and seemed to chuckle. "Goddammit." I arched back, ready to strike again as he came toward me. Even lying on my back, given the slightest opportunity, I would've knocked out his teeth.

"Get off me," I barked, hitting hard on his taut stomach with my left fist.

He grabbed my wrist to restrain my punches, his grip so tight my eyes flooded with tears. With one arm, he flung me against the window at the head of my bed. Then he wobbled around as if he were passing through a turnstile, and lumbered into the hall.

Fury gathered in me. I was trying to calm myself on the edge of my bed when I heard Pam whining. I leapt toward the door and saw Dad with Pam and Mary, the two in their nightgowns and bare feet, dazed and confused. Dad jerked Pam into a ballroom position, her nightgown rucked up in back, and flung her around like a rag doll. Her uncombed blond hair dropped into her eyes.

"Get off her, Dad," I shrieked. He was about to go after Mary, but I shoved him hard away from her and he stepped back, blinking a couple of times.

Dad twisted his head toward me. "You dance with Mike Grimmer. Why can't you dance with me?" Then he staggered to his room.

The three of us stopped for breath in the empty space of the dark hallway. Mary's eyes glossy, she reached out to Pam, her hair still in frazzled clumps. "Are you okay?"

Pam answered instantly, a low, brief, "Yeah." She could handle Dad. The one I worried about was Mary. Her mother had recently died in a car crash. She was the last one who needed a friend's soused parent groping her at a sleepover. Standing there holding Jacquie's door open, a surge of strength ran through me. My shoulders, arms, and legs felt strong. I felt aggressive. Swimming had done this for me. Swimming had made me strong enough to stand up to my father. And, ironically, so had the thyroid medication. The hormone they thought would "normalize" me had given me the strength to hit Dad hard enough to make a difference. Standing up for myself felt intoxicating.

"Sleep tight," I told the girls as I closed Jacquie's door. "I guarantee he won't try that again."

CHAPTER 18

It took almost four years, but eventually Mr. Bergen moved me into Pressure 1, the top practice group, just in time to prepare for the 1972 Olympic Trials.

Right away, I noticed there was something uncomfortable about Mr. Bergen's behavior with the older kids. For one thing, he amused himself by pitching pennies into some of the girls' cleavage. He'd pull out a handful of change and begin flipping coins in the air like we were trained seals. The guys snickered as the girls dove out of the way.

The penny pitching bugged me, maybe because it was too reminiscent of my father's brand of teasing, and I stayed clear of it. But Mr. Bergen singled me out anyway. Since I still hadn't developed breasts, I tied my straps with a shoelace in back, which hiked up the suit in front. As I gulped water from the drinking fountain between sets, he strode over like he was about to say something about my stroke. Instead, he said, "Peters, you're the only one I know with a turtleneck bathing suit."

I glanced at his hairy muffin-top roll, his old-man Speedo tied tightly over his hips, and I dropped back into the water, shaking my head. Mr. Bergen's age made him physically repellent to me, but there was something seductive about him too. He conserved his words, always leaving us to guess at what he really thought, and as a girl with a father who seemed to have no filter, the mind games intrigued me.

Most of the guys followed the rules and escaped his attention. But it had become clear to me that I no longer wanted to escape. I wanted *more* attention. I wanted to be asked to go down to the underwater window. I wanted to be called into his office. I wanted to be videotaped and held late for meetings. I wanted to do whatever was necessary to be closer to Mr. Bergen. And his pointing out my modesty made me feel something was wrong with me. The implication was that if I "fixed" the problem, I would finally receive the attention I so badly craved.

In the locker room, I took the risk of asking my friend Nuria, a freestyler whose breasts were as small as mine, "Do you think I'm wearing my bathing suit too high? Mr. Bergen thinks it looks like a turtleneck."

"He's a perv," one of the girls said, eavesdropping.

"Yeah, no kidding," others chimed in.

"If yours is a turtleneck, so are all of ours," Nuria said.

MR. BERGEN WAS STILL OBSESSING ABOUT how much we female swimmers ate and weighed that winter. He placed the scale outside his office on the back wall of the balcony, and every day we would climb the stairs so he could check our weight in front of the parents, the guys, everyone. If an average swimmer didn't make weight, Mr. Bergen would get ticked off and maybe say something to embarrass her, but if it was one of his star swimmers in Pressure 1, he'd get hopping mad. Usually, he'd punish the whole group by giving us a timed trial, requiring us to beat our best time, or making us complete some terrifying set of repeats with no rest. His inconsistency began to bug me. One minute he was touting team unity; the next he was dividing us into two groups, "winners" and "losers."

Coaches from left to right: Paul Bergen, Denny White, Debbie Reed, Darryl Wiesenhahn, Tom Keefe. Photo by Rob Paris.

I think it was Alice who shared with me that one of her weight-control secrets was chewing gum. The idea was it took more energy to chew a piece than there were calories in the gum. I bought extra-large packs and chewed constantly. I ended up with a twenty-two-foot gum chain, a mouth full of cavities and, eventually, a bad case of temporomandibular joint dysfunction.

I was not fat. Not even close. But I believed I was. With Mr. Bergen so focused on our performance, it is confounding that he went to such extremes to make us crazy thin. Maybe he thought the discipline of losing weight helped swimming; certainly, it seemed that losing weight meant to Mr. Bergen that we were serious about swimming.

Miserably, I intuited that I should strive for the cadaverous look of a marathon runner. I don't know why Mr. Bergen's demands made sense at the time, because many of the national swimming champions had broad shoulders and carried a fair amount of weight. Few were slender. But at the time, I didn't really wonder whether his goals were justified. His do-without-questioning approach comforted me. I was so greedy for intelligent direction from an adult that his totalitarian attitude didn't seem like a red flag.

Having to lose weight, on the other hand, was killing me. Looking for a weight loss miracle, I browsed the aisles of Walgreens with Pam and stumbled across a product called "Ayds" that resembled a box of Whitman's chocolates. "Look at this, Pam. Two chocolates to replace a meal. Maybe Jacquie would like these too."

Pam's thin face registered alarm. "If you guys are eating diet candy instead of meals, who's going to fix us dinner?"

"Don't worry," I said. "I don't plan to starve myself." I returned with a box of chocolate Ayds, hid the stash in the bottom drawer of my dressing table, and binged on them for most of the night.

Though I didn't lose weight, I could tell my sugar intake was helping: I had more energy in practice. When I heard Mr. Bergen shout my name I felt a jolt, like an electric prod. I would swim into the wall and think nothing of his antics. I had thoroughly brainwashed myself into believing he was right about everything, that he had no choice but to throw kickboards, or even stopwatches, to get some swimmers to listen. I told myself that these girls who didn't make weight needed to work harder. They needed to trust him, and to be more disciplined. So what if he had a temper and went ballistic at times? I knew I was working harder than I'd ever worked in my life, and he'd drawn that out of me.

To survive, I did what I had to. I did what we *all* had to. I rationalized.

LEADING UP TO THE 1972 DALLAS INDOOR Nationals, Mr. Bergen called us one night to the hard wooden bleachers. I glanced out at the water, the air overheated and muggy, and wished for a lecture that might shorten practice. He handed us a booklet he wanted us to take home to fill out. It was called an AMI (Athletic Motivation Inventory), and he presented it by saying, "This will identify those of you who are the most motivated." I sensed there was a correct answer to each question. His sleepy voice seemed a put-on, as if he were disguising his usual pent-up frustration, trying to convey calmness.

I thumbed through, reading a few of the multiple-choice questions, like, "I prefer people who a) are reserved b) are in between, and c) make friends easily." I preferred people in all those categories. I raised my hand.

"What is it, Twenty Questions?" I guess he was trying to be funny with his new nickname for me, but it smacked of impatience. He'd already made it clear: he didn't like questions.

"Some of these questions are, um, difficult," I said. I was afraid if I didn't answer correctly, he would embarrass me in front of the team.

"Don't agonize, Peters. Pick the first answer that comes to mind." I rolled my eyes as he snapped his pen against his leg. He wore a deep vertical crease between his eyebrows. Hardly anyone moved.

"Anyone else?"

I waited for an explanation, but none came. *What is he trying to do?* I wondered. *Mess with our heads?*

I know now that the divide-and-conquer approach was a way of closing the gate so he could control everything inside. At the time, though, this was the last thing on my mind. All I could think about was how I could prove in this written test that I was one of his stars.

DAD STOPPED BY MY ROOM THAT NIGHT to say good night. I'd come home late, so it seemed he'd missed our nightly conversation before dinner.

Sitting at my great aunt's cherry dressing table, flanked by drawers and straddling an upholstered bench, a mirror in front of me reflecting the open A.M.I. test and my woeful expression, I said, "Good night, Dad," opened a bottom drawer to my left, and popped a couple of Ayds in my mouth.

"What are you eating?" He sounded tired, and his face was red and puffy.

"Oh, um. Diet candies."

"*Diet* candies? What makes you think you need diet candy?"

By then, they were such a routine part of my day that I thought they were no big deal; I lifted the box out of the drawer and handed Dad a chocolate. He had put on so much weight by this point that his belly was a round mass in front of me.

He stuck the chocolate into his mouth and chewed for a while, reading the disclaimer on the side of the box. He glanced up every few lines, squinting. Then he lobbed the whole box into the trash.

"Dad!"

"That's garbage. You don't even know what you're eating."

As it turned out, Dad was right. Years later, Ayds candies were taken off the shelves, partly because of their unfortunate name, but also because the key ingredient, phenylpropanolamine, was known to cause strokes in women.

I scanned the questions on the AMI again, and this time it read like a trap. It was so much like our weighing-in: a lose-lose situation. If I answered that I responded negatively to yelling, I would sound like a wimp. If I said I responded positively, I would be encouraging Mr. Bergen to yell. *What choice do I have, since I have to take the test?* I decided I could answer the way I would on most days, or how I would on my best day. I chose the latter.

THE DAY THE TEST RESULTS CAME IN, rumor spread that Mr. Bergen was angry, that he had learned that some of us were "uncoachable." He often pulled Deena aside to talk, so I dried my hair with her that day, hoping to glean some information.

"Do you know what's going on with Mr. Bergen?" I stepped under the dryer and pounded the "on" button with my fist.

She turned her back to me, tossing her thin blond hair under the dryer with her fingertips.

"Seems like he's mad about the test," I said to the back of her head. I tried again. "Do you know why he's calling people into his office?"

Deena held up her hand to wave good-bye to some of our other teammates. "I have no idea," she said, her voice muffled by the whirr of the dryers.

Deena clearly knew *some*thing, but didn't want to say. Maybe she was under pressure. It seemed Mr. Bergen had been dividing every extra moment of his time away from the pool between Deena, Alice, and Paul—a few others too, but those three got the most micromanagement.

When a rumor spread to Mr. Bergen that Deena had been making out behind some bushes with a cute guy named Jim Atwater at the Upper Arlington meet, friends took bets about whether he'd punish us a team. He was constantly singling her and Alice out, forcing them to go down with him to the underwater window, presumably for a lecture about their stroke. Halfway through our set, he would climb out from below the deck, and whoever had been with him would drop back into the water with a flushed face and cheerlessness that made me uneasy.

The night Alice received her test results, she said little, facing straight ahead with her customary stoicism, as she drove home. Heidi seemed to block out the tension by focusing on finishing her homework by dome light. MaryAnn, at my elbow in the backseat, sat with perfect posture, her books on her lap, as high overhead street lamps rhythmically dimmed the interior light of the car. I was the only one tilting against the window, my head shaking with the bumpy Norwood Lateral, as early industrial and manufacturing plants streamed by, their hulking forms distant and stark.

CHAPTER 19

L eading up to the Olympic Trials, Mr. Bergen insisted we wear two or three bathing suits layered one over the other so we would feel the difference swimming in competition with only one. The idea sounded clever, a mind game that built my confidence when I discovered that even with the added drag, my times in practice weren't slower.

I was, however, concerned when he brought out shiny little orange "salt" pills the size of aspirin. Every night after practice, he'd been asking us to line up for a jelly bean like it was a big thing, and now the jelly bean had become a "salt pill" meant to replace salt we were losing through perspiration.

After practice on the first night of the pills, my parents were deep in conversation at home in their bedroom office when I trudged in and announced, "Mr. Bergen gave us pills tonight."

Mom whirled around in her office chair. "What kind of pills?" For the first time, she sounded suspicious.

"Salt pills," I said.

Dad leaned back on two legs of his chair, yawning, ignoring Mom. "They won't hurt you," he said. "You worry about the Olympic Trials, will you?"

"But Dick . . . he shouldn't be giving pills to those kids." Mom's forehead wrinkled as she cocked her head.

"Do they make you feel weird?" He did a funny wiggle.

"No."

"Then forget about them." He tapped Mom and nodded to show he wanted to get back to work. "We have enough problems without adding more."

DESPITE WHAT MY FATHER SAID, ALARM bells went off in my head every night before I popped one of those orange pills in my mouth. I didn't trust that they were "just" salt. Were they really some kind of amphetamine? Why didn't he ask us to pick some up at the pharmacy if they were so important? I didn't trust the swimming culture that said we needed to put our heads down, keep our mouths shut, and get the job done. But that's exactly what I was doing.

Along with the pills, Mr. Bergen announced a two-week diet of no carbohydrates: only meat, fish, and eggs.

One of the girls raised her hand. "Can we chew gum?"

"Sugarless," he said, "and diet soda. But nothing else. I don't even want you drinking milk unless it's skim. You're going to feel tired, but that's okay because in two weeks you'll switch to carbohydrates and no protein." He jotted something on his clipboard and placed the pen behind his ear. "If you follow this diet, you'll have a shot at the Olympic Team."

I followed the diet religiously. Within a short period of time, I was seeing stars after a main set and I could hardly lift my arms out of the water, they felt so leaden. To combat this lethargy, Mr. Bergen replaced the orange salt pills with huge chewable white pills that he said were fructose. "Your food is converted to glucose to provide energy to your cells," he said. "Fructose takes longer to metabolize. It stays in your cells longer so you'll feel stronger. Any questions?"

My eyes glazed over. Every night as I lined up for the fructose, I gave him a perfunctory smile, then chomped the tablet.

When I returned home, Mom would fill my plate with green beans or scalloped potatoes and I'd have to hand the plate back to her. "Sorry, Mom, but I can only eat meat."

Christmas morning breakfast, 1970. Photograph taken by my father.

Mom appeared to measure her words to keep Dad out of the conversation. "I don't mind if you need special food, Kim, but if you can't lift your head at the dinner table, there's something wrong with the diet." On some level, I appreciated that Mom was finally showing some concern and questioning Mr. Bergen's behavior, but she was too late. I was finally "all in," and nothing she said could trump what I was hearing every day at the pool.

I arched up straighter, thinking of ways to be argumentative. "I like the diet." Then I swallowed hard. Even as I worshipped Mr. Bergen, my gut told me I should question his behavior.

IN THE MEANTIME, PRACTICES WERE getting progressively crazier and more disturbing. In one practice Mr. Bergen yelled, "Hold it up."

Grimmer lifted his crotch out of the water to a chorus of girls shouting, "Oh, Grimmer, you're so gross." Mr. Bergen snickered along with the guys.

A prank we thought was funny at the time was to slap someone on the thigh with three middle fingers, creating a "W" mark that was known as the "Wiedemann Sign" after the popular Cincinnati brewery. I'd seen Mr. Bergen do this to others and hadn't thought much of it. Then one day I happened to pass by him on my way from the locker room to the weights, and with his three middle fingers, he wacked me so hard on the leg that I let out a yelp from the sudden shock.

Looking down at my thigh, I saw that his swat had left a red, three-finger welt.

"That's a "W" for winner," he said, smirking.

I continued along the edge of the pool to the weights, without reacting. We were getting used to this kind of thing, and didn't question it. The longer the red mark remained, though, the more I bristled. What did he think he was doing? I wanted attention, but not this kind.

Still, his overall approach seemed measured. Rational. Buttressed by scientific research. Sure, he had been inappropriate at times—kicking kids off the team, hurling those kickboards—but it was obvious he knew what he was doing. He had a plan, and he had done the research to back up the plan. At least, that's what I thought.

Some of the parents complained, "How are they going to compete if they're this lethargic so close to the Olympic Trials?"

Mr. Bergen came right back at them with, "If you want your child to stay on the team, you let *me* coach."

Ironically, his attitude made me feel safe. There is a fine line between manipulation and cooperation. Whether parents pushed him around or not, he gave the impression that they couldn't, which made me even more willing to trust his judgment and do what he demanded.

THOUGH I WAS ONLY FIFTEEN, I QUALIFIED for the Olympic Trials in the 200-meter freestyle, but here's what's bizarre: I don't remember qualifying. Not one moment. Did I make it on a relay split and no one mentioned it? Or was I so exhausted from the extreme diet that I don't remember it? For a swimmer to forget the moment he or she qualified for the first time to participate in the Olympic Trials it's like forgetting the day you got engaged to be married. I still half wonder if Mr. Bergen cheated for some of us, and if that's the explanation for my lapse in memory.

He was certainly capable of it. I remember that Charlie Keating III, the son of the Marlin president, had been trying for some kind of cutoff time. He had made several failed attempts and our whole National team was standing by the side of the pool, pushing for him to make it this one last try. The gun went off and Charlie entered the water. With a long, obvious swipe of his hand, Mr. Bergen started the stopwatch several seconds later. Naturally, Charlie made it.

So maybe he fudged a little on some of our times to create a more impressive Marlin presence at the Trials. Who knows? I was so happy to be on the team, I never asked.

Somewhere in my mind, I wondered if my doubts about Paul Bergen were due to my constantly doubting my father. With him, alarm bells had been going off for a long time. *He* was the one who was sneaky, who had lied to my mother. I wanted to dismiss Paul Bergen's cheating for Charlie Keating like I wanted to dismiss my father's affair.

I did the same with the pills. Maybe they were nothing more than the equivalent of drinking Gatorade or eating sugar. All I know is that despite my reservations, I complied with Mr. Bergen's training. It wasn't until some fifteen years later, in the late eighties, when he suspiciously and abruptly left swimming to train racehorses, that my curiosity about the pills and what they'd contained was aroused again.

THE OLYMPIC TRIALS WERE HELD IN Portage Park, Illinois, and with my first glimpse of the pool on the first day of the meet, I felt tingly, drawn to the water like a magnet. I had to hold myself back. The water was tantalizingly clear. Sparkly white lines flowed across its surface, and swimmers tumbled like colorful pieces in a kaleidoscope, dividing into mosaic patterns, reflecting light with each arm stroke, each kick, each breath and turn. A glorious sight.

How many of my teammates will make the Olympics? I wondered. I couldn't stop staring during warm-up at the celebrity women swimmers: Shirley Babashoff, Keena Rothhammer, Karen Moe—all from California.

The fifty-meter pool was relatively shallow, surrounded by a wide swath of concrete where swimmers rested on blankets and sleeping bags in front of a tall set of bleachers running the full length of the pool on two sides. In the corner, camera crews interviewed Doc Counsilman, the famous coach from Indiana, while his star swimmer—Mark Spitz once again—sauntered along the deck like a model in bare feet and a warm-up jacket, with a dry terrycloth towel slung over one shoulder.

This was before tech suits, head-shaving, or goggles in competition. Caps were only occasionally used by women—never men—and digital touch pads were in their infancy and prone to problems, so three timers with stopwatches on a catwalk above the blocks served as a back-up for each lane. To one side of the pool, a man with a microphone announced events to nervous spectators in the bleachers.

I wanted to swim my best, of course, but let's be real: making the Olympics in my event, the 200 freestyle, was as remote a possibility as my crossing the English Channel. My entry time was too far down the list to even consider it. But in four years, at nineteen, I would be at the top of my game. This was my chance to practice, to soak up what I could so that one day the Olympics could be a reality for me.

1972 Olympic Trials, Portage Park, Illinois.

But this wasn't the case for several of the swimmers on our team. Jenny in the 100 freestyle and Deena and Alice in the 100 and 200 butterfly each had a solid chance to make the Olympic Team this year. Jenny was two years older than I was, and Mr. Bergen had switched her from backstroke to freestyle like me. She waited ten feet from Mr. Bergen, watching the end of warm-up, looking more tense and nervous than I'd ever seen her. She gave me a weak smile. By the time she climbed on the block and shook out her arms and legs for the finals, I was holding my breath.

In the four years since Mr. Bergen's arrival, Jenny had transformed from a gangly backstroker to a hulky sprint freestyler with powerful shoulders and biceps and thick, muscular legs. She was lucky: in most events only first and second place made the Olympic Team but in sprint freestyle, due to relays, you could place sixth and still make the team.

From the moment she plunged into the water, Jenny's 100-meter freestyle was the race of a lifetime. With her powerful stroke and six-beat kick, she seemed to soar over the water faster than a peregrine falcon, breaking the American record and coming within one tenth of a second of the world record. When she hit the wall, she threw one arm in the air, jubilant. Her performance showed the rest of us we were ready for our events.

I was there, and not there. After Jenny's win, I watched for two days as Mark Spitz and Gary Hall set American and World records in the 200 butterfly and 400 individual medley. I kept thinking, *Dang, I'm so lucky to be here.* As the races unfolded in front of me, my mind drifted to the 100 butterfly between Deena and Alice. They would have to finish one–two in order to make the team.

I wanted *both* of them to win. Alice had been sweet, giving me rides to practice. Deena was only a few days older than I was, and we had joined the Marlins on the same day. Her winning would make me feel hopeful that this grueling swimming life could someday pay off.

*1972 Olympic Trials Finals, front, left to right: Kristie Rhodenbaugh,
Nuria Otero, Kim Peters, Connie Brown; second row, left to right: Kris
Odenwald, Kim Pahner, Emmy Bradshaw. Photo by Mary Keating Hall.*

I felt sure Deena would beat Alice and make the Olympic Team.
She was so gutsy and outwardly self-assured, and lately she'd been
walking with a bounce in her step. Her stroke looked fluid and
effortless. Alice, meanwhile, seemed to drag along with no energy
or oomph in the pool, like she was talking herself into it.

In the end, Alice missed qualifying for the finals by less than a
hundredth of a second and Deena won and made the Team. Later,
we learned Alice had been swimming with mononucleosis.

THE END OF THE THIRD DAY WAS MY 200-meter freestyle race.
I was rested, my limbs twitching with anxiety and exhilaration.
Looking up at the 5,000 fans in the bleachers, I hunted for my
parents but couldn't find them. I strolled over to Mr. Bergen, who
wore dark sunglasses over his dark sideburns and whose eyes were
glued to a heat sheet.

With uncharacteristic warmth, he stopped momentarily and said, "You up?" Then something odd happened. He placed his clipboard under his armpit, then slid his other arm around and onto my shoulder. "Get out there and swim smart," he said. "You're ready." His arm around my shoulder meant something to me. It was confirmation I'd finally entered his "inner circle."

I stepped up to the block and the conditions felt right. I was aware of the tense hush of spectators, the cool breeze, the still water. Rolling my neck and shoulders, I felt loose, almost giddy. I visualized myself plowing through that water, slamming into the turn, and pushing off with such force that I would smash into the wall.

The starter inspected his gun. "Swimmers, take your mark . . ." I placed my toes over the edge of the block, leaned forward, and grabbed the edge. Within seconds, my arms were churning the surface of the still water. *Stretch, reach, breathe, kick, hit that flip-turn, streamline, breathe, breathe, breathe . . .* I cut through the surface of the water and crashed into the touchpad: 2:12.36. Nowhere close to the finals, but at barely fifteen, my personal best. The extreme diet, the pills, our training regimen, all of it had worked. I slapped the water, elated, then grabbed my towel, flung my warm-up jacket over one arm, and took my time heading over to Mr. Bergen.

"Good job," he said.

I waited for a moment, my hair dripping from my pigtails, my red, white, and blue nylon suit sagging in front. I felt proud, like I'd hit the big time, but I was waiting for something more. *Was my stroke smooth? My body high in the water?* Mr. Bergen had his eye on Heidi, who was up on the block. With a stopwatch in his right hand, the clipboard in his left, he turned his back on me and stepped away.

CHAPTER 20

I t was early September, during our two-week swimming break, and in my usual semi-trance, I dragged myself to the front door after school and picked through the mail stuffed in our mailbox. On the top of the pile of mail was a postcard addressed to me from Mr. Bergen, sent from Europe around the time of the Olympics.

By then, I'd gotten over Mr. Bergen's snub. The Olympics were over, and though they'd been tainted by the horrifying report that eleven Israeli athletes had been abducted and killed by a radical Palestinian group, Jenny and Deena had returned victorious, each with a gold medal. Their success helped fix in my mind the possibility that with Mr. Bergen's help I could one day go to the Olympics myself.

So when the postcard arrived, at first I felt flattered. But as I looked closely, I noticed it pictured two Dutch girls wearing traditional laced caps and dark dresses up to their chins as they arranged tulips along a stream. On the back, beside my address, Mr. Bergen had written:

Hi, Kim. I got this card to show you how well you would get along in Holland (notice the height of the collar!) By the way, their everyday clothes double as swimsuits—you would be right at home in the swimsuits pictured on the front.
Love, Coach B.

Hi Kim,

I GOT THIS CARD
TO SHOW YOU HOW
WELL YOU WOULD.
GET ALONG IN HOLLAND,
(NOTICE THE HEIGHT
OF THE COLAR!)
BY THE WAY THEIR
EVERY CLOTHES DOUBLE
AS SWIM SUITS - YOU
BE RIGHT AT HOME
IN THE SWIM
SUITS PICTURED ON THE
FRONT - LOVE COACH B.

KIM PETERS

3314 OBSERVATORY RD.

CINCINNATI, OHIO, U.S.A.

4522

I stared at the card. What was he trying to say? That I should show more cleavage? Why would he use a whole postcard to tease me about my flat chest and bathing suit?

Mom was adding order totals at the dining room table and talking to herself about their exhaustive list of expenses. She looked weary, her gray roots in need of coloring. I handed her the postcard.

"Kim, I'm in the middle of something important. What is it?" She set down her pen and scanned the back of the card, then turned it over to look again. "What did he mean?"

"He thinks I wear my bathing suit too high." I was used to the turtleneck bathing suit comments by then but I hadn't found time to tell Mom. She handed the postcard to Dad as he hung up the phone.

I wanted to stretch my mouth, and didn't. I felt a bizarre rush of confidence knowing I could be aware of the desire and yet restrain myself. *How long have I gone without stretching my mouth? Months? A year, maybe?*

Mom pushed her dark glasses higher on her nose. "This is strange."

Dad flicked the card onto the dining room table. "What's strange?"

"Well, he thinks she wears her bathing suit too high, Dick."

"It's not strange." Dad rubbed Mom's shoulders. "She's like you, Beej. She's so straight-laced he's afraid to touch her."

Mom grinned at his joke.

"What is *that* supposed to mean?" I squawked. I yanked the card off the table and headed toward the stairs.

"Get back here. Where do you think you're going?" He came after me and grabbed the back of my shirt. "What in the hell is wrong with you?"

I stood, ramrod straight, and collapsed into tears. "You think you're hilarious, but you aren't."

"I was teasing your mother," he said, softening. "The comment had nothing to do with you."

"Well, what did you mean about his being afraid to touch me?" It bugged me that Dad was making the postcard about him. About something sexual. To me, the touching meant something. Maybe it was my own fault that I wasn't in Paul Bergen's inner circle. I jerked my shoulder away. "Stand back. You're in my zone, Dad."

"I'm sorry if I upset you, Butch. Kiss me." He pursed his lips and leaned forward, and I kissed him on the lips and squirmed a little, like I was swallowing Kaopectate. It wasn't the kiss but the *meaning* of the kiss that got me. A kiss wasn't going to erase what my father had said.

He gave me a lopsided grin and shook his head.

As I scrambled up the stairs, I heard Dad bellyache to Mom, "Is it the curse? She won't even let me touch her." He dropped ice cubes into a glass. They rattled like a question.

"Back off, Dick. You do the same thing with me. You push and push and you don't quit."

"I'm telling you, Beejay, there's something wrong with her. I can't say a damned thing without making her cry."

I slammed the door to my bedroom and burrowed under the covers. Mom and Dad had been away so much they didn't know Tom and I had broken up. I didn't feel like informing them. Grimmer had implied I wasn't affectionate enough. Maybe I'd kept Tom at arm's length too. Was that what was wrong with me? Was I wanting affection but keeping people at a distance? By now it was a regular thing: I would feel a moment of vulnerability and my brain would automatically take off and hover above me, watching my interaction from ten feet away. Maybe people were picking up on this.

I'd grown used to Mom and Dad's being gone and no longer blamed Mom for abandoning us. I believed she had to follow Dad around to hold the family together, and it seemed to be working. So why was I so furious with Dad? Maybe I wanted him to be somebody he wasn't, to read the postcard and immediately say, "That bastard had better keep his hands off you."

A FEW DAYS LATER, JUST BEFORE DINNER, Dad received a phone call from Mr. Bergen, and when he hung up, I knew from his sly smile he'd made a deal.

"What do you think of having Kris Odenwald live with us?" he asked me.

I felt a squeeze in my chest. "Not much." Kris was a year older and a teammate from Belleville, a small town east of St. Louis. Her parents had sent her to Cincinnati to train with the Marlins, and she had been living with the Bergens.

"I don't see the problem," he said. "You got a problem with Kris?"

"Dad, she's my competition. We swim the same events. You want her to *live* with us?"

He explained that Mr. Bergen's daughter, born with spina bifida, was around seven years old and about to have surgery. The Bergens thought Kris would be happier living with someone else for a while.

I threw my hands in the air. Kris's parents could afford Ursuline Academy, an expensive private school on the north side of Cincinnati. As the only daughter in her family, she was accustomed to more pampering than she would ever get at *our* house. Had she ever fixed her own meals? Washed her own dishes? Washed her own clothes, for that matter? Who was going to make sure she got to and from practice? Was this *my* new job?

Kris and I had been trading places in the distance lane lately. There were days when I wanted to wring her neck for clawing at my feet during a main set. If she was going to live with us, where was I supposed to hide on the nights that I wanted to strangle her?

Mom stood with her legs wide apart, her fist on her hip. She no longer sounded like her own person but a soft version of Dad, standing in front of me. "Her parents are paying a stipend, Kim."

"So?"

"So nothing," Dad said. "We can pay some bills with the money."

"Oh, honestly, Dick. That's not the reason."

"Like hell. Every bit helps, Beejay."

I shook my head, annoyed. "You guys are never home!" I didn't see how they could live with themselves, pocketing money from Kris's parents and taking off as usual, leaving us to fend for ourselves. "Well." Mom paused. "Your father and I are going to be home more often, right Dick?" She held her gaze until Dad nodded, then shook the ice in her rum and Tab and sipped.

Oh great, I thought, *just what I want: another person living with us and Mom and Dad around more to create chaos.* I was beginning to feel confident enough to stand up to Dad, even to shout back occasionally. With Kris there, I would have to restrain myself. Why couldn't he have talked to us about this first? He sure talked to us about everything else.

KRIS'S MOTHER SCHEDULED A VISIT TO inspect our "living arrangement" and we ran around like fools, madly hiding stains, vacuuming under furniture, and picking up stray glasses from our bedrooms. We even watered and cleaned up Mom's African violets and swept behind the fireplace screen. Anything to make an impression.

Somehow, we passed inspection. Kris moved into the guest room, adjacent to mine, and soon we were back to business as usual, but with one more kid in the family.

To make her feel at home, Jacquie and I kidded her for pronouncing forty-four like "farty" four and wearing blouses with the embroidered initials "KOA."

"What do the letters stand for?" we asked her. "Kampgrounds of America?"

Kris seemed amused, and I tried my hardest to make her feel comfortable. I couldn't blame her for being stuck with us. She was doing what I was doing: swimming with the best team around and trying her darnedest to make her efforts worthwhile. She was probably missing her parents too.

But the decision galled me. Mom and Dad tried to suggest we were upper class but we kids knew the truth. This was a step down for Kris. For her, our home must've felt like a low-end boarding house.

DESPITE THE BRIEF EUPHORIA FOLLOWING the Olympic wins, tension at the pool hadn't eased; in fact, the atmosphere had gotten even more outlandish. While Deena and Jenny were taking a break from swimming following the Olympics, Mr. Bergen was quoted in the *Cincinnati Enquirer* saying, "Deena simply isn't sharp physically since her layoff from the Olympics and Jenny is about 16 pounds over what she normally would weigh when competing." Even Dad admitted that Mr. Bergen had no business broadcasting his negative thoughts about our two best swimmers to the whole city of Cincinnati.

And what had he been trying to say with that postcard? I kept turning it over in my mind.

Then one day I arrived at practice to find a balcony draped in black fabric and Mr. Bergen pacing the deck in a black shirt, black pants, black shoes and socks, and even a torn piece of black fabric tied like an armband above his left elbow.

Too terrified to ask Mr. Bergen himself, I reached out to Denny White, who coached the St. X high school guys' practice right before ours. "What's going on?"

With his boyish face and perpetual smile, he seemed to be awkwardly ignoring the obvious. "Hey, Sneaky Pete."

I thought someone might've died—you know, the way you walk into a funeral home and you're not sure what to say?

Denny gazed at the black fabric slung over the balcony railing and sighed. "It's Black Monday."

"What's *that* supposed to mean?"

He didn't hear me. He was already headed toward the far end of the pool—trying to remain neutral, or maybe he thought the drama was amusing.

It wasn't to me. Black fabric over windows made me think of friends at school sitting shiva when someone died. He must be in mourning. Was that it? Or was this another version of trying to kill us? I didn't think of the violence of the Munich Olympics but of Nazi Germany.

Kim reporting to Dad after a race at the Marlin Invitational.
Photo by Peter Dernier.

Most of the guys on the Marlins were twice Mr. Bergen's size. "What a waste," one of them blurted out.

I didn't know what that meant. What was a waste? The black fabric? The intimidation? They did arm circles, around and around, stretching as though the drama had no impact. I watched as the girls arrived, most of them looking bewildered or fearful. I drifted off to watch the scene, a spectator outside of myself. I wasn't there. A shell of me was there—scowling, wincing, and trying not to feel.

Dad and Mr. Bergen entered my brain whenever it drifted. They peered at me when I changed my clothes. They screamed or issued threats when I imagined crossing them. The only place they left me alone was in the water—my time-out—where my brain shut down and my body took over. Where I didn't have to figure anything out.

As I stretched and circled my arms beside the block in my lane before practice, I began to feel a shift. I reminded myself of the situation: The Black Monday theatrics were freaky. They seemed obviously designed to instill fear. A fear I didn't have to accept. I power-plunged into the pool, concentrating on the black line and my breath. Breathe, stroke, stroke, breathe, stroke. The rhythm was meditative. Calming. It flushed out the noise.

Black Monday continued for several weeks, ending every night with a line-up for a single black jelly bean. Turns out Black Monday was some screwy idea Mr. Bergen made up. We never did find out what it meant.

DESPITE MY DESIRE TO BE SUMMONED to the underwater window or Mr. Bergen's office, when he finally said he wanted to see me, I panicked. The door to his office stood ajar and he appeared to be brooding: he leaned against a desk, his body stiff, and flicked his pen. Beside him was a miniature sculpture of the Greek King Sisyphus pushing a rock up the hill.

"Thank you for coming in," he said, hesitating for a moment, biting his fingernail. "Shut the door, please."

I closed it, then waited, fingering the goggles in my hand. He stared at a stain on the indoor/outdoor carpet.

"Was there something you wanted to talk to me about?" I finally asked.

"Yes," he said, his voice penetrating. "You are your own worst enemy. I want you to stop worrying and start swimming." He hardly looked up the entire time. Then, in a dispassionate monotone, he said, "That's all."

I backed through the doorway and headed for the stairs.

A few days later, he designed goal sheets for us. On mine, he wrote, "Start swimming more out of desire than fear."

Yeah, right, I thought. *Then quit trying to scare the snot out of us!*

MOM HAD BEEN TRYING HARD TO FIX delicious meals with Kris around, and they took more time, which allowed Dad to fire more questions while he filled up on rum and Tab. I didn't want to share my thoughts with Kris there—she was more comfortable with Mr. Bergen than I was—but if I wanted to talk to Dad, I didn't see that I had any choice. Kris and I plunked down on the floor, against the white metal cabinets. Some of the linoleum squares were kicking up on their corners and dirt had lodged underneath. The whole floor looked cheap and worn.

"Why did we pick a house with no chairs in the kitchen?" I complained.

"Bad day at practice?" Dad asked.

"Mr. Bergen thinks I'm swimming out of fear," I groused.

Dad glanced at Kris and then at me. "What do *you* think about that?"

"Well, I don't know what he expects when he tries to scare us." I twisted toward Kris, hoping she would back me up.

She was wearing her school uniform with her legs folded, her white blouse and pleated skirt spotless. "You have to realize it's bluster," she said. "He's trying to motivate us."

"Yeah, well, it's not working anymore. You call Black Monday 'bluster'?" I got up and dug in the refrigerator, hoping to deflect. I wanted empathy, not another logical explanation. And I sure as hell didn't want Dad siding with Kris.

Mom handed me a platter of roast beef to take to the table, and handed the salad to Kris. In the midst of the commotion of Dad's shouting for the younger kids to come down to dinner, Mom placed her hand on my shoulder and said quietly, "Kim, you have good instincts. Trust your gut."

I interpreted her comment as a message that my reaction to what was going on at the pool might not be too far off.

CHAPTER 21

A s soon as I turned fifteen, my parents bought a used turquoise
Impala so Mom could accompany me to practice. By the time
Kris moved in, driving had become automatic. But one dark,
densely foggy morning, I white-knuckled it, gripping the steering
wheel with my forearms, as I drove her to practice.

When we pulled into the parking lot, the natatorium was
cloaked in gray mist. Upon entering, a thin layer of fog loomed over
the water. Mr. Bergen cranked up the huge exhaust fan in the ceiling
but instead of sucking the fog out the fan drew more into the natatorium, creating a diaphanous haze similar to the Hollywood version
of heaven. I marveled at the irony. As the exhaust fan blasted and
the layer of fog grew denser, thicker, I felt the pressure on my lungs
as I inhaled the damp air. Goose bumps rose on my arms.

By the end of warm-up, the visibility was less than five inches.
We couldn't see our own hands. We could hear the deep splashing of
water, the gurgling of the backwash as we swam into the wall, and,
of course, Mr. Bergen's slow, droning voice.

I had the cynical suspicion he might cancel practice altogether,
like the day he wanted us to beat the national cutoff time in our
events and then, when we didn't, kicked us all off the team. I'd
looked around at the older kids that day and felt afraid. We're *all*

off the team? Was he out of his freakin' mind? As with so many of his mind games, he'd let us back the following day and hadn't mentioned our dismissal again. Now I was sure this was a drama he'd written and rehearsed the night before.

I had no idea why he had let in all that fog, but it was one of many bizarre decisions being made. When Mr. Bergen removed the doors on the stalls of the guys' toilets, we were told there were no doors at the state high school meet and he wanted to get the guys used to using the bathroom while others watched. Some of the guys suggested that maybe Mr. Bergen had become unhinged, that it was not the bathroom doors at all, and I agreed wholeheartedly. What was *wrong* with him? He was telling jokes before practice, jokes I never understood. I was too embarrassed to ask for an explanation when clearly most of the guys were getting their meaning.

One night, he had just finished lecturing us—apparently some of us weren't "dedicated"—and I was on my way to the locker room for my cap and goggles when he stopped us as a group.

"Oh, I forgot the joke of the day." Mr. Bergen smirked as he tapped one of the guys on the shoulder.

We gathered close so we could hear.

"What do women and frying pans have in common?"

We girls frowned at each other. One of the older guys said, "Tell us. What *do* women and frying pans have in common?"

"You have to warm them both up before you put in the meat." He did a two-step like he was proud of himself, and some of the guys coughed. Others howled hysterically. I didn't understand the joke at all.

I rushed toward the locker room, embarrassed by my ignorance, but Mr. Bergen picked up his pace until he was beside me. He wore a loose-fitting T-shirt over his tight old man Speedo and he forced his damp five o'clock shadow right in my face. "Did you get it, Peters?"

My heart raced. I tried to appear unaffected and outwalk him at the same time. Like my father, he kept following me, leaning in to get me to say something.

"Peters, you didn't get it; I know you didn't."

I smiled as I swatted the air. "You dildo."

Mr. Bergen nearly choked. "Peters, do you know what that means?"

I felt an instant panic. I'd heard the word in the locker room. Wasn't it like *goofball*?

Not wanting to expose my ignorance further, I didn't ask anyone what it meant. But he *did* back off, so it seemed to have had the desired effect.

OVER THE NEXT FEW MONTHS THAT FALL, Mom and Dad began traveling for the first time since Kris had moved in. It bothered me that we were no longer treating her like a guest. Was she going to be with us indefinitely? It seemed wrong that she, like the rest of us kids, was having to fend for herself, and I noticed she was calling home more often to talk with her mother.

One night after practice, as we walked through our front door, I asked her if she was doing okay, and she sort of moaned as we nearly fell over from the house's foul fishy smell.

"You homesick?" I asked.

Her nod was so slight I almost missed it.

I opened the broiler to see finger-size, perfectly rectangular filets, breaded and glistening, on a cookie tin. Jacquie had fixed dinner: fish, boiled corn, Pillsbury rolls, and tossed salad with iceberg lettuce and Good Seasons Italian Dressing. I was starving and thought the whole meal looked delicious.

Kris, her wet hair still frozen at the tips, looked tired as she reached for a plate in the cabinet. I handed her a spatula for the fish and as she set a filet on her plate, her eyes filled with tears. I'd confided to Mom that we needed more food but hadn't realized until then that Kris was unsatisfied with the quality of our meals.

Kris tried not to offend me. "The food is good," she said, "but I'm used to Mary Ann Bergen's cooking, and my mother is a great cook too."

Well shoot! I fumed. *My mother has five kids and works full time. How about Mary Ann Bergen? Does she have a full-time job? Or your mother?* Mom could prepare a lavish meal when she had to. She was a fine cook. She made sure we had milk, plenty of meat or fish, a variety of vegetables, and drawers full of fruit. What did Kris want? Turkey Tetrazzini? That wasn't Mom's style, even if she *had* the time. Mom had a lot to deal with: living out of a motorhome, selling gifts in five states, coping with Dad, five kids, and now a guest. Dad was the one who'd signed us up as a host family, not Mom. She didn't deserve the "bad cook" moniker.

That night, I finished dinner, strode straight to my room, and shut the door. After changing into my nightgown, I propped a book on my knees. Living with Kris wasn't a picnic. We had winter nationals to focus on, and all I could think about was how Kris was doing. What did she mean when she complained about the reading required at Ursuline Academy? Was she implying her education was better because I had less reading at Walnut Hills? Meanwhile, with my room next to hers, I found myself stressing over what I was wearing and how to keep everything spotless. There was less space in the house and less room in my brain. I posed at my dressing table, watching a fly on my mirror, and thought, *Dammit. My whole world has shrunk since Kris's arrival.* This wasn't what she wanted, and it wasn't what I wanted either.

EVENTUALLY KRIS BEGAN SPENDING more evenings in her room. I stopped in one frosty night after dinner, mainly to chat. Her room looked empty, devoid of any personal belongings. She was still wearing her school uniform, her knees crossed, a textbook in her lap. When she saw me, she leaned back against her headboard.

"It's probably hard for you with Mom and Dad drinking so much," I ventured.

Kris shrugged. "I'm not used to it." She told me a story about her parents and something about how little they drank, and my mind drifted. She said, *When I lived with the Bergens, this. When I lived with the Bergens, that.*

I was so sick and tired of hearing about the Bergens. Maybe it was manipulative of me, but I suggested in a nice way that she call her parents and tell them how she felt. "You should be honest, and don't worry about us," I said.

She placed a bookmark in the spine of her book. "I don't want you to get the wrong idea."

I broke into a smile. "You don't have to explain."

MR. BERGEN'S T-SHIRT READ SOMETHING like "Faith, Hope, and Love," and he was now attending regular Bible studies before morning practice.

"Something's happened," I said to Kris when I saw the shirt. "Something's bugging him."

Kris was carrying a huge stack of textbooks and complaining about how heavy they were. "Why do you want to turn a Bible study into something bad?"

"Well, *something* led to it. When you're working full time, you don't just think, *Huh, for fun I'll try Bible studies at four in the morning.*"

Kris sounded annoyed. "Leave him alone. What he does is none of our business."

Maybe she was right. But I had too many doubts to leave it alone. I'd witnessed his putting girls on his shoulders, and how he always stacked kickboards between the two front seats of his van and insisted that one of the girls sit there—and it was not just Deena who had to sit scrunched right beside him anymore. I told Kris one of the guys said he'd been in the backseat pretending to sleep when he saw Bergen in the driver's seat with this hand under a towel in the lap of one of the girls.

"I believe it," I said.

"Oh, come on, seriously?" she said. "Consider the source."

I wanted Kris to agree with me, but her loud defense of Mr. Bergen left me feeling isolated and disconnected from her. Was she willfully inattentive? Why was she so unwilling to see his flaws? I *wanted* to defend him—he had done so much to improve my swimming—but having seen what I'd seen, I couldn't.

THE DAY KRIS'S MOTHER WAS TO ARRIVE to help her move out, Mom washed the dishes while the rest of us lounged in the living room, our eyes fixed in a dead stare on the TV. There were shoes by the front door and stacks of papers and clean clothes on the back steps, waiting to go up. I didn't mind the clutter; I wanted to make it obvious to Kris's mother that Kris had made the correct decision.

As we said good-bye, Kris thanked Mom and Dad—she seemed genuinely grateful—and as I closed the front door, I leaned my back against the smooth wood and inhaled a huge, billowing breath.

My first instinct was to climb the stairs to Jacquie's room, but when I got there she had a pitiful look on her face, her pillows stacked high behind her head.

I draped myself on her extra twin bed in the opposite corner. "What's wrong?"

"I like her," she said, stony-faced. She seemed to be implying I'd chased Kris away.

"I like her too," I said, "but it's been hard having her live with us. Besides, we need Mom and Dad to go back on the road."

"Well, yes. That I agree with." She folded the corner of her page and closed her book.

Pam poked her head around the corner, a devilish smile on her face. "Now that she's gone, can I have her room?" She'd been sharing the attic with Ricky and David.

"Fine with me," I said, glancing at Jacquie.

Jacquie nodded. "Fine with me too."

That night, lying in bed, staring at the ceiling and listening to the rhythmic shush of leaves by my window, I felt a wave of vindication rolling through me. Kris had come in from the outside world and confirmed we weren't imagining our problems. Dad was drinking and yelling too much. Our home life *wasn't* pleasant.

And things weren't pleasant at the pool, either. They were downright dysfunctional. I wanted to focus on my swimming and tune Mr. Bergen out, but it wasn't easy.

THE DAY MR. BERGEN BEGAN ROARING around the parking lot on his Yamaha chopper, giving rides to some of the girls, I considered that he might be feeling bad about himself. He wore a T-shirt, a pair of navy corduroy shorts over his hairy legs, and the vehicle looked too big for him. Too big for the older girls to be holding on so gingerly. When he pulled up slowly in front of me, I stepped back, afraid he would drive over my foot.

A tiny part of me wanted to try it, to be able to say that I'd been on a motorcycle. But I didn't want to fall off—or, worse, have to touch him.

"Come on, Peters," he said. "You want to ride?"

I hesitated. "I haven't been on a motorcycle."

"So, this'll be your first time."

I hated the nausea creeping into my gut, especially since his words to me were about my being my own worst enemy and worrying too much. But there was no noticeable handle and I would have to hold on to his waist. Not only that, but I was wearing shorts; *would my legs stick to the seat?*

I awkwardly lifted my bare left leg over the black leather so I could slide in behind him. As I eased into the seat, my right calf touched the searing-hot exhaust pipe. I let out a screech and grabbed for my leg as tears shot out of my eyes. I was surprised my calf wasn't releasing smoke; the pink, sausage-shaped mark the pipe had made looked like a branding. The pain ran all the way to my groin.

"Be careful," Mr. Bergen said, which was not the proper response. I wanted something like, "Are you okay? I'm sorry. Let me look at the burn for a second." But instantly he revved the engine, and my head whipped back. All I could do was grab him around the waist with a silent prayer as he tore off around the parking lot, gravel sliding and dust kicking up on either side of us. I cringed with my arms around his hard midriff, squinting to keep the dust out of my eyes.

WHEN DAD SAW THE GIANT MARK on my leg, I frowned with embarrassment from my stupidity.

"What in the hell is that?" he asked.

"I burned it on Mr. Bergen's motorcycle."

"You *what*?" Dad, on the screened-in side porch with Mom, was wrapping up business for the day. He reached out to inspect the red mark, then grimaced at Mom. "That bastard. Were you wearing a helmet?"

I shrugged.

"You were a damn fool," he said. "What made you think you could ride a motorcycle?" Dad stomped off, presumably to pour a drink—not angry at Paul Bergen but at *me*. He thought I'd tumbled off.

I would've explained, but I didn't want Dad rushing to the telephone. And some of the other parents were already speaking out. When Mrs. Rust heard Mr. Bergen had slugged her son, Bob, she marched into the natatorium and got right in Mr. Bergen's face. "This is not going to happen again," she said. I appreciated that a few parents were beginning to draw a solid black line regarding what behavior was acceptable.

Mom heaved a heap of orders into a pile. "Don't ever ride a motorcycle again, okay?"

"He was giving rides to everyone, Mom."

"Would you jump off the Carew Tower if your teammates were doing it?"

I rolled my eyes. All my life, Mom had ridden behind Dad on everything: taking risks, not speaking her mind, putting us in danger.

"Would you? Would you jump off the Carew Tower?" she asked again.

"No, Mom." I set my foot on the nearest chair and rubbed around the burn.

"I would hope not," she said, her voice modulated.

Two weeks later, I was still nursing the burn.

CHAPTER 22

It still seems like yesterday. I drove into the natatorium parking lot and noticed there was no motorcycle. The sky was a rich robin's egg blue, the clouds fluffy and dense, and I felt out of place, like I should be on a picnic at the beach. It was the emptiness I felt whenever I arrived home from school or a swim meet and there was no motorhome in the driveway. I had developed a habit of disappearing into the far corner of my closed room, listening to the clock tick as I churned inside.

I entered the building and noticed the drawn curtains and the darkness of the coach's office. Sunlight cast long beams on the white concrete block walls behind the starting blocks. Something was off. Like a deflated balloon, I instantly felt less tense, but heavier.

Denny White sat on the single bench of the folded bleachers, the self-appointed greeter. "Hey, Sneaky Pete." He was missing his characteristic smile.

"Where's Mr. Bergen?"

"Gone," he said, shrugging.

"For how long?"

"For good."

"Whoa." I stopped for a second, uneasy. "What happened? Why?"

I wanted to know details, but he didn't seem to have any.

I drifted to the locker room—in shock, I suppose—and the first thing I noticed was the saturation of color: the bright white and marine blue walls, the red backstroke flags five meters from the starting end, the black overhead support beams . . . even the water seemed crisper, clearer. The cold damp of the concrete bit my toes and the metal lockers echoed in my ears. It was as if I'd been suffering from tinnitus and the hissing had abruptly stopped.

I put on my suit and sprinted back to prod Denny for more detail. "All I know is he spoke with Mr. Keating," he said.

"About what?"

"I don't know." He swallowed hard.

"You don't know *anything*?"

"Nope."

I lingered on the cold concrete outside the men's locker room, hoping Denny would think of something. But more swimmers began to arrive and nobody seemed to know what had happened. On impulse, I took the stairs, two at a time—I had so much nervous energy—and sped directly to Mr. Bergen's office. On his door, he had posted a quote by Thoreau: "If a man loses pace with his companions, perhaps it is because he hears a different drummer. Let him step to the music which he hears, however measured, or far away." I stood there and stared at the door. What was he trying to say? Thoreau was a proponent of individualism, of nonconformity. For five years I'd been hearing about team unity. About being a part of something big. Now he was saying he wanted to leave because he was some sort of Thoreau?

I wanted to kick the door in.

THAT NIGHT, DENNY COACHED. I CAN still recall the peculiar quiet over the pool. I could hardly pull my arms through the water. My kicking set was slower; my pulling set, abysmal. I was emotionally spent. Mr. Bergen's leaving was like driving into town after the death of someone close to you. People are going about their daily routine—rushing to work, feeding the meters—as if nothing remarkable has happened. Meanwhile, your whole world has collapsed.

I couldn't stop wondering what had happened. Had there been a misunderstanding? Everyone knew Mr. Bergen was as rigid and sharp-edged as a swimming paddle. Had he lost his cool with Mr. Keating? This didn't make sense. He'd transformed the team and just sent Deena and Jenny to the Olympics; why was he leaving now?

As abruptly as he had become a Christian, he had taken off without a meaningful explanation.

TO MY SURPRISE, MR. BERGEN SHOWED up at the pool the following day, presumably to remove some of his belongings from the office. I heard he was in the parking lot, so I ran out to see him. I was hoping to hear an explanation that made sense—that he had just gotten in an argument with Mr. Keating or someone else on the Marlin board, and would be back in touch with us. Some of us, at least.

"What happened?" I demanded. "You didn't say good-bye. Where are you going?"

Mr. Bergen placed a hairy hand on the hood of his VW van and glanced around as if checking to see if anyone was watching. Already he sounded distant. "I can't talk about it, Peters."

"Why not?" I dug my fist into my hip the way I sometimes did with Dad, hoping to convey my outrage.

He smirked. "I just can't."

"Well, who's going to coach us?"

"You'll do fine, Peters. Stop worrying."

A minute later, he was gone.

I watched his tires spew dust as his van shot through the lot. He turned onto North Bend Road, and then disappeared. *Geez, I thought. He sure has a nasty sting in his tail.*

I hated to admit it, but the crux of the problem was that although Mr. Bergen was abusive and a tyrant, just like my father, I was attached to him. Didn't he care at all?

I did a one-eighty and returned to the natatorium, gripped by a terrible, gut-wrenching anxiety. *Stop* worrying? Is that *what he thinks? I'll do* fine?

That night I drove home across the Norwood Lateral in choking congestion, grinding my teeth, feeling like I'd been duped. Swimming was the only thing I could do. I considered going home and living a more ordinary life—taking care of the younger kids as the oldest in the family—but Jacquie was already doing that. Why interfere? So I could cook and iron, wash the laundry, take phone orders, and manage Mom and Dad's incoming mail?

No, I thought. *Not doing it.*

I kicked myself for being so fragile, so unprepared. I had wished to be out from under Mr. Bergen's thumb for so long—but now that it had happened, I felt the worst, rawest kind of abandonment.

The trouble with swimming is, you're seduced into an unreasonable amount of work just to compete at the lowest level. Once you've made a decision to stay there, you're taking a risk. I felt as if I'd put all my money under the mattress and then gotten robbed.

THAT WEEKEND, I POKED MY HEAD INTO Jacquie's room, hoping to dull my disappointment in a conversation with her before practice. She was on her twin bed, her stocky shoulders slumped, her chestnut hair drooping. "Maybe it's not all bad," she said. "You might have more fun without him." She reminded me of the number of kids who had quit over the years because they couldn't get along with Mr. Bergen. "He was probably upset."

"What are you *talking* about?" I couldn't believe my ears. Jacquie had been swimming mostly for Darryl, not under Mr. Bergen. She had no idea how wacko he had become.

"Mr. Bergen called to see if I would quit the Marlins to play water polo for him," she went on, "and I'm thinking of doing it."

My mouth fell open. He would be hanging around Cincinnati? Coaching *water polo*? "You're going to play water polo for that man after he abandoned us?"

"It's better than staying with the Marlins."

"Oh, yeah? What's so *bad* about the Marlins?" I felt the heat rise in my chest. I hated that she was rewarding him for leaving. She didn't know the cause of his departure—nobody did—and given his sometimes scary and irrational behavior, I wondered if he'd crossed a line with one of the girls. "Why do you want to get involved? You'll be taking sides."

Jacquie's eyes bored into me. She seemed to be baiting me. "I have to think of myself for once, Kim."

"What did he say?" I stood at her door, waiting.

"What do you mean?"

"Mr. Bergen. Did he mention me?"

"No." Her abrupt tone sounded defensive.

"Fine." I stretched the gum out of my mouth and wrapped a wad around my finger. I could feel my resentment toward Jacquie building. Playing water polo for Mr. Bergen might be exactly what she needed to do to feel she was doing something for herself, but I saw her decision as another abandonment, indistinguishable from what was happening with my parents.

She set her book down, and for a moment her round cheeks relaxed and her eyes softened. She seemed to be trying to make me feel better. "He probably thought you'd never quit."

"Well, maybe I *will*." I bit the gum off my finger and continued to chew.

"You're disgusting." She returned to her book. "Close the door, would you?"

I grabbed my suit and towel and tore off in the Impala, headed for practice. I was so knotted up I had no idea what to do with myself. Overnight, the water had grown murky. I was circling on the surface in my own little lane, following an undulating and distorted black line at the bottom of the pool.

CHAPTER 23

I n May of 1973, within days of Mr. Bergen's departure, Charlie Hickcox arrived to lead the Marlins. At twenty-six, Charlie was scary good-looking, a boyish Mark Spitz type with dark, wavy hair and a mustache. He was also a rock star of the swimming world: he had set eight world records at the peak of his career, with three gold medals and one silver at the 1968 Summer Olympics in Mexico City, and he was married to Lesley Bush, a famous Olympic diver.

Charlie's five assistants—Gary Hall, Larry Barbiere, Jack Horsley, Bob Silver, and Bob Groseth, all former Indiana University graduates—had been hired by Mr. Keating, who was said to be edging his way in as an Indiana University "Team Dad" since his son, Charlie Keating III, would be attending there in the fall.

The laid-back, buff, and blond coaches wore sunglasses and shorts with their plaid boxers hanging out, and most of the girls began preening in the locker room before and after practice. I wouldn't say swimming was easier—in fact, the distance-lane yardage increased—but practices became an opportunity to flirt and tell funny stories, a strange departure from the shock-and-awe approach of Mr. Bergen. The pool seemed to go overnight from an intense

pressure cooker to the loose, undisciplined atmosphere of a frater-
nity keg party.

As much as I had feared and sometimes doubted Mr. Bergen,
nothing at the pool felt right without him. The sexualized atmosphere he'd brought didn't vanish with his departure, it just changed
tone. Every week brought a new scandal: coaches swatting swimmers
on the rear end, arms on shoulders, dirty jokes. And one coach liked
to touch me on the neck just before my races. I kept asking myself:
Was I just growing up and noticing more than I had before? Or was
there something *off* about all this?

The most obvious difference was the higher energy at the
pool. The guys were louder, more aggressive, and the coaches
accepted chronic tardiness, talking back, and any old excuse to
get out of practice. My reaction was to puff up my chest, lean in
with righteous indignation, and address each change as it arose.
I was determined not to push the memories of Mr. Bergen to the
back of my mind, because I believed in his authoritarian approach.
Some part of me imagined that if things got really bad, he might
even return to the team.

But all my pushing back against the changes at the pool was
really just my acting out of a fear of losing control of my life. It had
taken time to adjust to Paul Bergen and now I had whiplash. The
moment it hit me that I would have to accept the current regime—
right before practice started one day—I felt a wave of panic, realizing
I hadn't weighed myself in several days. Nobody had even mentioned
weighing in.

I stopped Charlie on my way to the scale. "Aren't we doing
weigh-ins anymore?"

He leaned over, smiling, as if he were talking to a child. "*You*
will monitor your weight from now on."

I took two steps back. *Is he serious?* All I could think was, *What
in the hell kind of loose ship is he running? If he is willing to let us
monitor our weight, God only knows what he might be loosey-goosey
about next.*

"I'm more concerned about your swimming," he said.

Fine, I thought, *I'll show* you.

The whole weighing-in thing was so ingrained by then, it was all I thought about. I decided I would check my weight daily and agonize without his help.

WHEN I RETURNED FROM PRACTICE THAT day, I was still outraged. I sat on the kitchen floor, giving Dad my litany of complaints about what I saw as a circus atmosphere at the pool.

"Charlie has no control," I told him. "The kids do whatever they want. You wouldn't believe how easy it is to get out of practice." I also went on a tirade about how it seemed Charlie had flung open the doors of the natatorium, and now swimmers from around the world were flooding in and landing at our pool like sea creatures after a tsunami. I couldn't understand why they were getting equal treatment. "He doesn't even weigh us!" I said.

Dad paused purposefully as he spun open his bourbon with the palm of his hand. "He's got no business weighing you. Look, you need to ignore it."

"Ignore *what*?"

"The problems. All of them. Focusing on the problems isn't helping you."

"Dad, are you saying I'm supposed to just go *along* with everything?" I heard myself whining.

"Just stay out of it," he said. "Stay out of *all* of it. You've got enough to worry about."

I leaned back against one of the metal cabinets and stared at the kitchen ceiling. This was a complete reversal of what Mom had told me about having good instincts.

"Fine," I said. I didn't know why I was confiding in him anyway.

LOOKING BACK, IT WAS STILL TOO SOON for me to realize how much of an emotional contortionist I'd become in order to function on Mr. Bergen's team. I have to admit now that the pool atmosphere with Charlie wasn't *that* reckless; without a doubt, the team was more functional than it had been under Mr. Bergen. So why was I angry all the time?

Maybe it was because with Mr. Bergen I'd convinced myself we swimmers were connected—that we were a team of performers, doing a difficult tap-dance in lock step with each other.

Of course, this was an illusion. We were all individuals in an individual sport and Mr. Bergen certainly had his favorites. But the amount of time we spent together, the dedication—the things we were forced to give up to be swimmers—and the daily pressure to excel had made me feel connected to my teammates. Sitting on the deck and listening to Mr. Bergen's lectures before practice every day had not been that different than sitting at the dinner table listening to Dad.

With Charlie, it seemed we'd gone from being a team to being a program with a doctrine of every-man-for-himself. And I felt it viscerally.

WITHIN A MONTH OF CHARLIE'S ARRIVAL, I received an invitation to the wedding of Mr. Keating's daughter, Mary, to Gary Hall, who was one of the assistant coaches and also an Olympian. I felt grateful to be included. The reception was held at Cincinnati's famous Netherland Plaza Hotel, a grand Art Deco structure, in the gold-plated Hall of Mirrors, modeled after the one in the Palace of Versailles in Paris. I was seated with other swimmers at a round table in the palatial balcony, looking down at the wedding party. The view reminded me of the ballroom scene in the 1972 film *The Poseidon Adventure*—the one that takes place just before the tidal wave hits the ship. Mr. Bergen was down there, mingling on the main floor, and I couldn't stop feeling a sense of impending doom.

DAD WAS THE ONLY ONE WHO NOTICED the change in me, which happened around the time of my sixteenth birthday. Charlie Hickcox's fame had attracted swimmers from around the world, and one of them, Susan Dickey from South Africa, gave me fits right away. She was a distance freestyler my age, short, with a broad, toothy smile and a faint trace of an early-nineteenth-century British accent clinging to her speech. She seemed sweet and polite and happy to be there, and I hated that. One night, swimming behind me in the distance lane, she swam right on my feet, tapping my toes, as if she were a car riding my bumper, flashing her lights in the fast lane of an interstate highway. I kept giving her the chance to go ahead of me, but she refused. As in a bike or horserace, it's always easier to swim behind. I sent her multiple angry visual messages that I wanted her to back the hell off. But she wouldn't.

About halfway through practice, the fumes from the chemical used to clean the concrete deck were so potent and we were coughing so hard that Charlie suggested we run outside between sets to clear our lungs. When we returned, Susan was instantly back on my feet, maybe two seconds behind me, and gliding into the wall, she ran right up my backside. Coughing and hacking from the acrid fumes, I barked, "Go ahead!"

I knew my reaction had nothing to do with her and everything to do with my own internal turmoil. I could've spoken more firmly and forced her to lead the lane from the beginning, but I wanted to be the victim. I wanted a reason to blame her. To blame *some*one.

After practice, when she climbed out of the pool and shot Charlie her broad, gleaming smile, my attitude was like the toxic gas. I could hardly look at her.

"Good job, Susan," Charlie said, wrapping his arm around her. "You're very talented."

I didn't know what to do with my envy. I was furious. Mr. *Bergen* would not have let her get away with this. I wanted him there to give her the cold treatment, to rant about "some" swimmers who weren't pulling their weight. Who weren't leading the lane when they should be. I wanted him to throw a kickboard or two. To make me justified in feeling so resentful. I wanted a return to the rigidity, a sense of the line I couldn't cross.

WHEN I ARRIVED HOME, I DUG THROUGH my drawer of team snapshots until I found a close-up of Susan, mugging for the camera. I taped the photo to the back of my bedroom door and hurled darts at her. "You bitch! You nasty little bitch," I spat under my breath.

"Hey!" Dad's voice shot up through the stairwell. "What are you slamming?"

"It's private," I yelled, daring him to come look.

A few minutes later, Dad poked his head around the door and examined the shredded photograph. An impish grin spread over his face. "Maybe I've been too hard on you, Butch," he said, "but I got no problem with the darts. I'm glad you found an outlet for your aggression."

A few weeks later, he was escorting his Bengals football friends to my room to see the shredded photo as part of a house tour. I didn't think anything of it; in fact, I relaxed. This was Dad's way of showing he was proud of me.

His was a bizarre version of encouragement, and it wasn't helpful. I'd gone into emotional shutdown mode twice in my life: as a twelve-year-old, after telling Dad about Ned, now again, with Mr. Bergen's leaving. Both events had caught me off-guard, shaken my sense of security.

I decided I'd go to the pool first thing the next day and speak to Charlie openly about my frustration, hoping to convey the trouble I was having adjusting.

I DRESSED IN A HURRY, MY HAIR STILL dripping down the middle of my back, and dragged myself up the stairs to the coach's office after practice. I was pumped and ready to lay out my gripes: coaches giving backrubs, kids skipping practice, and special treatment of kids with "talent." In the early '70s someone had co-opted Edison's quote about genius, saying that *athletic achievement* was 1 percent inspiration and 99 percent perspiration. I believed this wholeheartedly. It wasn't fair to treat "talented" kids as special. Talent was only a small part of it.

But five minutes later, alone with Charlie, I found myself stuttering like a star-struck groupie. He scooted so close that our knees nearly touched and I stopped in the middle of a sentence, unable to remember what I wanted to say.

"What is it, Kimberly?" There was a sparkle of mischief in his smile.

He began to say something about talent versus hard work but the words came out like warm chocolate and all I could do was stare at his thick, wavy hair. I wondered what it would be like to be married to him.

"Are you saying practice is too hard?" He waited for my answer and I was jolted out of my reverie.

"No. I'm saying it's too easy." What I couldn't say was that he had failed to create a structure for us, and with no structure at home I *needed* structure at the pool. He didn't seem to pay attention to our times, our moods, anything.

But he raised his hand to stop me. Sunshine, he said, was not a fitting word to describe our practice group, and he was sorry he had changed the name from Pressure I to Sunshine I. He was now going to switch the names again, this time to Gold, Silver, and Bronze, to focus on achievement. "If it were up to me, Kimberly, I would remove the kids with no talent. I would rather work with talent than hard workers any day." He rubbed his dark mustache as he searched for the words. "Kimberly, you're one of the most talented."

He spoke softly but his words sounded empty, reminding me of my parents' telling us they loved us and then leaving us alone for two weeks every month.

I knew Charlie was trying to support me, and he looked concerned, but he wasn't getting it. I believed I had *some* talent. That wasn't it. It was that he didn't have a firm enough hand on the reins.

When Charlie asked if I'd spoken to my parents about my frustration, in my nervousness, I launched into a defense of them. Then my mind moved directly to Charlie's telling us we needed to increase our consumption of protein. I told him there was no meat in the house because Mom and Dad were away on business.

I expected him to say, "Oh, it's okay, Kimberly. I understand you're stressed." Instead, he pulled out his wallet and handed me a twenty. "Use this to buy some meat," he said.

I had gotten something off my chest, but our chat hadn't gone the way I'd wanted.

I took the twenty dollars like a dope, thanked him, and skittered out of his office.

From left to right wearing caps: Kim Peters, Kim Pahner, Kathy Lukens; in water without caps: left to right Nonny Hartman, Sue Flerlage, Deena Deardurff; on deck, left to right: Kris Odenwald, Charlie Hickcox, Susie Hartman, Paula Koenig. Photo by Peter Dernier.

CHAPTER 24

On a Saturday afternoon, I lay sprawled on my bed, catatonic from a hard workout followed by too much nibbling on frozen icing from one of Mom's sale cakes in the freezer. Jacquie's water polo gig hadn't lasted very long and she'd decided to quit the Marlins, too. Now she and her friends, giddy in the living room, sewed clown costumes and chattered about how much money they would make throwing kids' parties over the summer. She had been accepted to an exchange program and would need money for her travel to El Salvador.

I wanted to earn some money too. Otherwise, how would I ever afford college? But with the swimming treadmill all summer, there was no way I could join the clown parties.

Dad, in the bedroom office, was in one of his moods, complaining to Mom. "What about the younger kids? How will Jacquie run the household if she's off throwing parties? Who will buy the groceries? Fix the meals? Put the checks in the bank when we're gone?"

"You have to let her work this out herself, Dick," Mom groaned. She thought the clown parties would pay so little that Jacquie would lose interest.

I shut my door, hoping to cut off the conflict, but Dad's voice grew louder. "She's unrealistic. How does she expect to find these kids with birthdays?"

When I heard Jacquie's last friend leave and then her puttering in her room, I poked my head in to see if she'd overheard Dad's rant. In a voice saturated with optimism, she listed the parties her group had confirmed for the summer. Then she paused. "Are you going to prom?"

I examined my nails. "Me? Not yet. Maybe Gary will ask." I was trying to impress her with my sophistication by name-dropping from my list of friends outside the swimming circle. Gary Robinson was a teddy bear of a guy in my art class. He was quiet, considerate, an attentive listener, and a talented artist, and I was interested in him—though I'm not sure he ever gave me a reason to think he might be interested in me. "I don't think you know him," I said. "He's on the football team . . ." I stopped when I heard Dad's heavy foot.

"*Who's* on the football team?"

Dodging Dad's scent—Old Spice and perspiration—I stepped into Jacquie's room and started to close the door. Lately, he'd provoked me just enough that I wanted to push back hard. "A guy named Gary, Dad." I clenched my teeth.

"Oh, yeah?" He threw his shoulder into the door and it flew open. I grabbed the knob so it wouldn't slam the wall.

Dad pulled up his belt and combed through his greasy hair with his fingers. "What *about* him?"

"Nothing, Dad." I blocked his way into Jacquie's room.

"What do you mean 'nothing'? Who's Gary?" Dad spat. He was at his worst just before the cocktail hour.

"I told you: a guy on the football team. Why do you have to know?"

"Aren't the guys on the team colored?"

My eyes narrowed and I jerked my head back to show my indignation. Though Cincinnati was a southern city in many ways, we didn't use the word "colored" anymore. Race relations were hobbling along—at best—but Walnut Hills High School was liberal, integrated, and, as I saw it, accepting of students regardless of race.

"Aren't they?"

"No."

"Well, is *he* colored?" Dad's booming voice rang in my ear.

I nudged his belly with my forearm. "What's the big deal, Dad?"

"What's the big *deal*? You want to know what the big *deal* is?" His nostrils flared like a gored bull's; I could see his teeth. I backed away as he swung, his first hit to my face a blast of light that knocked out my vision for a second. Then he was swinging and slapping so hard I couldn't react fast enough. I ducked into the hallway, covering my face, and he barged into me. I grabbed the rail but he kept coming. One wide swing, another, then a series of stinging smacks to the side of my face. The blood flooded my cheeks. I fought to grab the railing but his body was like a granite wall. With my back to the stairs, I stepped away, lost my footing, and stumbled down a few steps. He seemed to be right there, on me, shoving me down the stairs. I ended up on the landing.

"You ever go with a colored kid to anything…" He was gasping, six inches from my face. "You'll never live in this house again!"

Your house? I thought. *This is* my *house—I'm the one who's here all the time.* I was choking on tears of fury. I tucked my head in and hit back with all my force. *Is he really going to kill me over this?* Pam inched up the stairs toward the landing, fear locked on her face. Dad swiped at me again, just missing Pam with his elbow.

I glimpsed Jacquie's fearful eyes over the balustrade. "Leave her alone!"

Dad staggered away, seemingly weakened. I stumbled upstairs, past Jacquie, and tripped into my room. Pam and Jacquie tiptoed in, shutting the door.

"You shouldn't have told him," Jacquie said, comforting me.

"Go away," I sobbed.

"Where was Mom?" she whispered.

"Where she always is: with Dad."

"We should run away," Pam said. "We should wait until Mom and Dad are gone and take off, all five of us."

"You think he won't find us? Go away." The hurt was more emotional than physical. I curled to one side, pulled the sheet up under my chin, and listened to the moths hitting the overhead light.

Jacquie and Pam gently shut the door behind them and the house grew quiet. It was a cleansing chill that allowed me to sort out what was important in the moment and what wasn't. Jacquie and Pam were on my side. So were Ricky and David. The five of us had struggled on our own but we knew how to come together when it counted. Finally—*finally*—I would fight back. Seriously fight back. I would go to the prom with Gary if he asked me, and if I had to move out of the house because of it, I would.

It was 1974, six years since Martin Luther King's assassination, and national headlines about racism seemed to have been replaced by a constant stream about the Patti Hearst kidnapping and the Watergate coverup. I *thought* Mom was more enlightened than Dad and might come around to supporting me on this one. But later, from the top of the stairs, I overheard her rueful whispering.

"If you push too hard, Dick, you're going to end up with the exact opposite of what you want." She reminded him about how Jacquie had returned from a swim meet in Arizona, determined to open a Farrell's Ice Cream parlor, and had given up on it on her own. The implication was that ignoring Jacquie's idea had worked. She was now back to thinking about college.

I was furious with Mom. She wasn't exactly open-minded *all* the time, but why was she so unwilling to step in? There was no discussion of the morality of Dad's racism, the right or wrong of his reaction. Was this the *best* she could do? Imply that we were like toddlers, learning to assert ourselves? I wondered if she was afraid of Dad in some way. Afraid that he would come after her if she didn't toe the party line.

"Like hell," Dad said. "They shack up with some colored kid and they won't be members of this family anymore."

I wanted to march downstairs and wrestle him again, but I knew that wouldn't serve me. Mom seemed to be saying, "These kids are just pushing back. That's what kids do."

No! I thought. *This daughter is pushing back because she now has the strength to do it.*

How long could we survive in a house like this? Twelve-year-old Pam seemed to be the only one immune from Dad's physical attacks now. And he was getting so much worse.

AN HOUR LATER, I DUCKED MY HEAD into Jacquie's room. She'd heard Mom and Dad too. She lay curled in her twin bed, spooning her pillow. Their words seemed to have hurt her personally.

"One more year and I'm out of this hellhole," I said.

"Well, you better not go with Gary to the prom. Dad will kill you, you know, and I don't mean 'kill' as a figure of speech." She handed me a Twizzler.

I bit hard into the end of its leathery sweetness. "He won't kill me," I said. "If he tries again, I'm leaving."

CHAPTER 25

n the end, Gary didn't ask me, and as soon as I rode off to the senior prom with John Crosset—a guy from our white neighborhood—Dad's having knocked me down the stairs seemed to dissolve for him into a blurred memory as if it had been a disagreement over what program to watch on TV.

What amazed me was Dad's amnesia. I want to believe that he buried the memory because it was easier than addressing his own childhood trauma. It's breathtaking how trauma can keep us frozen for a lifetime, reacting like a child when tiny elements of those haunting memories return. But maybe the explanation for Dad's amnesia was simpler: it was easier for him to bury the memory than acknowledge the way he had acted toward me.

"We need to talk, Butch," he said one night as I came in after practice.

Six months had passed, and my anger at him over the Gary incident still smoldered. And now he was hounding me again, this time counting off the months until he'd have one less kid moping around the house or complaining about his drinking. I knew what he wanted.

"What are you doing about college?" he asked.

"I'm going to one," I said, coughing. I'd had a chronic sore throat and a chesty type of congestion for weeks now, but I put on an air of competence. Even though my senior year had started, college seemed a long way off. I told myself I would find time to apply when I felt better.

I was getting maybe five hours of sleep a night, waking up exhausted, dragging myself to practice, slogging through five miles in the water, driving to school fatigued, cramming for tests, and then returning to the pool for the toughest workout of the day, maybe six to seven more miles. I was barely coping.

"Just send out some applications," Dad said. "What's the problem?"

The problem was I was fumbling in the dark. Applications to *where*? Was I eligible for a college scholarship? Title IX had passed the previous year, calling for fair and equal treatment among men's and women's programs. Friends were talking about swimming in college, but it seemed most of the private schools, especially on the East Coast, didn't think the new law applied to them. Was I supposed to pick public institutions I knew had swim teams? This was before computers and Internet searches. I could go to the library and ask for help, but what would I ask for? And when on earth would I have the time?

"We've been cutting you slack and giving you breaks the other kids don't have," Mom said. "We don't care where you go, but we can't pay for it." The prospect of having one less kid to deal with had whipped them both into a frenzy.

I WANTED TO TALK TO CHARLIE ABOUT what he considered the best "swimming schools," but he always seemed to be busy. Then on November 17, 1974, it was as if a window cracked open and a blast of cold air rushed in.

The team was standing around near the locker rooms, some of the guys making farting sounds with their hands in their armpits and calling the girls ogres.

I hurried to put on my suit and return to the deck, where everyone was still milling about.

"Where's Charlie?" I asked.

No one answered, but we were all looking around at each other. One of the guys glanced up and rolled his eyes. In the corner of the balcony, the coach's office was dark, its curtains pulled and lights out. A chill darted through me.

"What's going on up there?" I exchanged a glance with Bob Groseth, one of our assistant coaches, as I gestured toward the office.

Bob studied me with unwavering attention, then arched an eyebrow.

"One day, I'm going to write a tell-all book," I said.

Bob was drinking a Sprite and he coughed it up in his mouth as he laughed. "No, you aren't." He seemed to be daring me.

"You want to bet?" I said. "You watch. I'm going to tell everything. All the Marlin dirt." I imagined a novel filled with accounts of coaches having affairs with swimmers, parents getting involved and threatening to kill the coaches, that sort of thing. I added that I wouldn't write it immediately. I had to attend college first. I needed at least until 1981.

Bob let out a raucous laugh, which made me even more determined. He grabbed a greasy paper plate from a trashcan against the wall, tore off a corner, and wrote, "I bet Kim Peters will not publish a book on swimming by January 1981." Then he looked at me again. "What are we betting?"

"Dinner at the Maisonette?" I'd never been there. It was the fanciest restaurant I could think of in Cincinnati.

Bob signed his name as Charlie arrived on deck to lead practice, his T-shirt rumpled and hair unbrushed. "We need a witness," Bob said to Charlie.

"For what?" Charlie took one look at the paper plate, then set the plate on one of the starting blocks, where he dashed off his signature.

"It's going to be an exposé," I said, my head cocked.

Paper plate bet, signed by Bob Groseth and Charlie Hickcox.

Charlie shoved the signed plate at me. "Sheesh!" Then he pounded his closed fist into his other cupped hand, placed his foot on the nearest starting block, and leaned over, his elbow on his knee. "Let's get started with a thousand warm-up: 400 swim, 300 hundred pull, 200 kick, and 100 swim."

I rushed off to my locker to save the paper plate document, then plunked into the water, swallowing my satisfaction. The idea of a book *did* interest me. Finally, Charlie knew *I* knew what was going on, and for once I didn't feel unaware.

THE DAY I SIGNED THE PAPER PLATE proved to be a watershed for me personally. Charlie escorted me to my car after practice. The turquoise Impala that Jacquie and I now shared was by itself in the giant gravel lot, and Charlie said he had something he needed to tell me. I hoped it was about college.

We stood on the driver's side of the car, and at first all I could do was smirk. "What?" I finally asked. "What did you want to say?"

He leaned down and with his silvery voice, said, "You don't know what's going on, so you shouldn't make assumptions." I think he thought I knew more than I did, but I knew *something* was going on. The outward signs were all there.

"I'm not making assumptions," I said nervously. "I have eyes."

"You think you know, but you're wrong." He sounded convincing.

"I'm not stupid."

"No, but you're on the wrong track." As I opened the car door, he put his hand on my shoulder. "You're doing a great job, Kimberly." With that, he squeezed my shoulder and left.

I watched the receding back of his white T-shirt and felt a familiar panic. *Wrong track?* What was he talking about? I flashed to my parents' plea about college. "Hey, Charlie . . ."

He stopped and glanced my way.

"Is there any way you could pull some strings for a scholarship?"

He was pensive for a moment. "You concentrate on your swimming, and I'll do what I can. Do we have a deal?"

I WAS STUNNED WHEN CHARLIE CALLED ME into his office two weeks after Christmas. Seated at his desk, he handed me a letter dated January 6. "I spoke to Pokey Richardson, the coach at USC. She'll be calling you."

I glanced at the typed letter, which read: "We would be pleased and honored to have such a great talent as Kim Peters as part of our family."

"Oh, my God!" My mouth hung open, tears filling my eyes. I didn't know what to say. *Me? A talent?* While I had never approved of Charlie's belief about talent being more important than hard work, I couldn't deny it felt good to hear the word applied to me. "What did you tell her?" I felt a mix of excitement and terror. "Tonight? She's calling me *tonight*?"

I gave Charlie a huge hug, and moments later I did a jackknife off the block. As I hit the water and threw my head back, my ears popped. The accumulated pressure had finally been released, and now I had to think like a student on her way to college. Swimming for USC? College in California? The idea sounded unbelievable.

PRACTICE THAT DAY WAS A BLUR. When it was over, I raced home to tell Mom and Dad, who were in their office giving Jacquie another sales pitch about working for them after college.

"USC might be calling me," I announced proudly.

"Southern California or South Carolina?" Dad didn't know where I'd applied.

"California, Dad."

He shrugged and handed Mom the stapler. "I wouldn't get too excited, Butch," he said. "People like to make promises they can't keep . . . like last night, right Beej?" He elbowed Mom.

I rolled my eyes as Jacquie left the room, but his attitude was still on my mind when I picked up the phone a few hours later.

Pokey's cheerful voice sounded like she was close by. "Charlie Hickcox has spoken to me about your swimming," she said, "and depending on your transcript, we may be able to get you some money."

The receiver shook in my hand.

"I don't know how much," she said, "but I'll talk with Barbara Hedges, the athletic director."

I don't remember a word after that. I was hearing a trumpet blast in my head. As I hung up, my pulse quickened, my fists clenched, and I screeched as I threw my arms in the air and hugged Dad.

His arms limp, he pulled away.

"What's the matter, Dad?"

He emptied the ice bucket into the sink. "Why didn't you let *me* talk to her?"

"I don't know. I guess I forgot." I rubbed my palms down my pant legs.

"You *forgot*?" He showed no enthusiasm. "You need to find out how much they're willing to pay. When she calls back, you let *me* talk."

I immediately began praying: "God, Jesus, Holy Spirit, guardian angel, Great Gramma and Pa Hodges . . . anyone else out there, I know you don't know me, but if you can pull some strings to get me a scholarship to USC, I would be grateful forever. Oh . . . and please don't let him get on the phone when they call."

A SHIVERING BUNDLE OF NERVES, I WAITED all week for the phone to ring. Finally, Friday arrived. I was in my room after practice, waiting for the cocktail hour to end so we could eat dinner. Dad's voice was so loud downstairs I couldn't shut him out, even with the door closed. The phone rang and he answered, "Abercrombie and Fitch." Back then it was a store nobody had ever heard of, but he recalled it from his childhood, having grown up near New York City.

"Dick," Mom called, "that could be the athletic director for Kim." But he had already hung up.

I squeezed my eyes shut, bracing for the phone to ring again. Sure enough, it did. This time, Dad restrained himself. I scrambled down the stairs and tiptoed to the kitchen to listen. He had a pencil behind his ear and was chewing the nail on his baby finger. After a few formalities, he said, "Well, with five kids we don't have a lot of extra cash."

Then came the bad puns, and laughter at his own jokes. My heart dropped. I was sure he was ruining my chances. I reached for the phone but Dad, holding the phone to his ear with one shoulder, silenced me with his index finger to his lips. I held on to the counter, five feet from him, ready to grab the phone if necessary and trying to glean as much as I could from the conversation.

When the call ended, Dad patted his round midsection and tucked his shirt into his trousers. "They'll offer you a full ride."

"Dad, you don't *know*." I felt sick to my stomach as I glanced at Mom. "Why couldn't you just act normal?"

Dad turned his back to me, opened the freezer, and dug into the ice with his bare hand.

"He did a fine job, Kim," Mom said.

"Well, what did she say?"

Dad pretended not to hear me as he poured bourbons and Fresca for himself and Mom.

"I'm sorry if I hurt your feelings, Dad, but . . ."

He handed Mom her drink and faced me. "You have so little faith. You have to give me *some* credit for knowing a thing or two." He bent over to place his bottle of JTS Brown bourbon on the bottom shelf of the butler's pantry, and for a moment I viewed him as a child in need of encouragement.

"I guess. It's just . . ."

"What?"

"I don't know, you sometimes . . . well, you embarrass me."

He leaned over and pursed his lips, and I kissed him. "It's a cold, tough world out there, Butch," he said. "You'd better get used to it."

A THICK ENVELOPE EVENTUALLY ARRIVED in the mailbox. I climbed the stairs to the house, ripped it open, briefly read the cover letter, and jumped around the front hall, squealing like a contestant on *The Price Is Right*. USC was offering to pay everything. Later, I learned that this was the second full scholarship awarded for women's swimming in the school's history.

Mom and Dad were traveling, so I raced to the pool, burst through the natatorium doors, and searched for Charlie. He sat in the bleachers, looking like a model for *GQ* with his dark, wavy hair and thick mustache. Nobody had ever done such a nice thing for me . . . ever. I wanted to kiss him.

"Congratulations, Kimberly." He gave me a sideways hug, then patted my thigh. "Let's go for a drink sometime. Would that be all right?"

"Yes—yes—definitely. Thank you *so* much. I can't believe it." At practice that evening, my mind raced so fast that I put my bathing suit on inside out and had to start over. The program I'd criticized for its chaos and toxicity was turning out to be a warm bath of sweet-scented oils.

Nobody said so, but I knew Pokey was taking a chance on me. I didn't know any girls on the Marlins who'd gotten a full ride, and it wasn't like I was winning my events on the national level. The offer was extraordinary, built on Charlie's convincing Pokey that I was a good investment. I couldn't help but wonder: *Have I really accomplished enough to be given this scholarship, or is it payment for keeping my mouth shut?*

It doesn't matter, I thought. *I'm doing this*. My world had shrunk to swimming, swimming, and more swimming, and for the first time I could see a future with my life in alignment. With the promise of a scholarship, I felt halfway out. Halfway out from living under my parents' strictures. Sure, there were problems at the pool and I had functioned better with the rigid rules, but with Charlie and Pokey's help I could build my own model for a path forward. The idea sounded delicious.

I would work as hard as I could, be a positive influence on the younger swimmers, and do as I'd been trained under Mr. Bergen's tutelage: hear no evil, see no evil, speak no evil. I would do anything I was asked without questioning or agonizing.

I jumped into the pool with a huge splash of relief. I'd overcome my biggest hurdle and now I had a plan. I pushed off the bottom and glided to the surface, stretching my arms through the cool water, twisting with each stroke, feeling the power of my body. Wow, did it feel incredible to have a way forward. Swimming had long been a hypnotic chug-chug-chug for me, but now whistles were blowing, boom barriers lifting. I was so nervous with excitement I felt like a runaway train.

I swam into the wall after a brief warm-up, then waited for Charlie. "Next, we're doing a mile breaststroke," he said.

Most of the distance freestylers groaned, but I was too elated to think much of it. I pushed off, and the laps ticked by so quickly I lost count.

About halfway through, I pushed off the wall, and as my knee whipped around, I felt a snap. I don't mean a slight twinge. A substantial snap. Acute and painful. Like something in my knee had come off the track. Fear shot through me. Had I dislocated a muscle? A ligament? On every kick I felt a click-click-click. Something was out of place.

CHAPTER 26

By the end of practice, I was in so much pain, I could hardly put any weight on my leg. Charlie saw me hobbling out of the locker room and wanted to know what was wrong. I pulled up my pant leg and he grumbled, "Dammit," which scared me. "Show it to your parents. Let me know what they say."

The next morning, as I limped to the locker room, Charlie hustled over. "Did you talk to your parents?" He looked wan and bleary-eyed, which sent a chill through me. "You didn't tell them, did you?"

"Well…" I hesitated. "They haven't been home. But even if they *had*, my father would go nuts." I held my cheeks to warm my hands.

"Like what?"

"Like screaming and shouting. He asks me about practice, I tell him practice was terrible, and he loses it."

"Why don't you *lie*?" Again, he seemed to be asking why I was so stupid. "Tell him practice is great."

"But it isn't."

"I don't give a damn. Tell him that anyway."

Alarm bells should've gone off for me, but they didn't. I thought, *Well, I guess it's worth a try.*

THAT NIGHT I LIMPED UP THE STAIRS to the house, my knee clicking and burning with each step. As soon as I entered, Dad called from the kitchen. "How was practice, Butch?"

I hesitated. "Great."

The house went dead still. I was sure there would be more to follow, but Dad said nothing. Nothing at all. It was like that tense moment of tranquility, seconds after a lightning strike. My whole world grew quiet. And I was overcome with joy. That Charlie Hickcox. What a damn genius! I wished he'd made the suggestion a year earlier. He could've saved me so much grief.

My lies didn't help my painful knee, however. I kept hoping the swelling would go down and the pain would dissipate, but from one day to the next, nothing changed.

AROUND THIS TIME, A CLASSMATE—Dan Angress—approached me about swimming for our high school, Walnut Hills. The school had just started a girls' team—Jacquie was its first captain—and I could swim faster than Dan and most of the other guys, so he asked if I would like to shake things up a little by swimming on the guys' team.

As he spoke, his eyes brimmed with humor. I loved his easy-going manner. He had olive skin and wavy dark hair that he left uncombed, and he wore a torn T-shirt with faded lettering over blue jeans that bagged at the ankles. A friend had told me Dan was the son of a Holocaust survivor; that his parents were divorced, his mother had moved away to take a better academic job, and he was living with friends. I'd had so much practice creating the appearance of a normal home life that I instantly thought I understood him. He was a work in progress I was sure I could help.

"We need you on the freestyle relay," he said. "Wouldn't it be fun to swim with the guys?"

I gave him a lopsided smile. "Fun" wasn't exactly the word I would use. On the Marlins I'd been swimming with guys in practice since I was eleven and mostly what we got from them were insults. "I don't know if I could miss practice," I told him. On the other hand, practices were killing my knee. Maybe with a day off every now and then for a high school dual meet, my knee would receive the rest it so badly needed. I wasn't sure how to respond. "Let me talk to my coach."

Dan nudged me in the waist with his elbow. "Catch you on the flip-flop, good buddy." His CB talk was so goofy, he made it hard to keep a straight face.

I HOBBLED INTO THE POOL THE NEXT DAY, hoping to ask Charlie about high school swimming, but as soon as he saw me, he said, "We need to talk."

I braced myself for a lecture after practice, though I was hoping for moral support. He asked if we could go for a ride, and when I climbed into his car, there was a wicked, icy breeze, wet ground, and dead leaves sticking to the windshield of his Volkswagen Beetle. Charlie was unusually quiet. Traveling west on North Bend Road, I turned toward him. "What is it you want to talk about?"

He didn't answer immediately, so I jumped in. "Before you say anything, would it be okay if I swim for Walnut Hills? Not practice, just their meets?"

Charlie cleared his throat. "If it'll help your attitude." He glanced over at me briefly, then continued to drive. "You're one of the leaders. You need to stop whining about a phantom pain."

I clutched my purse into my chest. Wait, *what?*

"Kimberly . . ."

"Do you think I'm making this up?" I barked.

He stopped on a hill for a traffic light and I glanced at his profile, his broad chin, and glistening eyes, staring straight ahead.

Calmly, he said, "This knee thing and your worrying are all connected. You have analysis paralysis."

"*Look*, will you?" I lifted both pant legs to compare one knee to the other, but he wouldn't turn his head. Instead, he put the car into second gear.

"You're hobbling on the deck like an invalid, Kimberly. You need to stop the whining or see a doctor." He glanced at me for a moment as a tiny puppy dashed in front of the car. He slammed the brakes, skidded on the wet pavement, and my knees smashed into his glove compartment.

Instantly, I shrieked. With tears shooting out of the corners of my eyes, I lifted my pant legs to examine my knee, which, after practice, was badly swollen.

Charlie looked scared. "Oh, my God, I'm sorry. Maybe you *do* need to see a doctor. Promise me you won't tell anybody about this."

WHEN DAD SAW MY SWOLLEN KNEE, he immediately grabbed the phone and arranged an appointment with Dr. Miller, an orthopedist known for his work with the Cincinnati Ballet and Bengals Football team. The son of a doctor, Dad believed in responding immediately. I didn't know how my parents could afford surgery if it were necessary, but they often seemed to wing it when it came to financial decisions. "We'll figure something out," they said.

Dr. Miller was humble, a man of few words, the consummate diagnostician. He seemed to think I had a sprained ligament before even examining me. Cupping my knee in his hands, he spoke directly to Mom. "This might improve on its own, so I'd prefer not to dig around."

I thought, go ahead, dig around. I'd been so euphoric over the scholarship and now, two weeks later, the symphony in my head had stopped, the music fallen away. He let go of my knee to write on his tiny prescription pad. "I'm recommending you ice this three times a day. After three weeks, if the knee still hurts, I'll operate."

I took Dr. Miller's advice: for three weeks, I snuggled in bed with a bag of ice in a dishtowel. By morning, exhausted, my bed drenched, I dressed slowly, grabbed a snack from the pantry, limped into the pitch-black morning, and shut the front door quietly behind me. The early morning air biting, my whole body downcast, I tucked myself into the car before the lights came on in the neighborhood. Driving through the darkness, I thought, *This swimming gig is hell. The birds aren't even up and I'm off to jump into an ice-cold pool with a sore knee and no decent breakfast.*

Charlie was right about my negative attitude. I wanted to be a dutiful daughter and teammate, but my world view had narrowed to the four walls of the natatorium.

I was at that point in high school when your life begins to feel minuscule. I wanted a way out. I also felt sad that graduation was in the offing and I hadn't done much in school. Classmates were expressing their opinion that the pendulum had swung too far in offering women athletic scholarships to college, which grated on my nerves. The pendulum *had* to swing wide to effect change. But it was also more than that. The thought of flying off to California had been such a rush; now, with my injured knee, it looked like it might not happen.

As a way of fighting back, I asked for permission from Mr. Brokamp, my school's tall, gentle principal, to paint a mural on the plaster wall facing the shallow end of the guys' pool as part of my advanced placement art class. When I handed him my design, he said, "You know, I like art and I like swimming, and you're combining the two." His long face radiated approval.

I was sure Mr. Brokamp would remember the angry call from my father when I ended up with a C in swimming because I had skipped eighth grade swimming class so many times, but he didn't mention it. He smiled as he looked over the plan. "You want to paint this on the wall of the *boys'* pool?"

I nodded. It was a twenty-foot-wide painting of girls diving into the water.

He handed it back to me. "I like it."

Mural on wall of boys' pool at Walnut Hills High School, 1975.

SO, DURING THOSE WEEKS, I CAREFULLY hobbled up and down a ladder, a brush in my mouth, painting female figures on the guys' wall. Some of the guys, incensed to see a painting of girls, didn't hesitate to confront me. "Who gave you permission?"

Dan was more diplomatic. As he dropped by the high school pool during class, he tipped his head back and took in the shades of blue surrounding the diving figures. "Good for you, Kimmy," he said. "You have every right to paint what you want . . ." Then he added, with a twinkle, "As long as you swim for the guys."

I did swim for the guys' team, several strange meets where spectators stared and shouted encouraging or discouraging cheers. And it could've felt like an amazing accomplishment—competing against the guys and winning. But instead it seemed a harsh reminder. Studies of female athletes and the impact of excessive exercise on fertility had been in the news. With my recent diagnosis of amenorrhea (a lack of normal menstruation), I stood on the starting block surrounded by guys, and despite feeling like I was some kind of pioneer on the Walnut Hills men's team, I also felt like a genuine ogre, like a male freak in a female body.

With my weight on my right leg to protect my sore knee, I was reminded of weigh-ins, of hurling my weight to one side, and hearing derogatory comments from the guys lined up behind me as Mr. Bergen glared. Dan, Jim, Cozzy, and others on the Walnut Hills team thanked me for participating, but more than ever I stood red-faced and uncomfortable on the block, wondering what I was doing there.

DR. MILLER RECOMMENDED SURGERY, which he said would involve a two to three-inch cut in the side of my knee and several weeks of recovery. The night after he told me, I lay on Jacquie's extra twin bed, my leg propped on a pillow, and told her how relieved I felt that I would be having a break from swimming.

"I don't blame you," she said. "Anything to get out of here." She said she couldn't wait to leave for El Salvador when the school year was over. She froze for a moment, stretching her neck toward the hallway. "Kim, Dad's on the phone with Charlie."

"What?" I jumped from her bed and, clutching the handrail, limped down the stairs. I heard the phone being placed on the hook right before I reached the kitchen.

"Dad, did you just call Charlie?"

He was blotto, greasy strands of hair falling in his eyes, red-faced, smiling without making eye contact. "I fired a warning shot, that's all. He injured your damn knee, so he sure as hell had better protect your scholarship."

I shook my head in disbelief.

"I was gentle; don't worry," he said. "You take care of yourself, Butch, and you'll do fine in this world."

CHARLIE WAS SLUMPED IN THE BLEACHERS, waiting for me, before practice the next day. My voice echoed across the water. "I heard Dad called you."

Charlie reached out his arm for a sideways hug, and I slid up close to him, noticing his tired eyes. "You have a lot to deal with," he said. "Your knee is a damn shame, Kimberly. I know you'll be out for two months, but I'll do my best to keep you from losing the scholarship."

Looking back, I think Charlie was a decent coach whose heart was in the right place, but he was extremely young and possibly not ready for that level of responsibility. Some days he seemed up to the task and others he had an almost glazed look, as if the job were too much for him.

I wanted relief from the pain in my knee, but even more I wanted a vacation from my parents, the Marlins, and, most of all, the pressure. I couldn't bear the thought of four more years in the water. I told myself that maybe with sleek white hospital linens, kind nurses feeding me healthy food on a tray, and absolute quiet . . . my outlook would change.

CHAPTER 27

The hospital stay lasted less than a week and Dr. Miller said the surgery was a success, though between the three-inch-long scar on my knee and all the added pain it didn't seem like one to me. He'd removed a dislocated fat pad, fitted me with a two-foot-long removable cast and a pair of crutches, and given me strict orders to ice and elevate the knee. With Nationals at the end of August, I still had a couple of months to recover, but he added one caveat: "It's important to take it easy. I don't want you testing that knee until Nationals. No all-out swimming, okay?"

I didn't have to push to my limit, but remembering the adage that a day away from training required two days to make it up, I was anxious to get back in the water.

At first, I did my best to at least complete the workouts. After a month back, I was still using only a pull buoy and not kicking at all. Every practice was painful. Climbing out of the water one night, I limped over to a metal chair by the wall. As I rubbed my knee, Grimmer stopped to chat on his way to the drinking fountain. "I hope you're not planning to swim at Nationals," he said. "It's not realistic."

The same day, as I limped to my car, another teammate, Monty, told me the only outcome of my surgery appeared to have been a nice scar. I tried to let the comments float away, but I'd put on weight— from 140 pounds to 152—which was too much to call water weight. I knew I wasn't hiding my state of mind.

I TOOK A FEW DAYS OFF TO ICE AND REST my knee, and when I returned, Charlie announced that he would be shortening our distance in practice to improve team morale. "Instead of doing three eight-hundreds, we will do eight three-hundreds, he said.

I didn't move from my spot on the floor. *Is he saying that swimming eight three-hundreds is easier than three eight-hundreds?* This was not sophisticated math. When I looked up, he had one hand on his hip and his weight on one leg, as if he were daring one of us to complain.

"One more thing," he said. "I want everyone to win. If you think the coaches aren't paying enough attention, I want you to come talk to me and not a friend. If I catch any of you gossiping, I will put you on the balcony with the parents."

I couldn't figure out what he was talking about. Gossiping about what? Was this about the rumors of an affair? He kept rambling. He said, "There is one particular person who has a slim chance of going to Kansas City Nationals because of the way she acted. This is going to end now. I want everyone getting along with everyone. Any questions?"

I had no idea what he was talking about.

That night as I worked up a sweat in practice, my knee throbbed. The more I ignored it, the more it felt like a sharp stab. Remembering Dr. Miller's advice about letting my knee tell me how much or how little to work, I got out during the main set and sat in the bleachers beside Jenny, who was picking her nails, defiant, as if she were waiting for round two of a fist fight.

"Are you sick?"

"My ear," she said. "It's killing me."

Charlie patrolled the deck, his shoulders stiff, a scowl on his face. He was beginning to remind me of Paul Bergen. Eight rows of swimmers, five deep, churned the water below him. It looked like a factory: rows of swimmers headed into the walls, flipping, splashing, gasping for breath. My knee had been through a grinder. Why was I so anxious to return to circling in a lane, over and over, like a machine? And for so many hours every day. With no conversation, no mental stimulation.

The thing about swimming is that you follow the ritual for so many days, so many weeks, so many months, that you forget what it feels like to have time to reflect, to have some distance from the sport to reassess if it's really something you want to do.

Jenny and I watched Charlie stomp across the deck in his saddle shoes. He wore a Hawaiian shirt and dress pants—dressier than usual—and something wasn't right. He shouted at the team with broad, sweeping arm gestures; I'd never seen him act this way before. Why was he so hostile?

"You haven't heard? He got a letter from Mr. Keating. He was holding hands with Deena at the World Championships Trials." Jenny launched into a chatty story, a version of the game of telephone, where Jenny told her mother, her mother told Mrs. Rust, and Mrs. Rust called Mr. Keating. I flashed to the May 1975 cover of *Swimming World Magazine*: Charlie's right arm was wrapped around Deena, who was snuggling up close to his chest as she clutched her gold medal and red roses, a childlike expression of vulnerability on her face.

Jenny's words began to blend with the harsh echo of Charlie's voice. She'd put on weight herself, and hadn't performed as well as she'd wanted at the World Championships Trials. Was Charlie really doing something wrong, or was this a jealous reflection of the attention Deena was getting? I didn't want to hear any more.

I limped over to Charlie, scrubbing my hands over my face.

He softened when he saw me limping. "Your knee still hurting, Kimberly?"

I nodded. "And so is my head."

Charlie scowled and strode off. I figured he thought I'd gotten an earful from Jenny.

I left practice in choking Cincinnati smog. As I peered through my dirty windshield at the yellow sky hanging over I-75, I switched on the radio to hear a reporter say, "President Ford was in town today, praising Cincinnati for its effort in pollution control."

What the heck is going on? This incredible hypocrisy! In my head, I kept hearing Dr. Miller's voice. I knew I was swimming too hard. I'd been limping around with a hot, achy pain, and my weakened performance showed it wasn't helping any.

IN MID-JULY, I RETURNED TO DR. MILLER, this time with Dad. I was still hobbling along, wincing with every step, and Dr. Miller spent at least an hour asking me about practice. He said, "Have you ever taken any anti-inflammatory pills?"

"No," I said, "but our coach has given them to some of the girls on the team for shoulder problems."

Dr. Miller stared at me. "I don't like hearing this," he said. "These drugs taken without special care can play havoc with a swimmer's bone marrow. They can even cause death."

Dad tried to smooth things over. "You don't know what they were taking."

I turned and cocked my head. "Dad, they said they were anti-inflammatory drugs."

Dr. Miller changed the subject. He prescribed Butazoladin for one week, and recommended I eat a special concoction of honey, Gatorade, salt, wheat germ, and syrup before Nationals.

ON THE WAY TO THE CAR, Dad sounded scared. "You got no business talking about the other kids to Dr. Miller."

"Dad, what did you want me to say?" The silencing bugged me, coming from *him.*

Dad shook his head. "What are you trying to do, Butch? Get yourself in trouble?" I think he believed Charlie was engaged in something illegal and afraid that I'd already said too much.

"They're calling them anti-inflammatory pills, and they *do* have shoulder problems."

"I don't give a damn. You need to stay out of the problems at the pool. They're way too big for you."

WITHIN A WEEK, DURING A SET of twenty 50s hypoxic (without breathing), I nearly blacked out. Hoisting myself out of the pool, blood pulsating in my kneecap, I told Charlie, "I can't finish. It's killing me."

He stomped away and I stood there, staring at his back. Then he pivoted and harrumphed. "You're finished in the distance lane."

"What?"

"You're finished with distance. That's it."

I looked around to see if anyone had heard him. Did he *mean* this? I hobbled off to change into my clothes and collapsed on a bench between the rows of lockers. I didn't know if he was trying to motivate me by giving me a break or if he was fed up. The chasm between us had deepened, and yet I was sure Charlie was angry at someone else.

BY THEN, DAN AND I HAD BEEN ON a few dates—my first non-Marlin boyfriend—and to celebrate our upcoming high school graduation, he invited me to the Celestial, a fancy restaurant in Mt. Adams, the artsy historic district with narrow streets of Victorian buildings and fancy boutiques overlooking the Ohio River. I don't remember exactly what happened. I have a vague recollection of being snubbed by the waiter and leaving even before we were seated.

We decided to head to my house, and when we walked in the door, Dad glowed. Having finished dinner—and, since it was the weekend, a few extra drinks—he was ready for debate. Mom pulled a left-over steak from the fridge and seared it on both sides as Dad quizzed us on Karen Quinlan, the girl in a coma who'd made headlines because of the debate over whether or not to remove her ventilator. Dad thought removing the ventilator was playing God. I thought it was showing compassion. Dan and I argued with Dad while Mom made potato pancakes with the left-over mashed potatoes, threw in some boiled peas, and forked the steak onto a plate. Dan's face lit up. He closed his eyes with each bite and told her it was the juiciest meat he'd ever eaten.

"Mmm-mm," Dan kept saying as Mom beamed. I'd forgotten he didn't have his parents around to enjoy home-cooked meals. He kept saying he didn't want Mom to go to any trouble, telling us, "I feel like such a chump."

I felt humbled. Dan and I had talked about his father—about how he had fled Germany, escaped to the United States, served as a paratrooper in WWII, parachuted into France on D-Day, been wounded, and was now working at Stony Brook University as a history teacher. He described the efforts he'd made to stay in touch with his father and how the distance had torn at their relationship. I rolled my eyes when I thought of my own father—the way he asked too many questions, insisting he knew stuff he didn't know, and the way he was so damned annoying at times. Still, he and my mother were also my biggest cheerleaders, doing as much as they believed they could to be a part of our lives. Despite their constant travel, they had refused to become just photographs on the wall.

Dan and I moved to the living room and stretched out on my parents' brown print sofa. I inhaled the sweet smell of his warm skin, and my heart fluttered as it pushed against the cradle of my own ribs. I lay on my side, squeezed against his body, with my head on his shoulder, one arm slung over his torso, and for a moment I forgot the ache in my knee.

Dan was so different. He seemed to care only that I was there, curled up against him. We were like two halves of a broken vase, glued together in a somewhat fragile way, with chips, fissures, weakness in the areas where we connected, yet I felt cherished and secure, like I was valued. With no demands. No requirements. No expectation. He helped me feel important with or without the swimming.

MONDAY MORNING, I ARRIVED TO A quiet natatorium, with Charlie pacing the edge of the pool like he was mentally working through something. I could hear the soft hum of filters below the deck.

"Are you upset with me?" I didn't want to make nicey-nicey; I wanted to get clear on what he expected. I was still unable to complete a full workout, and with Nationals only three weeks away, I needed a plan.

Charlie hunted down two metal folding chairs and flicked them open on the concrete, facing each other. "Have a seat." He sat down, then rubbed his chin for a moment as he measured his words. Then, all at once, the details poured out. Lesley had asked for a separation, then a divorce. He had slept in the park, received a forty-dollar fine, and she would no longer cook for him or clean the house. He fought back tears as I unfastened and refastened my knee brace.

I didn't know what to say. I'd dropped by for a tiny bit of encouragement and landed like a mouse in a sticky trap. I found myself repeating, "I'm sorry, I'm so sorry."

That night I drove directly home to tell Dad what Charlie had said.

All Dad could say was, "What a damn shame."

Charlie's disclosure made me more afraid than ever that he would disappear the way Mr. Bergen had. I couldn't handle it, so I banished the thought. I stashed the information in a dark corner of my mind, just like I had with the signed paper plate of my bet to write a book.

TWO WEEKS BEFORE NATIONALS, MY knee still sore, I was bouncing on one leg in the water at the end of a set when Charlie asked us to do an all-out time trial. "On the top, from a dive," he said, and the swimmers in my lane began to climb out.

I had been reminded by Dr. Miller not to dive, so I stayed in the water, which seemed to catch Charlie off-guard.

"I'm not supposed to swim anything all-out," I reminded him.

"Who says?"

"My doctor. Dr. Miller."

Charlie studied me with dead eyes. "I don't care what your doctor said."

"Charlie, I just had *surgery*." I was thinking, *Now this is getting personal. He's venting his frustration and making* me *the problem.*

He placed a foot on the step of the nearest starting block and glanced over at the pace clock. "First heat on the blocks," he said. Then he glared down at me in the water. "It's too damn bad, because if you don't swim the time trial, the Marlins aren't paying your way to Nationals."

"What?" I grabbed for the rung of the starting block as if to steady myself. *After all I've been through, Charlie is giving me an ultimatum?* How could he have gone from championing me for a scholarship to wantonly threatening about Nationals? I couldn't believe what I was hearing. Images flashed by in rapid succession— Charlie giving me money to buy meat; Charlie brokering a deal with Pokey; Charlie on the phone, assuring my father I wouldn't lose my scholarship. They swirled together like water around rock. At the same time, my mind raced through what I considered Charlie's errors of judgment: his focus on talent above hard work; his open physical contact with swimmers; the tension, the trepidation, the gossip. I wanted my pain and confusion to be somebody else's fault. I puffed up my chest, tore off my cap, and slammed it on the deck. "Fine. I'll find my own way to Nationals."

In a low voice he said, "Get out. You're done."

And that was my last day as a Marlin.

CHAPTER 28

It was rush hour when I left the pool hobbling on one foot—in a hurry, like I was running away from home. I didn't know who I could talk to. Still, I felt I needed to finish practice.

I drove straight to the University of Cincinnati—up congested Clifton Avenue, left on Martin Luther King Blvd, and right on Jefferson. The indoor pool was somewhere to the right. Where was it? I kept wondering what I was doing there, my body still shaking from the adrenaline. I was running down the checklist of daily chores like Mom. Maybe I was trying to be proactive, following the rules so the next big thing didn't get me. I'd pretty much blown it this time, though. I didn't see how I would get to Nationals. And what would Pokey think if I didn't swim? Would I lose my scholarship? End up living at home with Mom and Dad? Heavy thoughts piled up like the homework on the backseat of my car.

I considered Charlie's motivation. If he thought I was going to apologize, he was dead wrong. He must've known I would have a hard time swimming a time trial. Had this been a trap? Was he getting me out of the way for some reason? Why? Dr. Miller had been too upset about the casual use of Butazolidin not to have mentioned it to someone. Maybe Dr. Miller had called Mr. Keating and Mr. Keating had called Charlie. *Some*thing had put him over the edge. It didn't make sense that he would insist on a time trial against my doctor's orders.

I tried to summon the courage to get back in the water, and as I did, I let out a huge breath. I was through with that damn team. No more outrage. No more struggling to understand motives or morality. No more lowering my head, keeping my mouth shut, trying not to think.

I skidded into a parking space near the UC pool, a concrete block building in a sketchy neighborhood of Clifton. The place looked deserted, and for a moment, I hesitated. There wasn't a soul in sight. I'd been isolated by my knee surgery, and now I was completely and utterly alone.

I made my way to the swimming pool, my wet suit wrapped in a soggy towel. It was odd that it was unlocked, like a church sanctuary.

I'm trying to remember how I found a phone. I think a wall phone hung near the starting blocks. When I lifted the receiver, I must've been incoherent.

"What happened, Butch?" Dad's choked voice told me he was worried I'd been in an accident. And in a way, I had. Leaving the Marlins was the last thing I'd intended. It *had* been an accident, with all the accompanying shock and pain.

I stuttered out the details of my conversation with Charlie.

"Finish your workout at UC," Dad said. "Then come home and we'll talk."

The UC pool was twenty-five yards, with a diving well on one side and permanent spectator seating on the other. Light flooded through high banks of windows by the diving well as my damp flip-flops squished on the tile deck. I changed into my wet suit by the side of the pool. With cap and goggles in place, I fell into the still water and jumped several times—shivering, shaking, adjusting my goggles. I dropped to the bottom and pushed off on my right foot. I needed to soothe my mind.

Breathe-breathe-breathe. The water slid over me, each arm stroke, smooth. I stopped shaking as I sliced through the water. The bright light, the freshness. A warm-up had never been so satisfying. My whole body tingled. Nothing pulling at me. Nothing restricting. I breathed in, breathed out, breathed in, breathed out. The tension lifted and dissipated, then floated away. For that moment, the world felt in balance. I knew in my more relaxed body that I'd made the right decision to refuse to swim that time trial.

DAD CALLED ME TO THE KITCHEN AS soon as he heard the screen door squeak. He leaned against the counter, popping slices of salami in his mouth. "I just got off the phone with Mike Arata."

I shook my head, confused. "Why? Why did you call *him*?"

"You and Pam are starting with him tomorrow," he said.

"That was fast." The feeling of freedom an hour earlier seemed to dissolve. Mike was one of the coaches of St. X High School. He also coached Summertime, a team that practiced outdoors at the Jewish Community Center in the summer. A chemistry teacher and avid weight-lifter, he looked like a solid block, hard-edged and unyielding, with an Achilles heel of having to dot every *I* and cross every *T*. I'd finally adapted to Charlie's lack of structure and feared Dad had signed me up to work with another dictator.

"You happy?"

I shrugged. "I guess, but why didn't you wait so we could discuss this?" I wanted to be able to change my mind in the event Charlie called to apologize. "What about Charlie?"

"Don't worry about him. We'll get you to Nationals. Maybe we can call Paul Bergen."

"Mr. *Bergen*?" I grabbed on to the counter. "No, that's not a good idea."

By then, I was hopeful Charlie would tell me he regretted the whole thing. I resented so deeply his forcing me to the edge of a cliff, where the only thing to do was back away. Still, I wanted him to call.

BUT CHARLIE DIDN'T CALL. AND AS THE days passed, I didn't know what to do with my anger. Something about the idea of swimming for my old coach felt like a screw-you directed at Charlie. As soon as I heard Mike was unable to take me to Kansas City for Nationals, I decided to let Dad call Mr. Bergen.

DAD SAID MR. BERGEN SOUNDED SURPRISED to hear from him. He'd been jumping around from team to team and was now coaching the Nashville Aquatic Club in Nashville, Tennessee. He had said I would have to enter Nationals unattached, but he could coach me along with his team. "He promised to take care of you," Dad said.

"Take *care* of me? What's *that* supposed to mean?" Mr. Bergen hadn't taken care of me earlier, so I wondered how he would "take care" of me now.

"He'll be your coach for the Nationals. Isn't that what you wanted?"

"Not really."

Dad dropped his glass in the dishwasher with a thud. "I don't know what in the hell you want."

I held his gaze for a moment, frowning. I wasn't sure what I wanted either. No, I *was* sure. What I wanted was an apology from Charlie. I wanted to be back on the Marlins, feeling a sense of dignity and respect. I'd worked hard at trusting Charlie and the Marlin program. Now it seemed they hadn't trusted *me*.

What I didn't realize was that my massive internal defense system—the one I'd thought was so protective—had done more to sabotage my progress than anything else. The craving for structure I'd felt for so long was only a coping strategy that allowed me to function in the midst of my chaotic life at home. I'd become a sort of control freak, wanting all the rules in place so I wouldn't have to decide for myself. It would take years, if not decades, for me to finally realize how much I'd grown reliant on having someone tell me what to do so I wouldn't have to think for myself.

But at the time, I was still trying to hold it all together. I hugged Dad and thanked him, and when the time came I drove out to Kansas City Nationals on my own, planning to stay with Mr. Bergen's team, though I was still irritated with him for leaving and not particularly happy to see him. Three years had passed since he'd coached the Marlins, and the unanswered question of why he'd left had only grown bigger in my mind.

As it turned out, interacting with him couldn't have been more awkward. He put me in a room with Tracy Caulkins, a twelve-year-old and the youngest swimmer at Nationals that year. At eighteen, with the slowest entry times in each of my events, I swam in the first heat, inflamed my knee with every race, and bombed miserably.

I wasn't exactly there. I was watching myself from a distance, through the eyes of my former teammates and Charlie. I climbed out of the pool after each event, held my shoulders back, and limped with my towel over one shoulder past the Marlins to Mr. Bergen, hoping to provoke someone, anyone. I wanted the whole team to see me swimming for Mr. Bergen and feel betrayed. But nobody seemed to notice. I kept glaring at Charlie—that bastard!—wanting him to make eye contact, wanting him to convey that he wanted me back, that I still belonged in his talent club. He didn't glance at me even once.

When I reached Mr. Bergen, I expected some comment about my stroke or effort or *some*thing. But he had nothing useful to say. I felt pathetic, like a three-legged stray dog. I was sorry Dad had arranged for me to be there. Why did he have to jump in so quickly and fix everything for me? Couldn't he have listened to me for once? With more time, maybe I could've fixed everything myself.

It's funny to me now the way I'd chafed against the team for so many years and then overnight found myself pining for those days of belonging. It was similar to how I felt after Mr. Bergen left the Marlins, only this time *I* was the one who had left.

I felt wretched and lost, like I'd thrown away something important. I'd lost Charlie—his trust—and I'd lost the Marlins, my teammates. Most of all, I'd lost a belief in my own ability to recover. How would I ever get back to where I'd been before the surgery? Even if I could, how would I manage four more years of competitive swimming? I cried out three pounds of self-loathing on my drive back to Cincinnati, and when I ran out of tears, I imagined a beach in California: the sweet mix of salt and suntan oil, the expanse of sand, the glint of light on water, the advancing, the receding, an endless horizon.

CHAPTER 29

Dan was headed to Boulder to attend the University of Colorado, and Pokey reassured me that I could keep my scholarship, so Dan and I agreed it was only right—living a thousand miles away—to plan on dating other people in college. Still, I wanted to spend time with him during my one last week before leaving. Dad, however, wanted the family to visit his parents in Massachusetts.

As usual, Dad won. Against the family's otherwise unanimous agreement that we should do it some other time, he rode roughshod over us and soon we were on our way to Cape Cod.

Since Dad and Mom had to deal with last-minute business hassles, we didn't leave until late in the evening. By nine o'clock, finally on the road but still in Ohio and without food or alcohol, Dad was jacked up enough to bite the steering wheel.

"Come on, Beej," he cajoled, "I'm hungry. Fix me something."

But she was unrelenting. Maybe she imagined a leisurely meal with the seven of us seated in the motorhome, enjoying some time together before the stress of our grandparents. Or, I don't know, maybe she was hungry and irritable herself.

"I won't cook while you're driving down the road," she said, and Dad glowered.

"Dammit, Beejay."

Mom irreverently straightened her legs and threw them apart. "I'm not doing it, Dick." She reminded him that food and water shot out of the pans, turning the carpet into a nasty mess. "Have you noticed the floor?"

"Beejay..."

All at once, Mom shot up in her seat. "Stop the driving!"

Dad jerked to the side of the road and jammed the vehicle into park, sending our playing cards sailing off the table onto the floor. Then he bucked out of his seat and began swiping at Mom. She blocked him with her forearms and cried, "Stop, Dick!" in a tremulous voice as Jacquie and I bolted toward her.

We watched in shock as Dad backed off for a split second. I wanted to get between them, but with my sore knee, I was too slow. Mom ducked under him and out the door, and as she did, the oxygen emptied from the motorhome. I surged toward the steps and scrambled after her as she ran down the berm of the highway, Jacquie close behind us. We must've gone more than fifty yards with passing semi-trucks so close they blasted our hair and blew our clothes around like we were caught in a windstorm. Mom didn't slow down. I heard her sobbing over the crush of trucks.

"You have to come back," I yelled.

I wasn't sure she heard me. Then she screamed, "I'm not going back there."

"You have to," I screeched.

Mom slowed to a fast walk and stopped for a moment, like she was thinking of alternatives.

"Come on, Mom. Please?" I caught up with her, seeing stars. Had I stood up too fast? I was about to faint.

Jacquie shouted, "Mom, this is dangerous." The diesel-fueled air plastered our hair to our heads as passing trucks laid on their horns.

For a moment, Mom seemed to waver. Jacquie and I stopped, exchanging fearful glances. What was she going to do?

Mom took in one last fervent breath. Then she turned abruptly and the three of us dragged ourselves back to the motorhome. There was nothing said, but I knew Mom finally had drawn a line in the dirty shag carpet.

Jacquie and I broiled the chicken and chopped tomatoes for a salad as passing trucks rocked the vehicle. Mom wouldn't speak, just stared through the windshield in the copilot's seat. Eventually, she helped get dinner on the table.

When she finally calmed down, Dad put his hand on the back of her chair. "I'm sorry, Beej." He leaned down to kiss her on the lips, but Mom averted her head and pushed him away.

"That's the last time you'll ever do that, Dick."

Their eyes locked in a shared understanding.

And there it was. A recognition from Mom that this wasn't the first time.

He climbed back into his seat. Mom hunched over, not saying anything. As I watched the lights pass by, my first thought was, *Good for you, Mom. You held your ground, even though you weren't as strong as you could've been.* I wanted her to shake him up, maybe say she was leaving when the trip was over. And not just say it, but do it. I was so tired of Dad, the tyrant. Why couldn't he just get some food for himself if he wanted it so badly?

But as we drove on with dark clouds hovering over the motorhome on our way to the nearest Sunoco gas station to plug in for the night, I thought, *You know, Mom, your courage was too late. Too late for me, anyway. Seriously? Stop, Dick? Where were you when Dad knocked me down the stairs?* I was like, *You go, Mom. You get him. You tell him what you* really *think.*

I believed she meant what she said, but she'd been hiding the truth for a long time. Hiding it from us and hiding it from herself. I had no certainty this would be the last time—but I hoped things would change, despite evidence to the contrary.

THE NEXT DAY, WE PULLED INTO MY grandparents' driveway, climbed out, and tiptoed through the unlocked back door. "Hello, we're here," Dad called in his deep voice.

Peggy's hulky black Labrador retriever greeted us first; we leaned against the wall as he reared back on his hind legs and lunged at us with his wet nose. We entered the breakfast nook single file, the dog jumping up, slobbering, and nudging us in the ribs.

"Down, Lucky!" Pop-Pop called. "Ma? Peggy? They're here."

As soon as I saw Peggy's tentative smile, my swimmer's shoulders sagged and I tried to make eye contact with Dad. Peggy was born six years after Dad, in the year of the rabbit. He was the year of the rooster and according to centuries of Chinese wisdom the two signs were, to put it nicely, a difficult pair.

Oh, boy, here we go, I thought. We gave them lukewarm smiles and half-hearted hugs. Of the three of them, Pop-Pop appeared the happiest to see us, but that tepid greeting was the high point of the visit. We wandered toward their 1940s-style bar, with its full-length mirror and Art Deco detailing, and Pop-Pop propped himself on one of their vinyl stools, his belt up high around his belly, under his armpits. "Dick, you must get terrible gas mileage in that thing, don't you?"

There was no *How was your trip* or *It's wonderful to see you*. Instantly I realized where Dad got his bluntness. I followed Mom and the younger kids toward the living room, but Pop-Pop stopped me. "How's the swimming, Kimmy? We want to see you in the Olympics, you know." He raised his chin ever so slightly and I caught a familiar gleam in his eye.

"I'm a long way from ever making the Olympic team."

"Like hell she is," Dad said, his voice booming. "She's one hell of an athlete, and so are the rest of them." I could tell Dad was trying to win his parents' approval in the same way we kids tried to win his and Mom's. And like us, Dad wasn't making much headway. It was as if his parents were fixing him a special drink, thanking him for the lovely linoleum floor, with their minds longing for the moment when we would return to Cincinnati so their daily routine could return to them.

FOR SEVERAL DAYS WE KIDS CONGREGATED around our grand-parents' uncomfortable Victorian furniture, watching the flies land on lampshades or listening to their seventeen clocks ticking in the living room. *How are we supposed to have fun?* We wondered. They lived on a pond—"Triangle Pond"—and owned a pontoon boat, but didn't want us to swim. They owned a pool table but didn't want us to play. They had a TV but didn't want us to watch. There were no games, no puzzles, and we weren't allowed outside. Aunt Peggy was an amateur landscape painter and Mom-Mom had wall-papered the front hall, waist-high to ceiling, with Peggy's works in identical wooden frames. The highlight was examining those, Mom-Mom's collection of glass paperweights on her desk, and the photographs of unknown relatives on the wall.

WHEN OUR VISIT WAS JUST ABOUT OVER, and I thought we had followed the rules and were about to leave without incident, Mom-Mom stood in the foyer, arms folded. "Someone has taken one of Peggy's landscape paintings."

I was stunned. Mom and I were the only ones who had paid any attention to the paintings to begin with. Had somebody wandered in from the street? Or had Dad hidden a painting just to cause an incident? No. That was too far-fetched, even for Dad.

"Maybe one of the kids took it," Pop-Pop said, his nose wrinkling. The flat monotone in his voice told me he had something else on his mind. Was he disappointed in Dad? Or was he angry we were leaving?

"No, Pop," Dad said. "Nobody's taken a painting."

"Well, I know it seems strange, Dick," Mom-Mom said, "but one is missing."

Out of Peggy's earshot, Dad said, "Peggy's probably hidden the goddamn painting."

"Don't talk to me like that, Dick," Pop-Pop said. "The doorbell is also broken. Peggy saw Ricky take the doorbell apart and put it back together again."

Two minutes later, Rick (no longer wanting to be called Ricky) was standing in front of them, his cheeks rosy red.

"Did you break the doorbell?" Dad asked, his voice soft.

"No."

"Peggy saw you playing with it."

Rick began to explain but Mom interrupted, "You know darned well nobody took that doorbell apart. Why would Rick want to break something?"

"Because he's a troublemaker," Peggy said.

I wanted to throttle her. She stood with her nose in the air, blocking the light from the window. Mom had said for years Peggy was jealous of Dad for getting married and having kids and I had wondered if Mom was exaggerating. Now it seemed obvious Mom was spot-on, and that Dad was right: Peggy had hidden her own painting.

As Mom glared at Peggy, her reluctance to visit them in the first place, coupled with the terror of the ride and her accurate prediction that our visit would end in conflict, seemed to finally explode in one startling moment. Mom threw her hands on her hips and loudly declared, "He's not a troublemaker, and you have no right to call him that."

Pop-Pop didn't waste any time. He looked Dad straight in the eye. "Somebody took Peggy's painting."

Dad, uncharacteristically morose, interrogated each one of us. When nobody knew anything about the painting, he turned to Pop-Pop. "None of us would take it, Pop. It'll turn up."

"When it does, I want you to let me know," Pop-Pop said. He glanced away, signaling that his was the last word.

I felt sorry for Dad. After three days, our visit resembled every other: Peggy poised at the table, smug, her mouth a thin line; Mom-Mom with a serious frown; Pop-Pop disappointed.

Dad told him he wanted to leave on a positive note but Pop-Pop wouldn't back down. "This makes no sense, Pop," Dad said.

The seven of us climbed into the motorhome and waved with forced smiles as the bus left their driveway. Mom quietly said, "Let's not put ourselves through that again," and in our silence, I think most of us concurred. I did, anyway.

I waited for a response from Dad, but he was quiet. When we reached the end of Mom-Mom and Pop-Pop's short road, Dad turned the motorhome around, put the vehicle into park, and climbed out of his seat.

Mom seemed alarmed. "Where are you going, Dick?"

"Leave me alone, Beejay." He slammed the door, wandered around to the back of the motorhome, reached under the vehicle, and unscrewed the cap for the holding tank. We gasped, all six of us, covering our mouths with our hands, our eyes bulging, as forty gallons of human waste and toilet paper rushed onto the beach adjacent to my grandparents' house.

Mom sank down into her captain's chair.

A few minutes later, Dad climbed back into the driver's seat, and without looking at any of us, he put the vehicle into gear.

"Dick . . ."

"Shut up, Beejay," Dad said. "I don't want to hear another goddamn thing."

And for sixty miles, each of us sat alone, silent, staring out the window.

Dad must've thought he'd finally stood up to his parents. That they would go for a walk, notice the mess, and immediately suspect him. So maybe this moment of retribution would be his final act of dishonoring the family.

For me, it was the end of my ambivalence about swimming for four years in college. Everything that entered my brain could be summed up with two words: "Good riddance."

A week later, I was on a plane to LA.

CHAPTER 30

USC spread before me, a beautiful bubble of green lawns, palm trees, brick buildings, and fountains with fancy sculptures in the middle of a sea of sprawling concrete. I'd heard so much about the smog but the skies were cloudless, aquamarine; nothing like the stifling white humidity of Cincinnati. The mostly white students rode around campus on rickety bikes with wicker baskets, looking like the commercials for Wrigley's chewing gum. The guys wore Hawaiian shirts and shorts, the girls, skirts and matching tops, their hair tied in plaid ribbons.

In a 1975 letter to Dan, I wrote, "I feel too grubby. I've seen so few T-shirts on campus that I can count them on one hand. I know you think I'm exaggerating but I'm not!" I arrived wearing a removable cast on my left knee and a solid fiberglass cast on my right hand, having broken the fourth metacarpal when I blocked a playful kick by my friend, Emily, at a party.

Pokey already knew about my latest injury, perhaps from Charlie. "I have to wear this for a month," I said, holding up my arm.

She dismissed the problem with a wave of her hand. "You'll recover. You'll just have to take it easy for a while."

Whoa. *Take it easy?* No coach had ever said *that* before. Pokey was in her mid-twenties—about Charlie's age—attractive and tall, with an artistic flair, and exuding a grace and quiet confidence. She'd won Olympic gold medals and set world records in swimming, so I'd been expecting toughness, not warmth. Her positive outlook made me think I was entering a different sport altogether.

Pokey placed me in a dorm room with Cindy Schilling, a transfer student from a local junior college who was four years older and nicknamed "Mutha" because of her age. She had long, radiant blond hair and wore wire-rimmed glasses, peasant shirts, and bamboo flip-flops. In the California swimming world of the seventies, she was high fashion.

Pokey must've pulled her aside and convinced her I was a social project, coming from the Midwest as I was, because one of the first things Cindy did was organize a group of women swimmers to eat at The Red Onion, a popular local restaurant, to introduce me to Mexican food.

Some were merciless in their teasing—"You haven't *heard* of a quesadilla?"

"I haven't heard of a Mexican," I said, half seriously. The whole table roared. What I discovered was how fun it was to chow down on chips and guacamole, with no worries about counting calories. Everybody seemed to be having fun.

Within a week, I found out Cindy was a Democrat, didn't attend church, and had tried pot. I was like, *Okay, she doesn't go to church. No biggie.* I didn't like church either. And politics—well, I wasn't sure what I believed back then. But a swimmer who'd smoked pot? That didn't make sense to me. I couldn't let the topic go. I grilled her about every imaginable political and social subject that was hot in 1975. "How do you like Ronald Reagan? Do you think unions are good? What about premarital sex? Birth control? Gay rights? Equal rights for women?" I knew I was modeling my father's insatiable questioning, but I couldn't stop.

One night as I flopped on my bed to read Gardner's *Art through the Ages*, I glanced over as Cindy studied and interrupted for maybe the third time with, "What do you think of abortion?"

Cindy, smiling and squeezing her eyes shut, pretended to bang her head against the dorm room wall. "Don't you have reading to do?" she kidded.

I lay on my back, the book on my chest, staring up at the acoustical grid. So many ideas bounced around in my head that I couldn't concentrate. With classes so stimulating, and no tension or turmoil weighing me down, I felt like I'd been closed up in a cage all my life and now I'd finally been released to the world.

SINCE USC WAS SO CLOSE TO HOLLYWOOD, catching a glimpse of a movie star on campus was a common occurrence. I stood outside the entrance to Town and Gown—the philanthropy at USC that provided much of our scholarship money—and watched as celebrities arrived for a tribute to Fred Astaire. Mae West entered with her pink caked-on makeup and towering pile of blond curls, and Shirley Jones was there, looking like she'd walked off the set of *The Partridge Family*. Another time I poked my head through a classroom door to watch the filming of a scene in *Marathon Man*. I tripped Dustin Hoffman as he entered, he grabbed my elbow, leaned into me, and we both apologized, then laughed. I rubbed the spot on my arm for a week.

The USC men's swimming team were national champions and stood out on campus. I wouldn't say they strutted, but there was a noticeable swimmer-swagger with their tanned bodies and chlorine-bleached hair. For some unknown reason, most were members of Campus Crusade for Christ, and if they weren't, they kept it to themselves. It seemed the whole men's team resembled Bible-toting stars, hand-picked by God himself for membership in His club. I assumed that they aspired to the highest standards—no drinking, no pot-smoking, no sex—and that's what I wanted for myself, not because I believed what I'd learned in Sunday School (if I didn't, I'd end up in hell) but because I wanted to present a positive exterior. I'd accepted the idea that only "nice" girls end up marrying "nice" guys. I thought of school as a place where I might find the man I would marry.

AND THAT WAS MY STATE OF MIND, along with awkward, bland, and plain vanilla, when I found a seat in my first class—Drawing 1 with Keith Crown—and in walked John Naber, the most well-known of the USC swimmers, looking like his picture in *Swimming World Magazine*.

He gave me a confident grin. "You want to be locker partners?"

I wanted to pinch myself. *What am I doing in a class with John Naber?* He was tall and V-shaped, with a distinctive voice destined for television or radio.

I about died when he picked a chair beside mine, set his book bag on it like an ordinary person, and asked, "Have you ever taken figure drawing?"

This was the one class I could ace with my eyes closed, but I said, "Uh, well, um, no. Well, in high school . . . yes."

He seemed nervous about drawing naked bodies—odd, I thought, since as swimmers we saw naked bodies twice a day. I didn't mention being a swimmer, though, both from nerves and feeling delighted that he was treating me like an equal. I had the fried swimmer's hair, the parched skin, the body type—I looked like a swimmer—so maybe the casts on my hand and knee threw him off. Or maybe it was empathy: he was drawn to me because I was wounded. Whatever the reason, my intuition told me to wait, to mention the swimming only when I had to.

ON MY FIRST DAY OF PRACTICE, I SLUNK into the "dungeon"—the name for the USC indoor pool with its gray-green tile and gargoyles on every corner. I tiptoed across the worn tile, toward a group of swimmers, and felt strangely at home. Cindy introduced me to two other freestylers—Heather Greenwood and Laurie Edwards—and we stood there, looking nervous, as the guys churned through twenty-yard sprints across the width of the pool, the water swooping up like a tsunami.

I hadn't done short sprints like that in years, and the way the guys surged toward us excited me. The air didn't have that heavy, toxic chlorine smell that assaulted my nose either. The dungeon seemed healthier, more like a greenhouse. We laughed and made fun of each other when any of the guys noticed us.

USC Women's team, 1975-76. Left to right, back row:
Cindy Schilling, Kim Peters, Anita (last name unknown), Anne Ryan,
Heather Greenwood, Alicia Wolin; middle row: Cathy Kovacevich,
Cindy Foist, Michelle Kaye; front row: Jane Starrett, Laurie Edwards,
Stacy Carroll, Kaia Hedlund. Photo by Dan Avila.

AGAIN, I SENSED AN UNUSUAL LIGHTNESS, the kind I'd felt the day Mr. Bergen left. It began as a shiver that spread from my neck down—a reflexive, nervous excitement. I wanted college to be a do-over, a chance to heal my hand and knee, lose about ten pounds—I was still at 150—and swim a whole lot faster than I had before. I didn't think I had a chance to make the Olympic Team but if it happened, hey, that would be great. For once, swimming seemed potentially enjoyable. Was it just my age? The Southern California sun kissing me on the forehead every day on my way to practice? Or was it because there was more camaraderie and less teasing now that we were no longer coed? Whatever it was, I was less focused on smashing swimming records and more focused on healing the past and living the life that could've been—one where swimming was part of a wholesome teenage existence, not something that obliterated it.

John leapt out of the pool, water streaming down his lengthy torso, and pinched his nose as he spotted me. "What are *you* doing here?"

I stretched my arms to show I knew the drill. "Swimming," I said, smiling.

"Oh, no. You're a *swimmer*?" He sounded disappointed. "I thought you were a normal person."

"Nope, not normal at all," I said, smiling.

I DID END UP ON A FEW DATES WITH JOHN, and as soon as I mentioned the name "John Naber" to Mom and Dad when I called home, they swooned as if I'd said John F. Kennedy. My swimming at USC made my parents proud. And for me, it was a vacation. The team offered perks: fresh towels, team suits, and occasional all-expense-paid swimming trips for meets or exhibitions. Practice was significantly easier than Marlins practices had been; not because we were slouches—we had far more Olympians than we'd ever had on the Marlins—but because there were moments of rest.

In fact, I was told the guys' team and their coach, Peter Daland, had changed the swimming culture at USC. Some of the sprinters on the men's team refused to put up with endless miles of swimming every day, which influenced the coaches' opinion about appropriate yardage. For me, the difference was remarkable. I grew two and a half inches—to five foot nine and a half inches—eventually removed my casts, and even started having ordinary periods after six years of biannual menstruation. My body had finally stabilized.

I'm not saying swimming wasn't still tough. It was. But it was no longer torture. Even after a bad practice, I would leave the dungeon with sun on my shoulders and think, *Was practice really that bad? How could practice have been so bad if I feel so great?* I wondered if it was the sunlight and higher levels of serotonin, or that swimming was actually becoming more tolerable.

Since Cindy had a boyfriend living off-campus, she often left on weekends. I latched on to Heather, who was my age, shorter and bigger boned, and who swam with me in the distance lane. She had set a world record and placed second in the 400 freestyle at the World Championships in Cali, Colombia, and had been on the August cover of *Swimming World Magazine* a year earlier.

Funny and daring, Heather had a streak of wild abandon that drew me to her. She would invent funny names for other swimmers— like "Jaws" for a girl she knew who never stopped talking. The way she strung her words together, she could have me weeping with laughter. Like me, she struggled with her weight. And this wasn't the kind of weight that was in our heads; it was true extra weight we were carrying around. Her parents would send her vitamins and liver pills to prevent the "freshman thirty," then call and check to be sure she'd taken them.

On the rare occasion when she led the lane and I beat her in a set, she'd say, "You're on my feet, bitch. Go ahead." I'd shake my head, laughing, as I pushed off the wall. Later the same day we'd find ourselves in water fights with Laurie Edwards, pouring buckets under doors of the volleyball players in our dorm. Heather had a way

Pokey speaking to Laurie Edwards before a set. Photo by Dan Avila

of reinforcing my own belief that swimming wasn't everything—that it was only a means to an end and not the end itself.

SOMETIME IN EARLY DECEMBER WHEN CINDY was off visiting her boyfriend, Heather and I were in the EVK dorm cafeteria, on our third round of salad with ranch dressing. Though we were stuffed we were still hungry, so we finished by challenging our bodies' insulin resistance on two bowls of soft ice cream from the machine.

"Why do we do this to ourselves?" she asked me.

I slurped another glob of ice cream, shrugging. With important meets in the offing—UCLA, then Stanford, and finally Nationals in March—the indulgence wasn't helpful. Still, I enjoyed every minute. Pokey had been telling us we needed to focus, to stop giving in to temptation. I was having trouble. I enjoyed the freedom she afforded us so much that her warnings sounded like encouragement.

Heather wasn't so sure. "I don't know about you," she said, "but I *hate* swimming,"

"It's hell . . . but, well, what choice do we have?" I told her my body had gotten so used to the massive exercise that if I ever decided to quit, I'd have to stop eating entirely. Besides that, if I didn't swim I would lose my scholarship, and with no work experience, I wasn't sure I could find a job that would pay my college tuition.

"I don't know if I *want* to stay here," she said.

"Why not? What would you do for college?" Heather had the added pressure of a father who coached her, so moving back home meant moving back in with her parents.

"I'd go to community college. Maybe Fresno State."

I scowled. "What?"

"I could live at home for a while."

I shrugged. "*I* can't." There was no way I could live another day at home. My parents were, of course, part of the reason—well, my *father* was. Everything about my relationship with him seemed centered on my swimming. It was the one activity that made him proud of me as a daughter. And Dad enjoyed telling his customers about all the movie stars I'd seen on campus, too. For him, USC represented an achievement. But he wasn't the only reason I couldn't drop out. If I were to return home, *I'd* feel like a quitter. College was an achievement for *me*, too. I'd promised myself I would get through these four years, and I was determined to follow through on that promise.

I mentioned to Heather how I'd agreed to stay in touch with Dan but there were dozens of great-looking, intelligent guys on the USC team, right there on campus, and I had developed a bad case of out-of-sight-out-of-mind.

"We need to burn off some calories," Heather said. "We're not solving anything by just sitting here, eating and complaining. Let's go bodysurfing."

I shoved the last spoonful in my mouth. "I don't have a board or anything."

Heather made a funny face. "You haven't bodysurfed, have you?" She laughed. "I can see right through you."

WE HOPPED IN HEATHER'S LIME GREEN Mustang and drove west on the Santa Monica Freeway to an exquisite stretch of sand off the Pacific Coast Highway. The sun's heat mixed with the salty breeze pulled at the skin on my face, but there was no wide-open fish mouth. Something about California was working. My body was reacting to the miles of sand, the endless sky, the vast and furious ocean waves. I must've lost the need to grope for language.

Heather suggested that we run on the hard sand near the water and we did—about two miles. By the time we returned to the Santa Monica Pier, I had a swollen left knee and chub-rub between my legs and under my arms; I told her I wasn't sure about this body-surfing thing. I blamed my hesitation on the sores, not wanting her to know that my first experience in the ocean as a four-year-old with Dad was still vivid in my memory.

"Come on," she said, grinning, "It's fun; don't worry."

I followed her into the water on the north side of Santa Monica Pier. The water was cold, but nowhere near as frigid as the Atlantic waters from my childhood. "You take four or five quick strokes just before the wave comes," she said. "Then you glide in head-first, with your hands at your side. Watch . . ." She faced the beach, took a few short strokes, then disappeared in front of a wave.

I tried a couple of times to swim alongside her, but each time the wave poured over my head as she swam toward the beach. "I keep missing them," I said, spitting saltwater.

"You winner!" Heather liked to call everyone winners. "Only choose the waves that suck you in. Then swim hard. Also, you can use your hands as rudders." She demonstrated again.

The waves had a wicked pull and I was afraid one would dump me on the sand and break my neck, but I treaded water with an eggbeater kick as I retied my pigtails, waiting for the subsequent wave.

All at once, a mountain of water rolled toward us. "Is this a good one?" I could feel it sucking me in.

"It's perfect," she yelled.

I took three strokes. The water lifted me up, then down, and with a thundering glide—*woohoo!*—I rolled into the beach beside her.

We bodysurfed for hours. When we finished, I felt like a pro. I was no longer letting fear and dread immobilize me. My fingers now prunes, the icy saltwater tightening my face like shrink-wrap, I was exhausted but felt great.

As I looked back, I realized that although I'd enjoyed brief moments with high school friends—Mary, Pam, and Julie—swimming had absorbed so much of my time that I'd never imagined having such a close friend as Heather. Los Angeles had seemed as foreign as another planet when I'd arrived there, but now a bright new world had opened up before me. I wanted the euphoria to last forever. Well, at least four more years—long enough to get me through college.

All I had to do was keep on swimming.

CHAPTER 31

UCLA was our first big dual meet, and none of us was ready. I told myself I would psych up and do my best but something was weighing me down—something more than the extra bowls of ice cream. Despite the turmoil, the on-again, off-again with my parents, I was homesick. Mom wrote occasional letters and I sometimes called to share my excitement about college, but I was racking up huge phone bills as a result and, weeks later, crying to her that I needed money to pay for the calls.

I loved California, the newness of college, the comfort and playfulness I was experiencing for the first time in my life, and my knee had recovered and only occasionally pained me, but like Heather, I was still burned out on swimming. And when we arrived at UCLA for our first big dual meet in their outdoor pool, their fans filling the bleachers, my body went on automatic, my mind along for the ride. Despite our countless cheers of "UCLAter," we lost a lot of tight races that day, and the meet wasn't even close. UCLA slaughtered us.

On our way to the parking lot, Pokey looked the most downtrodden. "I don't know how we'll beat Stanford," she said. "Linda's quit."

"*Linda*? How could she?" We crowded around Pokey. Linda was our star backstroker—the national champion in the 100 backstroke, and also the first woman in USC's history to receive an athletic scholarship.

Pokey opened her car door, her mouth moving, no words coming out. "She wants to concentrate on the Olympics," she said, finally. "We'll just have to do the best we can."

WE LEFT AFTER THE EMBARRASSING DEFEAT, our heads down, our enthusiasm depleted. The Stanford dual meet—planned for the following week, Friday the thirteenth, in the USC dungeon— would undoubtedly be another slaughter. Of Stanford's fourteen swimmers, ten had already qualified for Nationals. Without Linda, we only had five.

We moaned and groaned for days about Linda's decision. What a sucker punch, having her quit like that in the middle of the season. But at practice, we began to notice something. Linda had often arrived late or quit workouts early. In her absence, we grew closer as a team. We began to say things like "Wouldn't it be mind-blowing to surprise everyone and beat Stanford?"

The only obstacle was our lack of a diver. Stanford had two divers and we needed someone to place at least second for the points. One of the USC song girls, a former diver, had been sick at the beginning of the season, but Pokey twisted her arm and she agreed to dive for us. Instantly, Pokey's tune changed. "As long as each of you swims out of your mind, we should be able to beat Stanford," she said.

By Thursday, we were gritting our teeth, shouting cheers in the locker room and telling each other, "We're gonna drown those Cardinal bitches!"

POKEY CALLED TO SEE IF SHE COULD GET the USC marching band to show up for the meet. "Will the girls be wearing the tight suits?" the band director shamelessly wondered out loud.

"We can arrange that," Pokey said. She handed out maroon Lycra suits that were meant for Nationals and on the day of the Stanford meet, not only did the band fill the stands but so did the men's team, which shocked us. We'd been urging the guys to come since the beginning of the season and only a few ever showed up. This time, the pool was packed. The men belted out the USC fight song and the Southern Cal cheer as if we were the football team. The walls, floor, beams—the entire dungeon—shook so mightily, it seemed the gargoyles at the corners of the pool had sprung to life even before we finished our warm-up.

Since none of us could swim a decent breaststroke, Pokey had made Heather swim breaststroke all week in preparation, which helped us squeak in a win by one second in the 400 medley relay. This spurred us to a one-two-three victory in the 200 freestyle. Next, in the 50 free, Cindy tied the national record. Our red-faced supporters drowned out Stanford cheers.

But the dungeon quieted as Stanford dominated the next few events. When the last backstroker finished, Pokey twisted toward me and said in a breathy voice, "You and Heather have to beat them in the 500."

The Stanford distance swimmer, Anne Brodell, was no slouch. She had set an American record in the 800 two years earlier, and was ranked sixth in the world in the 1500. I knew Heather could beat her, but I wasn't sure I could. And in twenty lengths, a lot could go wrong.

"Beat that bitch," Heather said on our way to the blocks, and I knew in my gut I had to do it. The meet was at our pool, at our school, with our fans. We were the Women of Troy, after all. A *family*, the men kept telling us. We had to show our toughness.

As the band finished the fight song, the cheering rose to a clamor and I stepped to the back of the block. "Quiet, please, for the start," said the announcer with the electronic gun. I glanced at Anne Brodell. She looked tired.

Seconds later, we were thrashing through the water.

I could almost feel the encouragement—the whistles, the screaming—of the fans in the dungeon. I focused on my breathing, my eye on Heather. I swam into the wall on the last lap, put my head down, and felt the energy of the fans. *Pull harder, kick harder, go-go-go*, I told myself. I slammed the wall and stood up as the crowd erupted. I'd beaten Anne by one tenth of a second, placing second behind Heather.

We had only two races left: the 200 breaststroke, which we knew we would lose, and the 400 freestyle relay. In a corner of the dungeon, Pokey huddled with Rob Orr, the men's assistant coach, compiling the points. A moment later she rushed toward us with a determined stride. "You girls have to win this. If you win the relay, we win the meet."

Knowing that every start, every turn, had to be perfect, my body tensed. In a tight zone of concentration, the four of us wrapped arms around shoulders in a group hug. "We can do this," Cindy said, and we all shouted a loud SC cheer.

Laurie, up first, stepped to the block, and my whole body began to shake. After her fifty we had a single-stroke lead. I shook out my arms, stepped up, and placed my toes firmly on the edge of the block. Laurie swam toward me, her arms hammering, her six-beat kick strong. She slid into the wall and—boom!—I sprang off the block and swam for dear life.

I gained another stroke. Heather, up next, gained a third stroke. Finally, Cindy, swimming for the anchor leg, hit the water, and the stands erupted.

We jumped up and down, screaming our lungs out. With more than a body-stroke lead, Cindy popped up from the last turn, and we knew we had it. As she hit the wall, the place exploded.

Pokey rushed to the back of the blocks and gave us each a hug. The band played the SC fight song as spectators sang at the top of their lungs, their feet thumping in the bleachers.

"You girls were five-tenths off the American record," Pokey shouted. "You swim like that at Nationals and you'll win!"

CHAPTER 32

Heather had been sick more than a week the day I returned to my dorm room carrying a cup of hot coffee after practice to find a note from her slipped under the door. "Hey, crab!" she wrote. "What's the matter? You on the rag?"

Hung over from too much reading, a difficult phone call with Dan the previous night, and morning practice, I dialed her number. "I need to get out of here," she said. "Let's go bodysurfing."

I had studying to do, and my ears were still ringing from Pokey's lecture that morning. She'd said we were "resting on our laurels" after the Stanford win and insisted we work harder if we wanted to swim well at Nationals. Tired and cranky, I'd wanted to push back, but hadn't been able to dredge up the energy. And yet the power of the ocean, its unpredictability, had been intoxicating before. Heather's invitation sounded like a nice diversion.

"Sure," I said. "I'm all in. Let's go bodysurfing."

We charged down the Santa Monica freeway, but this time Heather noted the dark clouds looming. I couldn't predict the weather since every day seemed sunny to me. In fact, I was feeling like a damn poor judge of the world around me. Why was I fighting with Dan? Measuring every word? How did I get to this place in my life where all I could think about was some boyfriend? The pressure of swimming only added to my misery.

I climbed out of the Mustang and scanned the beach, shaky. Heather had just recovered from the flu, I was tired, and Nationals was important. Was this smart? The hungry waves crashed with a deep, concussive resonance. Wind pounded the coast from north to south, and with no swimmers or lifeguards in sight and nothing but signs warning of dangerous surf, we stood on dry sand for a long while, debating.

"What do you think? Should we go for it?" Heather had to shout over the surf.

"I don't want to break my neck," I yelled back. "If the waves are too rough, we can quit, right?"

Heather smiled knowingly. "You chicken." She sprinted toward the waves.

I followed and tried to stay close. We jumped over the first bit of rough water, then dropped into an icy hole. The salt. The sand. The seething surf. We had no choice but to swim right away. We dove under a huge broken wave, and the chill gave me an instant earache and pounding pain in my temples. The surf tossed me violently, sand kicking up and pouring into my bathing suit. Heather pointed to another giant wave about to break. We dove under again, this time as low as we could. I felt the water thundering down on my calves. The next wave lifted us high above the sand, and we fought to keep from being hurled onto it.

"We have to get farther out," she yelled, so we swam, heads up, toward the huge oncoming waves. But even swimming at top speed toward the horizon, we weren't going anywhere.

"Are you sure this is wise?" I shouted.

Heather turned, her face stricken. "*Now* you tell me." She smiled and took a few quick strokes, racing head-up toward the beach. I followed and the wave immediately sucked us in. We rode the surge of water, the wave broke, and we must've dropped six feet. A rough mix of sand, shells, and seaweed tossed us like objects in a snow globe. We had to swim toward the horizon or get crushed by another wave.

We swam and swam, diving under wave after wave and gliding up higher than a two-story building. "I love this; I could stay here all day," I yelled. But then it dawned on me that we were stuck. The surf was too rough for body surfing. If we stayed much longer, we wouldn't have the strength to get out. And there was nobody to rescue us. At some point we would have to swim in to the beach. We were bound to get clobbered.

"We'll just have to pick a wave and go for it," Heather shouted.

I knew what she meant. We rode the next big crusher in, taking the huge drop and letting the wave slam us into the sand. I tumbled for a moment with what felt like glass in my mouth, covered in debris—sand, shells, and seaweed in my eyes and hair—and when I surfaced, I pushed into the swirling sand with the greatest leg strength I could muster. We screamed encouragement to each other and somehow scrambled up and out.

I was taking risks without understanding the danger. Those nights alone as a kid had made me think I could handle anything. Winging it in the aftermath of Ricky's accident had in some ways made me fearless. But so had swimming. Eleven miles a day and heavy weight-lifting had given me confidence, maybe over-confidence, in my physical strength.

Heather and I didn't talk much on our way home. I was counting off the mile markers, grateful I still had my limbs intact. As we exited the Santa Monica Freeway, she let out a heavy sigh. "I don't know what we would've done if something bad had happened."

"We have to be careful," I agreed. "Even when we're having fun. We still have to swim well at Nationals."

Heather rubbed her salt-sore eyes. "Hell, if I don't swim well, I won't be here next year."

I gave her a friendly shove. "You'd better come back. You're the best friend I've ever had."

"You winner!" she said. "So are you."

CHAPTER 33

On the day before our flight to Ft. Lauderdale, we finished practice to find spotted splashes of bright color resting on five of the dull gray starting blocks. Garbo, the men's assistant coach and Gerry, their manager, had left sunflowers, a gift from the guys to wish us luck at Women's Nationals. We scooped up the flowers, thanked the coaches, and launched into a spontaneous USC cheer.

The International Swimming Hall of Fame was outdoors, and when we arrived, women in sunhats, men in ball caps, and kids with popcorn and Pepsis filled the stands, clutching programs and shouting cheers. The sky was cloudless. The pool, clear as glass, sparkled with bright light on its surface, and its white lines reminded me of the early days at Mt. Lookout, the days I feigned illness and sat watching the squiggly lines create patterns and wishing I was somewhere else. Somehow the connection to those early years boosted my adrenaline. It was as if all the years of rigorous training were leading up to this one big meet.

Mom and Dad had driven down from Ohio in their brand-new Argosy motorhome and were huddled in the stands with other spectators. Though I was happy to see them, I felt pressure to swim well to make their trip worthwhile. I also couldn't help but think of

Jacquie—in her senior year of high school, alone at home, watching the kids. Coaches whistled and shouted. Blasts of static hit our ears as officials tested the microphone. On one side, a television crew for a local network grilled swimmers on how they expected to perform in their events.

I swam hard, but saved a little, in the prelims of the five-hundred yard freestyle. My body felt flexible and strong, higher in the water, and my arms seemed to slice through the water. I ended up in the finals in lane seven, three lanes over from Heather.

Just before the finals, I spotted Dad in the bleachers. He pointed to the television crew, and when I shrugged he rushed down to the deck and caught me on my way to the block.

"We drove all this way to see you win," he said.

After the eye-roll, I thought, "God give me the serenity to accept the father I cannot change."

Pokey met me behind my lane, her eyes determined, her shoulders tense. She seemed to fish for the perfect words, then delivered the advice she'd given us before the 500 at Stanford. "I expect you girls to go one-two." She hesitated, then added, "I don't care who wins." What I heard was that she believed I had a chance.

She patted me on the back and I stretched and did arm circles as I stepped to the edge of the block. Silently, I said a prayer—*Jesus, God, guardian angel*—then, in my head, I heard Dad's voice: "You get out there and do it." With both hands I squeezed the air out of a tiny wrinkle in my cap and adjusted my goggles.

"Take your mark," the starter barked.

I stepped forward, reached for the edge of the block, took a huge breath—and the electronic gun blasted, a sharp rip through the air.

I sliced through the water like a maniac and immediately gained on the girls to either side of me. Ever since my days with Mr. Bergen I'd tried to negative split my races—in other words, hold back a little on the first half so my second half was faster. *This is the moment to negative split*, I told myself. Then I just kept thinking, *Deep breath, two strokes, deep breath, two strokes.*

Before I knew it, I was on the last lap. I pushed off as hard and as streamlined as possible, and there was Heather, stroke for stroke, two lanes over. The cheering and whistles exploded and I was back at the Stanford dual meet in my head. I pulled with all my might, put my head down for the last few strokes, and slammed into the touchpad with my fingertips. I glanced up and my name on the scoreboard flashed with 4:52.48—a personal record, and I had beaten Heather by two tenths of a second, winning the race.

On the podium for the 500 yard freestyle,
Friday, March 19th, 1976.
Photo by Swimming World Magazine.

As spectators cheered, I jumped up, soaking wet, and threw my arms around Pokey in her fitted summer dress. Exhilaration washed over me; every nerve in my body tingled. I hugged Heather and headed toward my parents, who were waving wildly in the stands.

A reporter stopped me on the way. "Congratulations on breaking the national record," he said. I glanced at the scoreboard again and about fainted.

In the middle of the bleachers, a man shoved a microphone at my mouth; another man held a camera. "Can you talk about your race?"

"I don't know what to say." I was still wearing my USC cap, hugging my towel, and drawing in deep, heaving breaths, my nerves doing cartwheels.

"How did you feel?"

"Great. Really great. I'm just so happy USC could go one-two."

I picked out Dad's round face among dozens of spectators—the crow's feet around his eyes, his greased dark hair held back by a cowlick. He looked like he was storing up questions; he wore the face of the old Dad, from my childhood. This was the high-water mark of my swimming so far, and he was the proudest I'd ever seen him.

"What did the reporter ask you? How did you answer?" As he quizzed me, total strangers grinned at us.

"I didn't know what to say. I couldn't think."

"That's my girl," Dad said. He was squashed in the stands, his knees wide apart, with Mom in her dark sunglasses squeezed in beside him. "Come 'ere, Butch," he said, and he leaned over and kissed me on the lips in front of everyone.

I can still see Dad with his chest out, his hands tucked into his armpits. *You see this girl right here? My daughter*, he seemed to say, basking in the glint of light off the water and the enthusiasm of the spectators in the bleachers. I knew I had pleased him, and Mom too, which felt like a wonderful lift after all the uncertainty with my knee surgery.

Everything had come together in one race, and I floated through the next couple of days, contagiously jubilant. I ended up seventh in the 200 freestyle, and on the last day of the meet, Pokey's words proved prophetic: Heather, Laurie, my roommate, Cindy, and I won the 400 freestyle relay and set another national record, the perfect ending to a successful meet.

I'd overcome the injury, swum my best time, and felt terrific. I was drunk with relief. Finally, I could relax.

National Champion 400 yard freestyle relay, left to right:
Laurie Edwards, Kim Peters, Cindy Schilling, Heather Greenwood.
Photo by Swimming World Magazine.

MOM AND DAD WERE ANXIOUS TO GET BACK on the road. I wanted them to stay, but this was Jacquie's senior year, after all; she needed to have some fun and not spend all her free time babysitting the younger kids.

"Bye-bye, Mom. Thanks for coming." My tan cheek touched her soft white skin as I gave her a hard hug.

Dad lingered, wanting to say one more time how pleased he was. I hugged his large, round shoulders.

"Olympics, here we come," he said as he climbed into the Argosy.

I shook my head like Mom. Then I imagined myself on a towel on Miami beach, a book in my hand, glancing occasionally at crashing waves and soaking up the warmth of the sun's rays. Giddy with excitement, I imagined what I would do with a day to myself and no obligations, no specific plans, and hours to rest.

I WAS ABOUT TO CLIMB INTO THE RENTAL car to return with the team to the Holiday Inn when Pokey flagged me down, her face apologetic. "I hate to mention this, but several coaches have arranged to have a time trial tomorrow to make the cutoff time for the Olympic Trials."

"Oh, that's too funny. What do you mean? How can they have a time trial?" To enter the Olympic Trials, you had to swim a particular cutoff time for each event in a long course meters pool. With my knee surgery the previous summer and my recent times in short course yards, I still wasn't eligible.

Pokey explained that the Ft. Lauderdale pool could easily be converted from short course yards to long course meters. We just had to swim the length of the pool instead of the width.

"You're rested," she said. "You're ready. Just get out there and swim."

I massaged my eyes as I slowly shook my head. "I'm not ready to swim another hard race."

Pokey flicked back her dark hair and held her index finger to her mouth to quiet me. "Try to think positively. I know you can do it."

CHAPTER 34

Swimming a time trial the day after Nationals was like going into combat, winning, and then finding out you have to redo the battle a day later. I couldn't get inspired, no matter what. My arms and legs were leaden, and I failed miserably.

Fortunately, I would have one more chance to make the Olympic Trials at the Coliseum pool on USC's campus.

On the flight from Ft. Lauderdale to Los Angeles, I gazed out the window at the vast body of water below, the Atlantic's sandy beach, the greenish blue growing darker and darker, turning black at the horizon.

Cindy traded seats with another teammate on the plane so she could psych me up. "I'm not going to tell you what to do," she said, "but you should be able to make the Trials cutoff in all three of your events." I think she saw the fear and consternation in my eyes. "You don't even have to swim as fast as you did at Nationals," she reminded me.

"I know, I know," I told her. "I'm just so tired." My limited supply of energy had been drained to the last drop. Every muscle in my body ached. I wanted to crawl into bed and sleep for a week with no pressure from home, no pressure from Pokey, no pressure from anyone. But I had to prepare. The last time trial opportunity was just over one month away.

I SLOGGED THROUGH ANOTHER FOUR WEEKS of practice as awards for my performance at Nationals dribbled in. First was the picture of our winning relay in *Swimming World Magazine*. Then I was named USC Athlete of the Month for May. Most exciting was knowing that my name would go on a medal placed on the waist-high USC Honor Rail that snaked through Heritage Hall and bore the names of USC champions like John Naber, Buster Crabbe, and OJ Simpson. But two tenths of a second was uncommonly tight. I had won by a fingernail.

On my way into the locker room one night, Pokey stopped me. "Ricky Bell is speaking at the Vista Del Mar Child Care Center. I want you to go with him and say something inspirational."

I shook the water out of my ears. "Like what?"

She waved her hand through the air. "Just say something about what athletics and academics mean to you."

I wanted to make some joke—like, "You want me to tell them about physical and mental exhaustion, isolation, abuse, self-loathing, waking up so tired you hardly know what day it is?"—but I was too drained to come up with anything. So, a couple of days later, I stood at the microphone in front of the group of what seemed like twenty hyperactive kids and their teachers, swallowing an enormous knot in my throat. I couldn't think of a single thing to say. I'd been whipping through classes, doing the absolute minimum, and watching other students dazzle professors while I put in a mediocre effort, gorged on chocolate and apple fritters, and gained more weight.

The worst shock had come the day Kaia, another teammate, tested Heather and me in a four-foot tub of water to measure our percentages of fat for one of her classes. "You're both over twenty-five percent," she said.

I just stood there, disbelieving.

"That can't be right. Are you kidding? Twenty-five percent fat?" I took the test again.

"Twenty-five point six percent," she said. "Same number."

Heather and I headed straight to the bakery department of the 32nd Street Market and pigged out on apple fritters. I was living my life drifting between ravenous and stuffed, shaky and exhausted.

I tried my hardest to inspire those kids but I could hear myself babbling incoherently, unspooling a series of idioms about working until you hit the wall, until you're so exhausted you can't see straight. Barbara Hedges, the athletic director, sat in the audience in a tasteful tailored suit, a genuine smile on her face. I wanted to hide as soon as the adults started clapping.

I RETURNED TO MY DORM, LITERALLY SICK with dread, and examined my contours in the mirror. My face was pasty, and there were dark shadows around my eyes. I needed to perk up if I had any hope of making the cutoff time for the Olympic Trials in a few weeks. But how was I to do that when placing one foot in front of the other felt cumbersome? USC had been agreeing with me—I loved the sun and atmosphere at school—but I was so burned out. The injury, the exhaustion, the weight gain, and the high expectations had finally reached a critical mass.

As I slowly lifted a shirt over my head and wearily shoved an arm into a sleeve, I turned toward Cindy, my shoulders slumped. "Do you think I might have something wrong with me?"

"Yes," she teased. "Definitely something wrong."

"No, seriously, I mean like something physical. I have no energy at all."

She rubbed my shoulder, then gave me a hug. "You're okay. Go to the health center. Find out."

I WAS STILL TAKING MY THYROID PILL daily and assumed I had my condition under control. Were the levels low for some reason, or was I just too burned out? I made multiple visits to the USC Health Center and the doctor checked my vitals, so although I don't remember, he must've checked my thyroid.

"Do you have a lot of stress in your life?" he asked me.

"Well, I have to make the Olympic Trials. I didn't swim last summer because of knee surgery, and . . ."

He didn't wait for me to finish. He wrote a prescription for an acid neutralizer. I tucked the prescription into my purse and never used it. I knew that what ailed me ran deeper than heartburn. It was the day after day, week after week, year after year. You don't admit it to yourself, but your body tells you. You toss and turn at night, your appetite changes, your energy levels reduce, your concentration is scattered. Plain and simple, depression had changed the neural circuitry of my brain. All I wanted was to try once more; if I didn't make the cutoff time this round, I hoped I could just go home and be with my family.

SINCE OLYMPIC TRIALS CUTOFFS NEEDED to be swum in AAU-sanctioned pools, with three timers and certified officials, there were limited opportunities to make the Trials. This absolutely was my last opportunity.

As I walked across campus the day of the time trial, I soaked in my surroundings. I strode past the fountain in Alumni Park, the trimmed boxwoods in front of Bovard Auditorium; past Tommy Trojan, the life-size bronze sculpture of a Trojan warrior; then past the Student Union and down the street till I made a sharp left toward the modern School of Art, with its glass and concrete.

As I waited at the light on Exposition, I noticed I was calm, not jittery with excitement, like I wanted to be. The weather was perfect, warm with a pleasant breeze, and I'd slept like a lead weight the night before. I kept telling myself repeatedly that I was ready, even though I sensed I wasn't. I decided to at least try.

When I arrived at the Coliseum, Pokey took one look at me and said, "Get out there and do the best you can." She knew in one glimpse this wasn't my day.

I overdid my arm circles, shaking out the guilty ache in my legs, knowing I would disappoint her.

I shouldn't have bothered to swim at all. Diving in, my arms and legs ached. The strain of pulling through the water was like holding my body weight in a handstand for more than four minutes. After the eight lengths, I was so far off the cut-off time for the 400 that it made no sense to try for any other events. I climbed out of the water and knew what was next. I would quit swimming for good, go home, and get the rest I so badly craved.

I CALLED COLLECT FROM MY DORM ROOM to tell Mom and Dad I would be coming home.

"What do you mean you're coming home?" Dad said. "What about the Trials?"

"Dad, I didn't make the cut-off this time."

He paused for a moment, cheerless. "You still have opportunities, though, right?"

"No, Dad. I'm finished. I tried today and missed it."

"But you swam in the Trials four years ago."

"Even if I had made the Trials this time, I doubt if I could make the Olympic Team."

"But you *could* make the Team. Your converted time places you in the top three."

It happens sometimes in swimming that you can be stronger in short course or long course, depending on your training, and I tried to tell him that before reiterating, "Dad, there are no more opportunities."

And there *were* no more opportunities. With Olympics only once every four years, this had been my last chance to make the Trials. I knew I didn't have another four years of swimming left in me. In fact, I wasn't sure I had *any*.

I glanced through our dorm room window at the parking structure, and my mind flashed to memories of my earliest years—his taking me into the ocean, the water slamming my face. He was the proud father, pushing me to succeed. I was the little girl wanting him to pull me through the waves.

"You can't come home, Butch. I've told people you'll be on national television. Stay there until you make it."

Again, I tried to tell him this was not negotiable. I wanted him to say, "I'm sorry, Butch. You must be disappointed." I didn't need his pressure; I wanted his compassion. I twirled the telephone cord around my thumb, unsure of how to persuade him. I'd been struggling with myself over whether or not to keep swimming. Though I knew Dad was enthusiastic in his support for me, I had thought his main interest was saving on the tuition and living expenses of college. After my win at Nationals, however, he seemed to want the Olympics far more than I did.

There was an expressive pause. Then I heard Mom's disembodied voice on the end of the line: "Your time at Nationals was fast enough. Why can't you use that time?"

"Nationals was a yards pool, Mom. It has to be fifty meters."

I could tell she wasn't devastated. Something in the sinking of her voice. Maybe she was reading my determination. But she probably also thought Dad was way too invested, and this was my life, not his. I asked to speak to Dad one more time, and she put him back on the phone. I heard a quiet whimper and wondered, *Is Dad crying?*

"I'm coming home on Friday, Dad, and I want you to understand that I'm happy with my performance this year." I kept telling myself I was. What did I have to be defeated about?

"But you must feel terrible you didn't make the Olympic Team."

I tilted my head back and stared at a gouge in the acoustical tile. "No, Dad."

"You've never been a quitter."

Instantly I hardened. "Quitter?" In a stern voice I didn't know I had, I blurted, "What's wrong with what I've done? I did *well* at

Nationals. I'm a national champion! An All-American." I ranted about every honor I'd received, blasting my outrage into the receiver. When I paused for a second, I heard Dad's crying. It was only the second time in my life I had heard him cry. In the background, Mom pleaded with him.

"We're not ready for you," he said.

I heard how brittle his voice was, and I softened. "Why not?"

"I don't know, Butch. We need at least three days to let people know. Are you certain you can't try one more time? Do you have to come home?"

"I'm sorry, Dad. I did the best I could." Tears flooded my eyes, but I didn't let on.

Dad inhaled so deeply I heard his breathing. "Okay, I'll pick you up at the airport."

In that moment, I knew what was going on in his brain. It would be just like him to make a huge, theatrical announcement. I didn't want to be thought tragic when it had been the best year of my entire life.

"Please, Dad, do me a favor. Don't make a big deal out of this, okay? I feel bad I disappointed you, but it would kill me to come home and have you depressed."

The air throbbed with Dad's silence.

"Did you hear me? I know how you are, Dad. Will you promise you won't plan a pity party? Please?"

"Don't worry, Butch. I'll see you on Friday."

KAIA WAS WORKING AS POKEY'S ASSISTANT and she offered to drive me to the airport. As I climbed into her car, I slammed the crown of my head into the door frame. "This is what the last month has been like," I said, rubbing my head.

"You had a great year," she said. "Go home and rest."

By then, my apathy had given way to relief. I was thinking I would go home and rest and then decide to either swim on the local team with Mike Arata or, more than likely, quit swimming for good. I would have to figure out if I could stay at USC for my last few years of college. It was a calculation of whether the burden of swimming was worth the free tuition.

I felt a sense of dread as I hugged Kaia, in her Hawaiian sundress and bamboo flip-flops, at the airport. I believed I had reached a level of acceptance, but I knew my parents—especially my father—hadn't. I would be returning to my old life. How would I deal with living at home? Dad? Mom? The fam-damn-ly?

The flight from Los Angeles to Cincinnati was arduous with two stops and long layovers. By the time the plane landed, I was dreaming about crawling into bed.

Dad waited for me at the baggage claim. He stood there with his hands at his side, a sweet, cautious smile on his face. As much as I'd dreaded returning, it was wonderful to see him. And for most of the half-hour ride home—across the bridge, along Columbia Parkway, and wending our way up Delta Avenue—he chatted about the Olympics, how I still had three more years to prove myself. "What a damn shame," he kept saying, shaking his head. "You were so close."

I listened without a word.

We turned onto Observatory Avenue, and I felt a strange freedom. Geraniums and verbena, creeping jenny in window boxes, antique rocking chairs on porches, residents arriving home with their briefcases or groceries . . . I was home. I felt grateful to Dad for driving the thirteen miles to get me.

Then I noticed that cars, crammed nose to tail, lined our street. The closer we got to the house, the more congested the parking. Was there an event up at the Observatory?

The answer hit me like a sudden blast of heat. Dammit! The center of gravity was our house.

"Dad, I asked you—no, I begged you—to help me feel proud of my achievements."

"They're here to support you, Butch," he said.

He pulled into the driveway and I saw vacant eyes staring through the living room window. "Are you kidding, Dad? Now I have to deal with *this*?" I swallowed a scream and, climbing out, fought an urge to slam the door. "This is not support!"

The house was filled mostly with Jacquie's friends—three deep—all of whom pushed toward me to hug and tell me how sorry they were. It seemed everyone I knew had been invited over to comfort me for not making the Olympic Team. I had no place to hide.

One girl hugged me with tears in her eyes. "I'm so sorry. You must feel terrible."

Yes, I thought. *I do now.*

The Stoehrs, the Lumbs, and other friends of Mom and Dad were there too. One after another tried to inspire me—"This is only a bump in the road; next year you'll do better"—but they didn't understand.

Our house was a damn funeral. I knew Dad meant well. And so did Jacquie. As the two biggest extroverts in the family, they loved having people around to charge them up. They thought it might help me feel better. But that wasn't me. To some of the guests I explained that I was happy—not sad at all—but they wouldn't believe me. Before the last guest left, I had to excuse myself to find a place to sob. I poured a glass of water and nearly retched when I sipped the Cincinnati chemicals.

I'd been telling myself it was okay, that the Olympic Trials hadn't meant anything, but now I felt I had disappointed my parents, my siblings, my friends, and even people I hardly knew—I hadn't done enough to uphold my family's honor.

Before I'd even unpacked my suitcase, they'd convinced me I was a failure.

CHAPTER 35

I had returned to a hell house. The whole family was unhappy for various reasons, and Mom and Dad's strategy was to stay home until our attitudes improved. By then I had given up on waiting for life to return to normal and was sick of Mom and Dad's singing from the same page of the hymnal. It would've been easier if they had just left.

Jacquie had been accepted to Bowling Green for college, but was still locking horns with Mom and Dad about how she would pay the tuition. I had missed her Walnut Hills graduation, which, for the first time, had taken place at Riverfront Stadium instead of Music Hall. "It was a sporting event," she groused as she crouched on her bed with a book. Then she flashed me an odd gleam. "As a gift, Dad told me to do something for myself."

"Like what?" A statement like that seemed off the wall, coming from Dad. Had he softened?

"I'm getting my ears pierced," she said, her eyes wide and determined.

"What?"

"He told me to do something for myself and that's what I'm doing."

Dad had been telling us for years if we got our ears pierced, we would have to get our noses pierced, too. This was before tiny nose rings. He meant the thick metal ring they used to control livestock. "He's going to beat the hell out of you, you know."

"I don't care," she said. "I'm doing it."

WHEN DAD NOTICED THE TEENSY-WEENSY gold balls in Jacquie's ears, he wouldn't even look at her. "Couldn't you have *not* pierced your ears as a favor to me?" He was still fuming about an impromptu party where Rick and his friends had raided the liquor cabinet and then, after using the Victrola, had flung Jacquie's favorite LPs around like Frisbees on the front lawn. Rick had been afraid to throw the scratched records in the trash where somebody might see them, so he'd burned them in the fireplace, which had filled the house with dense smoke and created a sweeping patch of soot up around the mantle.

"The whole goddamn house is going to hell," Dad said. "Jacquie with her ears pierced, Rick trying to burn down the goddamn house, and what's with Pam? When did she start wearing slutty clothes?"

"What slutty clothes? You just don't like John." Whenever Pam's boyfriend came to the house, she crawled into his lap in the living room, which enraged Dad. She'd been Dad's so-called "cuddle bunny," and now this teenage boy was grabbing all her attention.

I don't think Pam was aware how much this aggravated Dad. She asked Mom and Dad if she could drive John to college and Dad's response was, "What? Are you pregnant and want to run off and get married?"

Pam erupted. "You have no right to talk to me like that. I'll get married if I want to."

Mom said, "That's not a respectful way to talk to your father."

Pam snapped back, "Well, he's not respectful to me."

The whole family was fed up with Dad's offensive behavior, but there was no curbing him. I was beginning to wish I'd found an excuse to stay at school for the summer.

Due to fear of getting fatter, I returned to Summertime Swim

Club, half-heartedly, my system like a clogged drain. Meals backed up on a regular basis and my chest ached like never before. I was still holding my breath, waiting for something bad to happen.

I trudged through morning workouts and spent afternoons on the living room couch, my back arched, my head back. Yet I didn't quit swimming. Maybe I didn't have the backbone to face Dad's rejection. I knew my distress was as much mental as it was physical—that my swimming would improve once I began to feel better mentally—but how was I to accomplish feeling better in this pressured situation? I didn't seem able to recover at home.

MOM HAD GROWN COLD AND UNFEELING. She'd held a couple of garage sales, and when I asked her what happened to my white Marlin warm-up jacket with the red and blue trim and my name embroidered on the front, she said, "Oh, I sold your jacket to a sweet bar owner on the west side of Cincinnati. She was so tickled."

I wept.

Mom, sifting through more clothes, stopped what she was doing, and looked surprised. "Aw, honey, you're never going to wear that jacket again."

"Yeah, no kidding. You made sure of that." I curled into a fetal position on the living room couch, clutched a throw pillow, my elongated fingers sporting the nails I'd bitten to a nub. Where had my childhood gone? I was nineteen years old and felt like I was twelve again.

A few minutes later, Dad stormed in. "Where is the little pain in the ass?"

"Who are you talking about?"

"Who do you *think*?"

David entered the room. He had developed acne, a problem that had plagued Dad as a kid.

"What in the hell is wrong with your face?" Dad yelled. "You need to scrub with soap."

David, with tears in his eyes, left to wash with a cloth until his face was raw. When he finished, he marched into the living room, smelling like rose petals. Dad was still bracing for a fight. I adjusted my pillow and dramatically rolled away from them, waiting for the tirade.

"Why don't you go back on the road?" David yelled.

Dad stopped in his tracks, shocked. Now even David was shouting back. Dad grabbed David by the shirt and snaked him over to the Victrola, where he turned down the volume to make his point more dramatically. He thrust his fingers into David's sternum. "You want to fight this battle like a man?"

David took two steps back. "No."

"Sounds like it."

There was dead silence for a moment, then Dad let go of David with a little shove. "I don't need you to tell me what to do. You worry about your face. I'll worry about the business."

David left to sulk in his bedroom. Years later, he would discover that it was the soap that had given him the pimples.

Nothing calmed Dad. Did drinking produce his anxiety? Was it the business? It seemed we were embarrassing him because he'd wanted us all to be superstars and we weren't.

I lay with my back to the TV, trying to block out the tension, but grief from feeling trapped doesn't get up and leave. It sits on your shoulders, weighing down your heart. I knew I could escape to California, but unlike the first time I left home, the realization was finally sinking in that this was my family. My life.

The television blasted pre-Olympic coverage, loud enough to shake Dad in his seat two rooms away. A pillow over my head did nothing to muffle the sound. Our dog, Mustard, barked incessantly. The metallic screen beat the front door frame as vehicles rumbled down Observatory.

The minute I heard Mom and Dad arguing, something inside me snapped. I was grappling with the perceived wreckage of my swimming career, and all I could do was wander off to the refrigerator and devour anything palatable until the food wedged against my ribs. I hyperventilated, stuck my finger down my throat, and vomited in the toilet. Later, I tried laxatives. Everything I ate turned my stomach into a watermelon.

Some part of me realized I *had* wanted to make the Olympic Team. Otherwise, I wouldn't have been hooked by the sad faces when I returned home. Without realizing it, I was behaving like Mom: hiding behind my own wall of disappointment, a wall that kept others out—and now, was crumbling.

Looking back, I see that I believed I was married to swimming and felt my failure to at least make the Trials had been a betrayal of that relationship. But quitting wasn't an option. Quitting would be like leaving the overweight wife with the five kids and the dog and the cat and the house and the motorhome to go off with the pretty brunette with the shiny red fingernails who doesn't know shit.

I told myself that my body had broken down because my emotional breakdown seemed to have no impact on anyone. This was the narrative I'd constructed because the implicit blaming of other people felt better than the truth, which was that my body had broken down because my mind was tied in knots, and because I was treating my body like a garbage can.

At practice, I was so weak that I could barely pull my arms through the water. Afterward, I would walk in the door at home, walk straight to the refrigerator, load up on cheese and crackers or scoops of ice cream, then collapse on the couch. I joined the family at dinner, gobbling crumbs of guilt. After dinner, drained of color like dried celery, I puked a little in my mouth. All evening I lay, clammy, on the side porch, listening to moths pop against the screen and thinking about swimming.

Dad, drink in hand, wanted to debate any number of political or social issues, as if everything were the same as it had always been. I couldn't deal with him. I slipped into the downstairs powder room, stuck my finger down my throat, and hurled up most of dinner. I hated my life.

To Jacquie's friends, I insisted I didn't know what was wrong with me—but, of course, I did know: I was bulimic and hiding it.

I have trouble recalling when the vomiting started. For a long time, I denied it even to myself. *I'm nauseous*, I thought. *That's why I need to vomit. If I get this greasy, high-carb, high-fat food out of me, I'll feel better.* We can tell ourselves any old thing to cope with reality, but the body always keeps a checklist.

The more I whined, the more friends and family said, "Get over it."

I decided I would continue to do what was necessary to convince them I had. I deflected, I questioned, I tried to act cheery as I continued to purge.

ON JUNE 22, I OPENED MY MOUTH AND noticed that my gums and tongue were a bright cherry red. My stomach bloated, still screaming for food, I'd developed white spots around my ankles that I hadn't seen since I was a little girl out playing in the snow. I curled into the hollow of my parents' worn brown sofa and faced away again. I had reached the point where vomiting was automatic and I couldn't stop.

"Can't you get off that damn couch?" Dad shouted. "What's wrong with you?"

All at once, I heard a piercing cry and crash. Mom and Dad glanced up and saw glass and other debris falling in front of the picture window, landing in the leggy yews, and shattering.

Dad leapt to his feet. "What in the hell was that?" Debris was still falling.

We heard shouting from the third floor—Pam's voice—as Dad slowly climbed the stairs. Rick, who was now thirteen, had shoved Pam through the third-story window. After she'd been dangling by her legs a few seconds, the reality hit Rick: *Uh-oh, I'm about to drop her twenty-five feet!* Luckily, he'd registered that in time and pulled Pam back in unhurt.

Dad returned to the dining room, staring at Mom—speechless, which was a novelty for Dad. Then he said, "Those goddam kids. We need to get out of here, Beejay, before I kill one of them."

His words seemed to grab me around the neck. *You* want to run away from *us*? *We're* the problem? Watching from the couch,

I noticed Mom's shoulders drop. Her pen flipped in the air and landed on the table.

"What are you going to do, Dick?"

"About what, Beejay?"

"What do you think I'm talking about? The window. What are you going to do about the window?"

"I'm going to have Rick repair the damned thing," he said.

I began to cry. Rick had just turned thirteen, the age I had been when swimming had reached a point of no turning back. My tears became heaving, choking sobs, then gasps and panic. I didn't know what it was, but it was drowning out everything around me. Before I knew it, I was frighteningly light-headed.

In a flurry of shouting, my father and sister, Jacquie, hustled me to the motorhome and we dashed off to the doctor. Desperately gasping for breath, I slumped beside the green Formica table as Jacquie held a paper lunch bag over my mouth. Dad kept shouting to her from the captain's chair, "Is she doing okay? Hold the bag tightly." To me, he yelled, "Try to calm down, Butch. We're getting you help." The window and door across from me lost their form.

In a medical office that looked like a galley kitchen, Dr. Ebersold gave me a painful shot in the left shoulder. And as the lights in his office flashed, my thoughts ricocheted like the silver balls of a pinball machine. I wanted out. I wanted to be mentally ill. To have a strong enough excuse to not swim, to be finished with the gasping, choking exhaustion of swimming. And the isolation.

"You'll be okay, Butch," Dad said with his hand on my back. "Dr. Ebersold will fix you up."

I was gasping so hard I could only nod.

"I'll take care of her," the doctor said.

A few minutes later, I was unconscious.

CHAPTER 36

I woke in a cavernous room of Good Samaritan Hospital with *Days of Our Lives* blasting and a strong smell of disinfectant. I was in bed. Diagonally across from me was a slender Black girl about my age wearing a gown—floppy in front, ties dangling—her eyes barely open, her head tilted toward the window. I briefly glimpsed an older woman in the next bed, staring at me.

They finally did it, I thought. *They've put me in a loony bin.* I pushed myself up using the adjustable side rails and fumbled with the button to raise the bed. How had I gotten in this hospital gown in a room with seven beds and two other women? Curtains tied against the wall were tangled up with the IV poles that stood by each bed. The voluminous room seemed clinical and cheerless, like hospital units in World War II movies.

The animated woman beside me was petite, with intense blue, almond-shaped eyes, thick eyeliner, and a trace of red lipstick. Her frizzy hair fell in loose waves around her heart-shaped face. Judging by her silky pink nightgown, I figured she'd been there awhile. She asked what I was doing there.

"I don't know." I understood my being placed with the other girl—she looked depressed—but why this energetic old lady?

The woman began gesturing, eyes wide, talking about theater this, theater that, and how she'd been acting most of her life. She wanted to talk, and I wasn't in the mood.

"Have you ever heard of Lillian Gish?" she asked me.

"No," I grunted half-heartedly.

"Look up the name."

I glanced past her and caught the girl in the corner bed shaking her head ever so slightly. Since I still wasn't sure if I was in a psych ward, I didn't know what to think. *Is Lillian Gish a famous actress?* Maybe she was a demented woman who thought she was Lillian Gish. She definitely had too much energy.

"How do you like the room?"

"Fine."

"And the nurses?"

"Fine." I lay there like a lump, answering in single words and fractured concentration. I could feel my brain not wanting to work. I hated being so joyless, but her curiosity made me defensive. I kept thinking, *This woman won't shut up; is she channeling my father?*

When a nurse entered, the two exchanged compliments like neighbors in a grocery line. Lillian seemed to be the kind of person who had to banish any negative thought. I kept waiting for her to say something provocative so I had an excuse to tell her to stop.

"Mother taught me that if you blah, blah, blah . . . and she taught me blah-blah-blah-blah-blah . . ."

"I'm sorry, what?" I crooked my neck and gave her a withering look, hoping to convey the full impact of my misery.

Lillian was polite, and spoke with long pauses. "Forgive me for asking, but why are you here?"

I rolled toward her on the bed. "I didn't make the Olympic Team, and my father's devastated. I don't know . . . I guess I had a breakdown."

Lillian paused as if about to tell me something important, then said, "If you please yourself, you please your audience."

"Okay . . ." I waited, but she didn't say anything more. Please my audience? What was she *talking* about? I began to describe the welcome-home party, trying to win her over. I added a few moans and groans and let my hospital gown slip off one shoulder, then curled into a ball, facing away, to emphasize my sorry state.

I was broken and lost, and wanted empathy.

Lillian wanted to keep talking. In my mind's eye I could see her almond eyes flickering. "That was a loving thing he did for you," she said.

"I'm sorry, but I'm going to have to sleep. I'm tired."

Oh, my God, I thought. *Why can't she keep her damn mouth shut?* Dad was wonderful and caring? Bleh.

A FEW HOURS LATER, STILL NO ONE HAD come to tell me what was going on. Aides wheeled Lillian out of the room and I could feel my body relax. I was so distressed I wanted to throw the sheets over my head and sink into my wretchedness. The woman in the corner stared out the window at nothing. Her face was drawn, her hair pulled back in two short braids behind her neck. I introduced myself but she didn't respond. She looked stricken. I worried that I was behaving like Lilian, sucking away her limited energy.

"They took my baby," she said suddenly.

"What?"

She rearranged her legs to get comfortable as we listened to a metallic rumbling from a cart rolling down the hallway. The racket seemed to add to the weight of her sadness.

"Are you okay?" I asked.

"I have cancer," she said.

"Cancer? Shoot." I didn't know what to say. "They couldn't do anything?"

One of her eyelids drooped and she looked like she'd been suffocating in the unhappiness in the room. She shrank under the blanket.

"I'm sorry." I tried to think of what I would want someone to say to me if I were in her position. "Maybe you could have another one. Another baby."

She wearily tugged on the sleeve of her gown. "No ... no more."

I could feel my eyes well up. I had so much going for me, and here was this woman with real life problems. Not self-created ones like mine.

Voices of hospital staff drifted in from the hallway. The woman said her name was Carla and she asked why I was there.

"They're doing tests, and um, well, I don't know ..." My problems were worlds away from cancer, a dead baby, or a hysterectomy, if that's what she'd had. I wanted to punch myself as I hemmed and hawed.

I felt guilty about everything. Guilty I'd disappointed my parents. Guilty I'd disappointed friends. Guilty I'd disappointed myself. I must have, right? Otherwise, why would the Olympic theme song make me nauseous? If I truly had wanted to quit swimming so badly, why was I still practicing? Was I that gutless? That afraid to quit? I had done this violence to myself and was letting the victim in me run rampant. *Stop!* I told myself. *Swimming is giving you a college education, dammit.*

I reached below my bed and pulled out a pad of Arches archival paper that Mom had dropped by the hospital for me. "You mind if I draw your picture?"

"I don't care," she said. "You good?"

"You mean as an artist?" I shrugged. Carla was a mature woman. I was such a kid.

A nurse moving at high speed rolled Lillian in from her treatment, and Carla reflexively closed her eyes.

"She's angry, that girl," Lillian said when she noticed.

Instantly, I wanted to cut her off. Why the commentary? Did she even know what was ailing the poor girl? She sure had no idea what was ailing me.

"We need to be involved in life," she said. "Active and involved. Not passive."

When she said this my eyes bored into her, and the nurse hurried over and closed the curtain between us. Lillian was hitting some "Dad nerve" in me, and my father's voice was coming back like acid reflux.

I began writing a mental checklist of the traits I hated about Dad. His insensitivity, his meanness, his blistering insecurity, his abuse. My list included moments he shouted at one of us and moments he wasn't even home. I was target practicing with arrows aimed directly at him, yet somehow missing him each time.

Another part of me spoke in my mother's soft voice, rationalizing his behavior. "Oh, Kimmy, your father didn't mean what he said. The business is a struggle. We've been working hard and not making any money and . . ."

As her words trailed off, I defended myself. This arrow was for dragging me into swimming. That arrow was for abandoning us. My voice became louder and brasher, and soon I was shouting. And swearing. And punching. A forceful slug straight to his gut. Dad backed away and held himself, then swallowed hard. He caught his breath, asked me to kiss him, and like a robot, I leaned over and kissed him on the lips. The whole scene happened entirely in my head, but somehow it settled me. It was as if the imaginary scene rearranged my emotional circuitry, releasing the last bit of tension and blame directed at my father. Lilian had unwittingly helped me let go of the emotional stranglehold my father had on me.

OVER A COUPLE OF DAYS, AN AIDE WHISKED me off for various tests. I was relieved to find the curtains beside my bed closed as she wheeled me back to the hospital room each time. But on the third morning, as soon as I began to stir, Lillian pushed the curtain back with her forearm.

"Do you mind taking an observation from an old lady?"

I sighed. "No."

"Well, then. They'll find there's nothing wrong with you."

Thank you, Dr. Lillian, I wanted to say. I don't think she saw me shudder.

"Your struggle is between pleasing yourself and pleasing your father," she said.

For a moment, I felt understood. She was spot-on about my father.

I was nodding in agreement when Dr. Ebersold entered the room. He stood by the edge of my bed and spoke calmly. "The test results are back and they were all, as I suspected, negative."

A lump formed in my throat. Did he mean the stomach pain was imaginary? He hesitated for a moment as I glanced over at Lillian. She'd just applied some bright red lipstick and was wide-eyed and smiling, her ear cocked in my direction.

Dr. Ebersold pulled the curtain shut between our two beds. He reached for a chair and sat down. "I've given your situation some thought and I believe I know the cause of your breathing problems and stomach pain."

As he rubbed his chin, my abdominal muscles clamped tight. Dad and he were friends. Had he contacted Dad and discussed what Dad thought was wrong with me? Would I have to go to Longview, the sprawling brick mental hospital I'd passed every day on my way to Marlin practice? How long would I have to stay there? A month? A couple of months? My mind raced.

He folded his hands in his lap. "Do you want me to say what I *think* your problem is?"

I nodded and coughed up some phlegm. Then I sat as still as a mannequin as he searched for the words.

"Well, I could be wrong, but I *think* . . . I um, well . . . I think your problem is your parents." He cleared his throat as he waited for my reaction.

I was dumbfounded. Wow. For the first time, someone had noticed.

"You know," he said, "I'm fond of both of them. I know they love you; I've heard them talk. But you need a break. I'm going to prescribe a medication. We'll move you to a private room where you can have guests any time of day, but no parents. Would that be okay?"

I stopped breathing. Then I took a ragged, bottomless breath. "What will I do?"

"You will read. You will watch TV. You will rest. I'm going to call your father and explain this to him."

I let out a satisfied sigh for the first time in weeks.

The doctor opened the curtain, and I glanced at Lillian, who wore a heavy-lidded look of satisfaction. I wanted to throw my arms around the doctor and shower him with words of gratitude, but all I managed was a soft-spoken, "Thank you."

DR. EBERSOLD MOVED ME TO A PRIVATE room for a couple of weeks and Jacquie arranged for a steady stream of smiling, cheerful faces, mostly her friends who had attended my welcome home party. I learned later that my father had asked Dan not to come, saying that it wouldn't be good for me. I hardly registered anyone's presence anyway. Maybe the drug was an anti-anxiety drug. I'm not even sure. I couldn't sleep. I couldn't stay alert. My life had become dull gray, no highs or lows, like I was sandwiched between two worlds: the world I wanted and the world I was living. I was self-conscious enough to remember I needed to keep my shoulders back and appear cheerful, but I couldn't sustain it.

By the time my parents checked me out of the hospital, I felt more rested but was also a zombie, just alert enough to notice the added layer of cellulite on my upper thighs.

"Try not to feel bad about the Olympics," Dad said. "There's always . . . what's the other one?"

"Pan-Am Games?" Mom answered like I wasn't there.

Dad glanced over his shoulder at me. "Right! You can make a team next year."

I gazed out the window of the backseat, trying to feel some emotion, as Dad kept firing: *What's your plan? When do you leave? Do you think you're in shape to go back to school?*

To every question, I mumbled, "I don't know."

Our house vibrated with the Olympic theme song, but I had no interest in who made the team, and who didn't. Mom told me Gary Hall, my former assistant coach—Mr. Keating's now son-in-law—had paraded his infant son in his arms around the Long Beach swimming stadium when he won at the Olympic Trials. I was too detached to care.

What mattered most was that I'd stopped vomiting. Something about being in the hospital—possibly the food or perhaps the medication—had fixed my bloated stomach, and my urge to vomit had turned off like a switch. I knew the physical danger of bulimia and no longer had a desire to use laxatives or gobble up everything in sight. Dr. Ebersold had handed me something that felt like control over my life. I would return to school and swimming, and with Heather as my new roommate, my life would get back on track. I decided to block out the hospital stay; I wouldn't mention it to anyone. It would be as if I hadn't been there.

CHAPTER 37

I landed at the LAX airport, buoyed by the sunny, expansive California sky and the vast distance from my parents. I also felt excited at the prospect of leaving the dorms and moving into an apartment for my sophomore year. I had so much to tell Heather and had been so busy blocking out the world that I had no idea how she or anyone else had swum in the Trials or Olympics.

Kaia had agreed to pick me up at the airport. I spied her broad smile in a crowd of onlookers as soon as I stepped off the plane. She looked Hawaiian, with a faded yellow tank top on her narrow torso, a long floral skirt, and a flower in her wavy blond hair. I bounded over and practically knocked her to the ground with my enthusiastic hug. I couldn't wait to hear what I'd missed during my so-called "vacation."

"What do you want first?" she asked. "The good or the bad news?"

"Good news," I said. "Definitely good news."

"The team is going to Japan," she said. "That's the rumor, anyway."

"Woo-hoo!" I did a little jig.

She explained that the trip was going to be a fun publicity trip for us, but also for the Japanese. In order to go, we had to qualify at Nationals. She added that I wouldn't have any trouble. "And the bad news?"

"I'll be rooming with you this year." She gave me a hangdog look. "Heather won't be coming back."

I dropped my shoulder bag on the concrete floor as people scurried past us. "Say what?"

"That's all I know: she's not coming back," Kaia shouted over the rush of travelers—something about Heather's parents—but my mind became a blur.

This was impossible to fathom. Heather not coming back? She *had* to come back. How was I supposed to get through another year of swimming without her to create fun? We had done everything together. Who would I chum around with?

Dammit, I thought. *What is it about me? Abandoned again.*

AS IT TURNED OUT, I ENDED UP ROOMING that year with Anne, a quiet girl on the team I hardly knew, and Kaia roomed with Perucha, a butterflyer from Indonesia. The four of us shared a cozy second-floor apartment with a galley kitchen, combination living room–dining room, two small bedrooms with twin beds that shared a bathroom, and a narrow balcony.

I hadn't seen Dan all summer but he'd promised he'd visit me at school, so once I'd settled in for a week or so, I called him. I told him about my weight gain and difficult summer, and when I mentioned Heather, I started to cry. "Can I come visit?"

"Sure. When?" He seemed distracted.

"I don't know. Friday?" I wanted to leave that minute.

"You mean like this *weekend*?" Then he said, "Sure, why not? We'll work it out."

I loved that about Dan. He was the one person in my life who would be there for me no matter what.

I skipped a day of practice and used money intended for my phone bill to buy a plane ticket to Colorado.

WHEN I ARRIVED, DAN GAVE ME A TOUR of the University of Colorado campus, where we passed Willie Nelson with his ponytail and red bandanna, followed by a handful of adoring fans. He showed me the pool where he practiced, introduced me to a band of intellectually handicapped men he taught in his part-time volunteer job, and took me to The Sink restaurant for dinner. I'd never been so happy to see someone in my life.

That night, with butterflies in my stomach, I snuggled with Dan on the floor on his twin mattress and explored the limits of Catholic sex. I told him I felt unattractive. I clutched his blanket around my torso and as he wrapped his arms around me, I confessed, "I'm still gorging on apple fritters and thick chocolate bars."

By then I'd realized my eating was emotional and had nothing to do with hunger. I told him I was grateful for the scholarship but I was so burned out on swimming—so exhausted—that I couldn't control my eating. Even in that moment I was mentally parsing every calorie from dinner, my brain moving too slowly to draw out the words.

"Do you think you're the only person who's ever pigged out?" he asked.

"I know." With my index finger, I caressed a clump of his hair.

"Look, your weight will come off," he said. "Try not to think about it."

Just then, there was an explosive pounding on the door. "Dan, I know you're in there," a female voice shouted.

He gently withdrew from our embrace. "I've been meaning to tell you," he whispered. "But it's not what you think."

"Are you serious?" Of *course,* it was what I thought. A woman knows this intuitively.

"Kimmy," he whispered, "remember, we talked about dating other people."

The door pounding continued. "Open the door!"

I felt a tightening in my chest. To me this was a big deal, and difficult to reconcile. I heard movement, and felt certain the girl had pressed her ear to the door. Dan put his hand on my leg and I froze for a moment, pushing him away.

"Open the fucking door, Dan," she shouted.

Dan leaned closer, rubbing my shoulder.

"Don't!" I shook him off.

We lay there listening for a while. If I hadn't felt so pathetic, I might've jumped up and swung open the door myself. But I didn't know what to do. Call a cab? Force him to drive me to the airport right then? I'd flown to Colorado for emergency medicine and discovered an overcrowded ER.

The following morning, Dan drove me to the Denver airport, where I gave him a hug and a brief pat on the back that translated as "I wish you the best" and then I entered the terminal.

By the time the plane landed in LA, I thought I'd overreacted.

KAIA WAS AMUSED BY THE STORY, IMAGINING hot and heavy sex on Dan's dorm room floor.

"Okay, if you say so," she said when I told her that wasn't the case. I was still a virgin—a strange club to belong to, since everyone I knew seemed to be having sex by then.

She suggested we plan a party and invite the Canadian swimmers from the men's team—Steve, Michael, and George—who liked beer and were less intense than the Bible-toting contingent. She made several pitchers of margaritas and some nachos and guacamole, and by the end of the evening Steve and I were on my twin bed, in prone position, whispering I-love-you lies in each other's ears.

Kaia, tipsy herself, walked Steve to the door. As soon he was gone, she stood there, her back against the door, wanting details.

"Nothing happened," I said.

"You're full of it. I could hear you."

"Oh, could you hear the *ooh-ah* you're so handsome, *boom-boom-boom*, I love you so much? Did you hear *that* too?" She was beginning to get on my nerves.

Kaia doubled over, laughing hysterically. "I don't know what happened, but it was something."

"It was *some*thing all right," I said.

And before I knew it, I was trying to explain to her that swimming had stunted my emotional development. With a series of coaches as surrogate fathers, swimming had held me hostage. The early structure of swimming had given me a sense of control in my life. Now with Pokey as a real coach—not a stand-in daddy—and a more relaxed structure, I finally had time to think, to explore, to imagine a life that wasn't defined by swimming, and I was overwhelmed.

"There are so many choices out there," I said. "So many things I could do." I told her swimming felt like a job.

"Because it *is* a job, you knucklehead," she said. "You're working for your education."

A MONTH LATER, IN EARLY OCTOBER, Pokey pulled those of us on scholarship aside and said, "I realize this is a lot to ask, but I've received a request to have you girls attend a cocktail party fundraiser for the Orange County Trojan Club in Santa Ana. You will need to wear appropriate clothing—a skirt, a nice blouse. I don't want to see anyone in tennis shoes or T-shirts."

I thought it was funny she needed to remind us, but then she added, "They may ask you to demonstrate."

"Demonstrate *swimming*?" I shuddered.

"We'll see," she said, sighing. "But bring your bathing suits to the party just in case."

I dreaded that party for a week. I didn't own a cocktail dress and had never been to a cocktail party, unless you count serving drinks for my parents' Bengals football friends. The idea of donning a bathing suit in front of an audience of partygoers was too cringe-worthy to imagine.

ON OUR WAY TO THE PARTY, I remember hoping beyond hope that our maturity would make them too embarrassed to ask us to swim.

An older woman escorted us to the backyard, where I stopped abruptly at the sight of twenty-five or thirty guests all gathered in small groups around a tiny, kidney-shaped swimming pool. Men in silk Hawaiian dress shirts and women in cocktail dresses sipped drinks as uniformed women offered canapes on silver trays. Smoke billowed from the corner of the patio where a man turned thick slabs of greasy steak on a grill.

I nudged Laurie. "Was Pokey kidding? Do we really have to get in that pool and demonstrate?" I pointed to the water.

"God, I hope not," she said with an unsteady chuckle.

I hiked over to Pokey, who introduced me to one of the women donors. When the woman got distracted, Pokey leaned over and whispered, "Mingle, will you? And try not to look so pained. I'll see what I can do."

The whole scene brought me back four years to a family trip to Barneveld, New York. My grandmother had died of cirrhosis of the liver, and we were there to visit my mother's father and meet his new wife. While the adults sipped their gin and tonics, my father had insisted the five of us kids show off our great swimming talent in the slimy little pond that was visible from my grandfather's porch. There had been an ugly scene and a fair amount of crying before and after the demonstration, which had shortened our visit. I knew these people donated big bucks that were important to the success of the USC women's program, but that didn't make this situation any less embarrassing. *Why do we treat women athletes like this?* The guys didn't have to put on their skintight Speedos and show off *their* body curves. I hated the double standard. But I thought of Kaia's comment about swimming as my job. Jobs required that we do things we didn't enjoy. Sometimes they could even be degrading. The workouts, the performance at meets, and now swimming like a trained seal in a pool the size of a bathtub—these actions were the currency that allowed me to get my education.

The fake smiles and superficial talk at this party bore a strange resemblance to the façade we had created at home every time Mom and Dad entertained. Their Bengals gatherings, like this cocktail party, had involved their drinking and telling jokes in an alcoholic haze while we kids, when asked, served drinks or engaged in superficial chit-chat with their guests about school or our love of swimming.

Pokey couldn't convince the Trojan Club to drop the demonstration. "I'm sorry," she said. "Just get in and don't think about it."

Easy enough. It was what I'd been doing for years.

They escorted us into one of the bedrooms, where we removed our cocktail attire and donned our bathing suits. Then, under the tiki torches of the fancy Santa Ana patio, we stepped out to an audience applauding like we were circus performers. The demonstration was ridiculous, since the most we could swim were two strokes before hitting the wall, but when we finished I tried, just as I always had with my parents, to spin it in a positive light. At least we weren't knocking on doors, begging for money.

OUR TRIP TO PROVIDENCE, RHODE ISLAND, for Nationals my sophomore year began with a spate of bad luck. First, we missed our plane. Then, after arriving to more than a foot of snow and ice and without enough rental cars, we were too late for warm-up and ended up paddling around in the tiny, over-chlorinated Marriott hotel pool. In the lobby, a Marriott clerk handed me an envelope with my name on it:

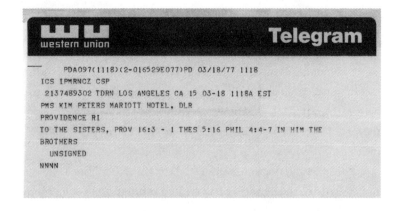

```
Telegram
western union

     PDA097(1118)(2-016529E077)PD 03/18/77 1118
ICS IPMRNCZ CSP
 2137489302 TDRN LOS ANGELES CA 15 03-18 1118A EST
PMS KIM PETERS MARIOTT HOTEL, DLR
PROVIDENCE RI
TO THE SISTERS, PROV 16:3 - 1 THES 5:16 PHIL 4:4-7 IN HIM THE
BROTHERS
    UNSIGNED
NNNN
```

Cindy stood next to me as I read. It was a Western Union telegram with three Bible quotes about rejoicing, signed, *In Him, the brothers.*

I looked askance at her. "Why did they address the telegram to *me*?"

"They were trying to be nice," she said. "To wish you well."

On several occasions, I'd attended non-denominational prayer meetings with the Christian contingent of the Men's team—partly out of feeling pressured, but also because I'd hoped to improve my attitude about swimming. None of it had helped. I didn't want to talk Bible quotes or even attend church anymore. The telegram felt like a warning—like an implicit judgment that I was out of step in some way.

And I guess I was. The meet was a disaster. In the 500 freestyle that I'd won the year before, I swam the most painful 500 ever. Forget negative splitting—that wasn't even a possibility. I knew halfway through I couldn't hold back or I wouldn't make the finals. I ended up third in the consolation finals (eleventh place), and seven seconds slower than the previous year.

That evening, sometime in the middle of finals, Pokey grabbed the wrong stack of entry cards for the next day and meet officials insisted our team would have to scratch our events the following day.

That night at the hotel, Pokey called Barbara Hedges, the athletic director, who called some USC attorneys, who got all jacked up and ready to jump on a plane and fly to Providence to file lawsuits. All night Pokey paced the hallway of the Marriott, waiting for the phone to ring. Only a few of us got any sleep.

By morning we were still unsure whether the officials would let us swim. I slogged through warm-up—a few hundred yards and some twenty-five-yard sprints—just in case the meet officials changed their minds. For the longest time, we watched from the bleachers as Pokey, all in navy blue, stood amongst a group of sour-faced Rhode Island officials, all in white.

Spectators began to grow restless as the officials argued in a semicircle around Pokey. Swimmers from other teams approached us, wondering why the events hadn't started. "Maybe we can do something," they said.

A few minutes later, the word came back: other coaches had interrupted the officials' conference. "We will withdraw from the competition if you don't allow USC to swim," UCLA warned. Soon Arizona State and Miami joined the protest.

A part of me hoped we wouldn't have to swim at all—that we could blame our troubles on the bad officials and enjoy the rest of our trip to Providence, then go to Japan without the trouble of earning our way.

But as the announcer got on the microphone, welcoming us to the second day of Nationals, the group of officials disbanded and Pokey rushed toward us, her stride determined.

"They're fining me and putting all of you in the first heat of your events," she said, meaning in a heat with the slowest competitors. It wasn't the worst situation, but not the best either. And now I would have to swim.

MY LIMBS FELT LEADEN IN THE 200. I couldn't get up emotionally for the rest of the meet. I placed fifteenth in the 200 and fifteenth again in the mile. When I hauled myself out of the chilly water on the last day of Nationals and Pokey said I'd earned a place on the USC swimming trip to Japan, I about fell over. I'd misunderstood what it took to qualify.

Pokey walked me to the locker room with an arm around my shoulder. "Every year isn't perfect. You had a great year last year, and next year you'll do better."

My eyes watered as I thanked her.

CHAPTER 38

A gaggle of cameramen waited for John Naber at the Tokyo arrival gate. There were about ten US and Canadian Olympians on the Men's team, but with the four gold medals he'd won at the Montreal Olympics, John was the most famous. Our Japanese hosts escorted us onto a bus to customs, where we grabbed our bags and were driven to a press conference. All US male Olympians were directed to sit with the coaches on long couches; we girls looked on as cameramen flashed bright lights and snapped pictures.

The photographers followed us onto a modern bus with transparent curtains, comfortable chairs, gigantic windows, and a giant clock in front. The American organizers drove beside the bus in a Rolls Royce. By the time we arrived at our hotel to a crowd of friendly greeters, my cheeks ached from all the smiling.

I had imagined a typical American room but with a sparse, contemporary Japanese design. The Akasaka Shampia was nothing even close. An attractive boutique hotel, each of its rooms bore a remarkable resemblance to a fancy motorhome.

Inside of five minutes, we were out in the hall, modeling the tiny kimono-style robes we'd found in our closets. "Love your outfit," we told each other as we posed.

Small USC team group upon arrival in Japan; standing left to right:
Laurie Edwards, Kim Peters, Joe Bottom, Scott Brown, John Naber,
Bruce Furniss, Michael Ker, Laura Tyrrell, Ron Orr, Sam Stein, George
Pearson (USC trainer), Linda Kimura; front row left to right: Gerry
Geraghty, Mike Nyeholt, Mike Bottom, Rod Stewart.

Word traveled up from the lobby that we had ten minutes to prepare for dinner, so we raced to get ready. I pictured an authentic Japanese meal with sushi and delicate fish dishes. Instead, our Japanese hosts chose a Chinese nightclub a block from the hotel, where we gathered around tables with lazy susans and dined on Mongolian beef and shrimp fried rice; perhaps it was their way of making us feel at home. Several demonstrated how to eat with slippery chopsticks. We elbowed each other and poked fun when Ron Orr, seated across from me, gave up a few times and reached for the shrimp with his fingers.

That night I lay in bed and thought of my own family at the dinner table—the way we all sat in the same chairs, uncomfortable, awkwardly listening to Dad's jokes and Mom's reactions. There had been something familiar that night in the Chinese restaurant. Like my siblings and me, we were in this adventure together. Having a devoted boyfriend, a sleek body, and extra time to enjoy my life seemed unexpectedly less important. Japan was allowing me to forget myself and enjoy the swimming family. Somewhere in the back of my mind, I realized, I'd believed it was important to quit swimming on a high note—and this trip was beginning to look like the perfect way to leave.

OUR TOUR GUIDE TOOK US TO WHAT he said was "the cheapest in all of Tokyo," a string of shops selling shiny electronic equipment of every kind imaginable. After a fifteen-minute sales pitch, I settled on a single-lens reflex Pentax camera for 47,000 yen ($173.00), the most I'd ever spent on a purchase for myself.

With the camera slung over my shoulder, in a collage of geometric blinking neon, I stumbled into a high-tech watch store where I bought an expensive blush-colored Seiko with a crystal lens for Dan, a bittersweet gift in light of our last visit. I wanted the watch to be an implicit message: *I forgive you*; *I still care*; and *Sure, let's start over*. But even as I placed the yen in the clerk's open palm and watched him wrap the watch, I doubted that I was honoring myself. A voice in my head kept asking, *Why am I holding on so tightly?*

Since my visit to Denver, Dan had been trying to win me back; I was tempted—he was special to me—but also uncertain if I could trust him again. And I was still noticing other guys who were geographically closer and equally interesting and good-looking. Ever since Heather had returned to Fresno, I'd been longing for a best friend to connect with, and yet I couldn't really say what or who it was that I wanted. I felt like I was pushing my heart around in a shopping cart.

The Japan trip turned out to be a whirl of flirtations with guys on the team. There was John Naber, who walked me back from the Baptist church; Tim Regan, who accompanied me to several ancient spiritual sites; and Yukichi Miyazaki, a Japanese swimmer who followed me around as a kind of tour guide for part of the trip. I was up for anything, but I also felt disembodied, unfocused. I couldn't stop thinking about Dan—*Should I have called him before*

I left? Do I really want to stay with him?—and I was trying to fill the void with something. Anything. An hour after accepting an invitation from Michael Ker—one of the three Canadian guys—to join him in his room and ending up in a heavy make-out session, I lay on my own bed, curled in a confused knot, full of a gluttonous revulsion at my latest rebound guy.

The Japan trip hadn't been a reset at all. It was all related: the food, the swimming, the guys. Trying to fill up had made me emptier.

Kim with Yukichi Miyazaki

TWO DAYS LATER, MIKE BOTTOM PULLED me aside in the hallway of the Shampia Hotel and invited me to the rooftop. Arrestingly handsome—but not an operator—quiet, and one of the devout Christian leaders on the team, he wore a cross on a chain around his neck even when he swam. He and I had shared a seat on a bus trip to an uncomfortable Pentecostal service in Long Beach, where the congregants had waved their hands in the air and some of the members had spoken in tongues. Before the Olympic Trials I'd run into him at the USC medical center, where he'd kindly handed me a brochure about I.B.D (inflammatory bowel disease), suggesting that this might be the cause of my stomach pain. Other than those two occasions, I hardly knew him.

I checked my hair and brushed my teeth, wondering what could be so important that he would invite me up there alone. We hiked to the roof and squatted on a four-inch-wide piece of concrete, like a curb at the edge of a street. At first, we marveled at the Tokyo commercial district, so exotic compared to what we were used to—the geometry of its tall, narrow buildings, its sparkling lights, its dull gray backdrop. The wide-open expanse, the way it blurred at the horizon, was staggering.

My hands clammy, I reached for my Pentax, snapped a picture, and waited. Mike's letterman jacket stretched across his broad shoulders; his arms were slung loosely over his knees. He turned to me with those bushy brows and cerulean blue eyes. "Do you know why I invited you up here?"

Nervous, I squirmed. "I have no idea."

He sat up straighter. "Well, I'd like to talk to you about Jesus."

I shrank back a few inches, staring. "Jesus? Why?" Were we about to have a Bible study? I noticed he'd said talk *to* me, not *with* me.

He rambled about his girlfriend, and a touch of frost entered me. Then he added, "But she and I are going steady."

I twisted away from him. "I'm going steady, too."

"You are?" He seemed surprised. "With . . . ?"

"My boyfriend, Dan." I was surprised by my white lie, but I knew what Mike was getting at. He could sleep with *his* girlfriend—they were "going steady"—but he believed, based on gossip, that I was engaging in a few too many extracurricular activities.

Mike fidgeted for a moment like he didn't know what to say. "My girlfriend and I are practically married," he said, seemingly to reinforce his point. "I think you should ask yourself, 'What would Jesus do?'"

Suddenly, I didn't want to talk with him anymore. What would Jesus do about *what*? I'd been trying to fit in with the Christian guys on the team, but clearly I wasn't measuring up. I was sure he thought I was sleeping around. Had he heard something about me in the Men's locker room? *Those damn Canadian guys. Kaia and I never should've invited them to dinner.*

I wish I could have been confident enough to ask Mike if he was also sitting down with Michael Ker and telling him he should think about what Jesus would do. But I felt too hurt to say anything; he didn't know me well enough to judge.

Like my mother seven years earlier, feeling she'd outgrown the neighborhood after my father's affair with Anne Boyle, I wanted to find a new community—one where I could start over as a nice person with a good reputation and self-esteem. I told myself I didn't care, that I was just confused about what I wanted to do with my life. I knew it was more than that, however. Swimming and I were struggling, but inside I was struggling too. And Mike somehow knew that.

I SEARCHED FOR TIM IN THE STERILE Shampia cafeteria at breakfast. He was alone at a metal table, hunched over his tray in a rumpled plaid shirt, his eyes downturned, his hair resembling a Brillo pad. He looked the way I felt.

I set my bowl of steamed rice and raw egg next to him and pulled out a chair. "Mike Bottom had a little talk with me last night."

"*Now* what did you do? It must've been bad," he teased. His contagious laughter relaxed me instantly.

I rehashed the conversation, leaving out the part about Dan. "What was he trying to say? That I'm a bad Christian?"

"Who *cares*?" he asked, laughing. "Well, I guess *you* do." He chuckled again.

"This isn't funny, Tim." I shifted in my chair.

He set his chopsticks on the edge of his bowl and lowered his voice. "You shouldn't let one guy's opinion influence the way you think of yourself."

I appreciated that he believed Mike represented only one guy, but I still cared about all the other Christians on the team and what they thought of me. And somewhere in the back of my mind was a dim memory of Mom's telling me I had good instincts, that I should trust my gut. I thought, *You know, maybe I could do this thing. Maybe I could quit swimming and have my life back. I could be free. With no more demands. No more starvation diets. And no more façade of being a "good girl" so others won't judge me. I could eat all the steamed rice and raw egg I want. I could stop worrying. Tim is right. I don't have to let others' opinions influence me. I could get out of this swimming bubble and move on with my life.*

Mike's version of Christianity had blended with swimming. Focusing on what Jesus would do, like swimming for my life, was somebody else's idea of what was best for me.

Ron Orr with a tour group of Japanese students.

FOR DAYS I OBSESSED ABOUT MIKE'S WORDS. At the Imperial Palace, when strangers stared and approached us for autographs or whole tour groups of schoolgirls wearing navy sailor suits and matching gold hats mobbed the men's team, crying out in their high-pitched giggles, I played Mike's tape in my head. And then I argued with myself. I told myself I wasn't *in* his club. I was my own person. *Thank God I live in America*, I thought, *where it's okay to be different.*

"What Jesus would do?" He'd preach about a wooden beam in your own eye, wouldn't he? Or was that one of his disciples?

Oh, hell. I didn't care. I wanted out. I wanted college to be more than chlorine and double daily workouts.

I made up my mind.

WHEN WE RETURNED TO SUNNY LA, with its clear skies and lush green palm trees, I unpacked my bag and set the souvenirs—the camera, watch, Japanese flags, folded paper birds, business cards, rolls of film and colorful bookmarks—on my gray wool bedspread as if they were ribbons and medals. As I admired each one, I let out an inaudible sigh; then I picked up the phone and dialed home.

When Dad heard my cheerful voice, he seemed uneasy. "You sound happy," he said.

"I am. And before you say anything, I want you to know I've made up my mind. I don't want you to talk me out of this."

I could sense Dad's discomfort. He wanted to hear about Japan; this was clearly about something else.

"Bee-eej, get on the phone," he yelled. "Let me let you talk to your mother." I was sure he wanted Mom to deliver the "sensible argument"—the softer, Mom version of *What in the hell do you think you're doing?*

When I heard Mom's voice, I said, "I know you're not going to like it, but I've decided to quit swimming." I continued to explain, but in her silence, I could tell she'd stopped listening.

She sounded tired, matter-of-fact. "Your father and I can't live your life for you, Kim. If you want to quit swimming, quit." I was sure they'd already discussed the possibility.

She then asked if I'd like to talk to Jacquie. I happily agreed.

Jacquie tried to convey her support without making it obvious to Mom and Dad. "They're sick of hearing you complain." Her voice was low.

"Are they right there?"

"Yes."

"Are they being jerks?"

"Uh-hunh. But try not to let this bother you. Know what I mean?" She was deliberate and slow in finding the words. I knew she meant well.

When I hung up, I glanced through my window at the neighboring apartment balconies. Happy music blared from someone's stereo. For maybe an hour I stood there staring. I'd stunned myself. For so many years I'd dreaded telling Mom and Dad I wanted to quit; now the moment had finally arrived, and although I was hot all over, sweating at my temples, maybe even nervously scratching my legs, nothing worse had happened.

I jumped up and made a list of classes I would take—psychology, oceanography, maybe criminal justice or cinema—then left the apartment to enjoy for a solid day a sense of hope and calm, imagining life with freedom to do what I wanted. I would write letters, make art for the walls, cultivate new relationships. Somehow, I would find a job. And my life would reflect a less predictable rhythm.

But before I did anything else, I wanted to tell Pokey.

I HOPPED ON MY BIKE AND CRUISED across campus. The wind was fierce for an LA afternoon, and I felt as if the strong gusts were sweeping through the emptiness inside me.

I was pedaling toward the pool when I spotted Kaia leaving the rec building.

She waved and called, "Have you heard the latest?"

"No, what?"

She seemed to bubble with her secret as I skidded to a halt in front of her.

"You've been voted team captain."

CHAPTER 39

It was as if I had gotten a marriage proposal from the wrong guy. This wasn't supposed to happen. I didn't see how, after such a mediocre sophomore year, I could be voted team captain. Maybe they were rewarding me for my freshman year performance—which I appreciated—but it seemed every time I tried to escape swimming, the universe handed me yet another reason to stay exactly where I was.

I flopped on my bed and called Mom for advice. I wanted her to prop me up, to reassure me that quitting was a good decision.

But as Dad listened on the upstairs extension, I detected a renewed hope in his voice. "How will you pay for your last two years if you don't swim?"

"I can work," I said. "Get a job during school."

"A job that pays thousands of dollars? You're kidding yourself."

Kaia had mentioned a swimming tryout for LA County Beach Lifeguards, a gig that paid more than any other lifeguard job in the world. If I was determined to pay for school without my scholarship, I knew there'd be a way.

"You have to decide what you want," Mom said. I could sense her hackles going up too.

"I want to quit, but I was voted team captain. What am I supposed to do?"

"Well, you have to decide how you feel about disappointing people," she said.

I should've been quick with a retort, since Mom and Dad were often disappointing us. But I couldn't think. I felt torn between happiness and commitment. I didn't know if I could be both happy *and* honor the commitment. I was still swimming for the family. The USC family.

"Whatever you decide," Mom said, "you'll have to live with the consequences."

My mind drifted for a moment. What *were* the consequences? Weren't they all positive?

Except for the money, of course. Not swimming would mean years of paying off two years' worth of college loans. I allowed myself a few days to think it over.

A COUPLE OF NIGHTS LATER, AS KAIA mixed vegetables in our galley kitchen, tossing them into a salad with her olive oil and rice vinegar dressing, I slouched against the counter, ruminating.

"Do you realize how much better I feel since I made the decision?" I asked her. In my mind, I had already quit. In just two days, I had become more engaged in my classes, doing extra research and trying hard to impress my professors. "I'm loving my classes. With swimming, I had no time."

"Nobody has time," Kaia said, pressing. "That's how it is in college."

The prospect of losing the team friendships—my only friendships—scared me. My whole world had been swimming for so long. I also doubted my ability to live a normal life. If I was having trouble maintaining my weight now, how would I maintain it without all that extreme exercise?

I hated the thought of continuing, but even more, I hated the thought of quitting as team captain. Being chosen had made me feel special and connected to my teammates. I wanted to hold on to that feeling. Overnight, it seemed possible that I could please Pokey, please my teammates, and please my parents. There wasn't a single person in my life telling me I should quit.

In that moment, I made a conscious decision to please everyone else; hopefully, I'd please myself by osmosis. I turned to Kaia, my voice cracking. "Okay. I guess I can do one more year."

The future me would have made a different choice. I could have spent that year enjoying my classes without the added pressure of swimming. But swimming and my family had taught me to get through the difficult situations. I wasn't ready to take a stand. I'd promised the school four years and I intended to finish. I told myself to buck up, behave like a trustworthy adult, and follow through with my commitment.

THE FALL OF MY JUNIOR YEAR, DAN transferred from Boulder to UC Irvine—in part, he said, so he could be just forty minutes away. I wasn't ready to decide what I wanted with him, so I tabled the news as if I'd never heard it. I would deal with my uncertainty if and when he showed up.

But not to decide is to decide. Wanting to surprise me, Dan arrived at my apartment on a day when Tim and I had been watching the USC football game in a beer-fueled haze—and instead of introducing Tim to Dan like a mature adult, I suggested that Tim hide in the closet. I had nothing to be ashamed of, but the appearance embarrassed me. Inside the closet, Tim accidentally knocked over a bottle of bleach, which spilled out, visibly and odorously, across the floor. Dan swung the closet door open, and Tim stepped out.

"Uh, sorry. I was just leaving," Tim said as he shook with laughter and skittered out of the apartment.

I apologized, but nothing I could say seemed quite enough. And that was the end of my relationship with Dan.

I hated myself.

I called Kaia to tell her what had happened, and the story sent her into convulsive laughter.

"Why don't you come out to my parents' house?" she suggested. "We'll do something fun."

I DROVE MY YELLOW OPEL KADETT to Kaia's childhood home in Arcadia and there, in her parents' kitchen, she cut me a piece of her famous carrot cake and made light of the situation. Then she suggested that I try for a beach lifeguarding job so I wouldn't have to go home over the summer.

"They're all men," she said, "and there's no interview. It's a race." She stabbed the cake with her fork. "The water is freezing cold, but with your excess fat, you should be able to beat most of the guys . . . God, what did Dan say when he saw Tim?"

I put my hands over my chubby cheeks, trying to think of a comeback, but nothing brilliant came. I looked down at the carrot cake. "I can't eat this."

"Why not?" She was half-teasing, half-serious about the weight gain, but she'd gotten me thinking. Compared to most swimmers, I *could* tolerate cold water. And thanks to Heather, I felt confident in the ocean. Maybe lifeguarding would allow me to quit swimming and not slum it as a student.

"When is it?"

"A couple of months."

The job sounded easy—even glamorous—for summer work. I would sign up for the race and try for the job.

CHAPTER 40

The night before the lifeguard competition, I was up all night, gorging on cinnamon toast, thinking the added weight might help me. By morning, I was still stuffed.

When I arrived at the beach, cold, sticky air came at me with a frightening force. It was freakishly cold and damp, but I felt elated.

Tanned bodies mobbed the registration table. The beach was full of stereotypical Southern California surfer guys with dark, leathery skin, sun-bleached hair, and blue eyes—the kind I avoided.

When I reached the front of the line, the guy at the table was in rare form. "You're going to have to take off those clothes to compete," he needled.

I squinted daggers. I had survived Paul Bergen, Charlie Hickcox, and Dick Peters. Distance swimming through dysfunction was my specialty. I slipped my jacket off one shoulder and let the lifeguard write a number on my upper arm in black permanent marker. I covered the number and zipped my jacket back up with a sense of purpose. Regardless of what anyone thought, I was doing this thing, and I didn't care who I had to climb over to succeed.

No wetsuits allowed, men in Speedos assembled twenty deep in a mass fifty meters wide. I followed one swimmer to the edge of the water and dipped in my feet, a habit that seemed wise until I lost feeling in my toes. I counted around fifteen women among the over three hundred tanned and muscular men.

How did Kaia talk me into this? I asked myself. The water was around 55 degrees Fahrenheit, colder than the coldest pool I'd ever swum in, and these waves were not ankle busters. I planted myself in the monstrous shoal of men, precisely spaced from each other and hugging themselves as they wandered about like a school of yellowfin tuna.

A man with a megaphone offered some encouraging words. There was a loud blast, then deep, resonant splashing as the entire mass scrambled through the surf in a tangled rush, shoving on either side of me. I leapt over one glacial wave and then another, then dove into the frozen water and headed straight for the horizon. Guys jostled me on all four sides; looking down, I realized one was caught underneath me. He struggled to come up for air. I pushed him aside like a tethered buoy.

The mass of swimmers took a sharp left turn around a marker and swam parallel to shore. I could feel my lips, hands, and feet going numb. I kept going. Gradually, swimmers dropped away.

It was 800 meters to the second marker. About halfway, I gagged on some bilious saltwater, and for a moment something else—I didn't know what—stuck to my face. Shades of gray and deep olive green clouded my vision as I rolled like a log over the giant waves.

Rounding the second marker, I imagined the final lap of the mile at US Nationals. An adrenaline rush, a few strokes, and suddenly I knew where I was. I lifted my head and took a couple of quick strokes—and all at once was swept into an enormous wave.

Guys bailed to either side. I took the huge drop, shaking but holding steady, and kept my arms at my side as I cruised into the beach.

Thank you, Heather, I kept thinking. All that bodysurfing had paid off.

I climbed up the hard sand to the finish line, my skin stark white and pinkish like a frozen shrimp. I was sure my lips were blue.

A massive crowd of lifeguards in red swim trunks and navy jackets grinned at me. One said, "You made it," and a wave of heat poured through me. He handed me a popsicle stick with my number. I had finished in the top thirty and would be one of the first female lifeguards in the history of LA County Beach Lifeguarding.

Maggie Van Oppen, Kim Peters, Theresa Van Oppen, and Kiff Kimber. Promotional photo for Real People *TV show, 1979*

I DON'T REMEMBER MUCH OF MY JUNIOR year, but I do remember that toward the end of the season, one of my fellow swimming sufferers, Lauri Siering, reached out to me after practice and offered to walk me home.

Lauri was a brilliant swimmer—an Olympian with a silver medal—and she also had the courage to speak her mind. She wanted me to know that she recognized my pain, and she confided in me that a few years earlier her mother had awakened in the middle of the night, tripped over the family dog on the way to the bathroom, broken a rib which had punctured her spleen, and, shockingly, died from the accident.

I nearly collapsed when I heard the story. I had two parents, two brothers, two sisters, and friends. So much to be grateful for.

Lauri was seriously considering quitting herself. "Swimming can suck the life out of you," she said. "But some of your pain is yours to own." She handed me a pocket-size navy-blue book of affirmations called *One Day at a Time in Al-Anon.* "This has helped me. Maybe it'll help you."

I skulked into my apartment, plunked down on my roommate's tattered sofa, and browsed through Lauri's little book, smoothing back the dog-eared pages.

"Okay, fine; I get it," I said to myself—too quickly. My siblings and I had complained about our parents' drinking for years. Their dependency was no secret. What I hadn't told people about was the massive amount of time we kids had spent alone. What would people think if they knew that Jacquie—my younger sister by a year—had been my stand-in mom; that we saw so little of our parents? That swimming had been a way to get their attention when they were around?

I stared through the dirty living room window. Then I rifled through the Al-Anon book again, and this time my eyes landed on a section about reliance on other people for approval and identity. This was me to a T: depending on others for my happiness. Swimming was so deeply ingrained in me, and winning so tied to my worth as a person, that I was afraid I would have nothing left if I stopped. Would I have to drop out of school? Return to my parents? If so, I'd have to confront their abandonment and its impact on me. Without swimming, people would find out the kind of person I really was.

Between the pages, I felt a shock of recognition. I *did* want to determine my own life. To really own it. I wanted to feel proud, loved, tough—not like a quitter. I wanted to live my life on my own terms, without the prerequisite of reassurance from everyone around me. And I wanted to feel safe in drawing my own conclusions about religion and God.

More than anything, I wanted to feel a part of my family without the compulsion to please them. Freed from the compulsion to please Dad.

I'd devoted so many hours to swimming and hadn't worked hard in my classes; now I thought, *How could I?* My whole life had been swimming, swimming, and more swimming. I had blamed my parents for dragging me into the sport, but I was the one who seemed incapable of getting out. Is that why I'd held on so strenuously to my childhood story of my father's hurling me into the ocean to teach me to swim?

Stop being a victim, the book seemed to say, *and think of your own mental health*. The message landed—but unfortunately, the first try at really standing up is often not pretty.

THAT AFTERNOON, I STROLLED INTO practice, late, and when Pokey saw me donning my bathing cap, something about her relaxed posture rubbed me the wrong way. She pointed to the end lane. "You're too late to join in. You'll have to finish the warm-up by yourself."

I crossed my arms like a four-year-old, telling myself, *You can do this, Kim*, and blurted out, "I'm not swimming the warm-up."

Standing there in her navy flare pants, one leg perched on a starting block, Pokey faced me as my fellow teammates swam into the wall. "Go home!" she said.

For a moment I cowered on the edge of the pool, my mouth hanging open. It was too early for me to realize that asserting myself was a learned art, that first attempts can be shaky, and also had consequences. I knew on some level that Pokey's demand was exactly what I'd wanted. I didn't want to be there.

When she continued to ignore me, I thought, *I'll show her!*

I stomped back to the apartment to fill myself with raw cookie dough.

The following morning, I arrived at practice early to apologize.

I WISH I COULD SAY I HAD IT ALL FIGURED out, but I didn't. I believed that I could quit swimming and with a little finagling, still make my family proud. The truth was, I couldn't. Swimming was my part in saving the family—my own nuclear family *and* the USC family. Quitting was going to disappoint people. Period.

For two months, I swam my hardest, my mind focused on the end of the season, but this time, I didn't make Nationals. After winning there two years earlier, sitting at home while the team flew off without me was difficult. But I'd be lying if I didn't admit I also felt relieved. Finally, my rational mind was telling me something my body had been telling me all along. The mouth-stretching, the hypothyroidism, the weight gain and lethargy—they had all been warning signals that something wasn't right. My body had been shouting and I'd talked back, rationalizing about how swimming was the problem. It was swimming that was too exhausting, too demanding, too dysfunctional. What did my body expect?

But sitting at home, my legs propped on the arm of the sofa, my head on a cozy pillow, with no responsibility to swim, I was forced to cut through the fictional narrative I'd created. Yes, swimming could be crushing and backbreaking in many ways, but my anxiety was built on hiding who I really was, which was what I was doing when I focused only on pleasing others. I'd been hiding when I swallowed the pills, when I didn't scream and shout about what I saw as craziness under Paul Bergen. I'd been hiding when I kept the secret that we kids were left alone. I'd been hiding from Charlie, from Pokey, from my teammates, from everyone.

Finally, I saw that quitting could be a win-win. A win for the team but also, more importantly, a win for me. I no longer had to hold myself accountable for protecting my family. I could step away from my hiding place and begin the arduous process of living more honestly. My departure from the team would leave a spot open for another, more motivated, swimmer. Quitting also would give me time for more joyful activities. I told myself this was a generous act.

NOT LONG AFTER NATIONALS, I ARRANGED TO meet Pokey in her office—a cramped, windowless box near the starting blocks at the corner of the dungeon. I knew I shouldn't be nervous, but I shivered as I entered.

The water was still, the deck dry. I told myself to put one foot in front of the other. The meeting would be over soon, and not long after swimming, the team, workouts, everything, would be nothing but a distant memory.

Pokey cheerily pointed to a chair across from her wooden desk. I felt the hair rise on my arms as I sat down. "It's as if I've been majoring in swimming."

Pokey's warm smile comforted me. I expected her to say something about how I'd gained weight or how I'd brought this on myself. That morning, as I folded clothes and placed them in boxes for another move, I'd tried on my cardinal and gold USC warm-up jacket and cringed at the tight sleeves. But Pokey seemed unwilling to rehash the disappointments.

"I want you to know how much I appreciated the scholarship," I said, "and I'm sorry."

For the briefest moment, it seemed she was about to lecture me. Then she said, "You need to stop saying you're sorry. You did a lot for the team. I'm sure you'll make a success of yourself, whatever you do."

These were scary words and I could feel myself trembling. Even then, there was a part of me that didn't want to quit. I knew the torment of abandoning my family, and now I was abandoning my swimming family. Swimming at USC had been less structured than swimming for the Marlins, sure, but somebody had still been looking out for me, telling me what to do. Now I was giving that up for an uncertain future. I felt guilty and wasn't sure what I would do.

But Pokey waxed nostalgic. Maybe she identified with how difficult it had been for her the day she stopped competing. "Swimming lasts only so long," she said. "You've had a great career."

I hugged myself. *Was this a career? It sure hadn't ended well.* Still, her words blanketed me like a blast of warm air. What enormous gifts she had given me: first the gift of a college education, and now the gift of leaving with dignity.

I rose and gave her a clumsy hug. "Do I need to sign something?"

"No, I'll do it." She was wreathed in smiles. "Good luck."

We hugged again. Then I practically skipped onto the dungeon pool deck, past the first gargoyle.

The dungeon was tranquil, the water still, the thin black lines of the lanes motionless, as I measured my steps on the tile floor behind the starting blocks. I knew this dungeon like I knew my parents' house. I turned the corner and headed for the double doors.

I wanted to remember everything, beginning with that first cold day at Mt. Lookout when Bill Behrens accepted me on the team. I wanted to remember Will Keller's focus on fun, Mr. Bergen's hammering on hard work, and Charlie Hickcox's emphasizing talent. Mr. Keating on the microphone. Susan Dickey on my feet. The camaraderie, the pressure, the teamwork. The feeling of accomplishment at the end of a great workout. The fear at the end of a bad one. Weights, kickboards, pull buoys, timeclocks, weigh-ins, hypoxic training, underwater windows, and touch pads. The Thoroughbred Invitational, the Olympic Trials in Portage Park, the Nationals in Ft. Lauderdale, the trip to Japan, the close friends, the college scholarship, and Pokey's encouragement.

When I got to the doors leading to the courtyard, I paused momentarily and turned, hoping to store one last image in my mind. I soaked in the smell of fresh cotton towels, glanced at the water, glistening like crystal, and glimpsed the painted USC block letters on pillars at the deep end of the pool. I could hear the echo of Pokey's footsteps. I wanted to pinch myself. These had been some memorable years.

I pushed through the door, out to the bright sky and the broad expanse of practice field beneath it, and thought of Dad's words that day when I was four and he'd dragged me through the ocean waves. Ironically, the words he'd used to soothe me then gave me a boost as I was leaving swimming for good. "Look out, not down," he'd said.

I did that now—and for the first time in my life, I felt free. Truly free. To fulfill my own dreams and not somebody else's. I didn't have to spend one more minute looking down at the bottom of a pool. The rush was exhilarating.

EPILOGUE

IT'S REQUIRED AN ADDITIONAL FORTY years of intermittent therapy to deliver the "tell-all book" I once promised I would write. Truth be told, I've needed every one of those years to process and make peace with the swimming life I shared with my teammates and the one I battled alone.

I'll forever feel the luster of having been a part of two extraordinary programs, and I feel especially indebted to Charlie Hickcox, Pokey Richardson, and Barbara Hedges for providing me a scholarship to an outstanding university. Relationships are held together by tough moments, and swimming side by side with my teammates for thirty hours a week, forty-eight weeks a year, through sometimes traumatic and painful events, created deep bonds between us.

I've spent a lifetime getting over Paul Bergen. His special blend of abuse and attention during those impressionable years I swam for him made it hard to sort what was his legacy and what was my father's. Perhaps in the same way that a young tree forced to bend will forever retain its shape, we swimmers retain a kind of bodily and mental imprint from our early years of the sport. I still have eating issues, occasionally stretch my mouth, and gorge on a full stomach. And every now and then someone will look me in the eye on a perfectly lovely day and ask, "What's wrong?" But I know I'm strong, both physically and mentally. All those years of pulling myself through cold, chlorine-drenched water did that for me.

Fortunately, a lot has changed since my years of competitive swimming. Swimming has become one of the most followed sports in the world, and swimmers at the elite level now have the opportunity to earn prize money, national funding, and endorsements. With this added attention, the culture of swimming has changed dramatically. Studies of the coach–athlete relationship in elite athletics have shown that verbal attacks, excessive yelling, or physical acts of aggression like punching walls or throwing kickboards can lead to psychological and emotional harm that can last a lifetime. I can't help but wonder how much I was changed by those years of having the living daylights scared out of me on the Marlins. What if I hadn't experienced the humiliation of daily weigh-ins, the razor-sharp focus on weight, the extreme diets, or the soaking in chlorine and other toxic chemicals four to six hours a day? Would I be the same person? Still weighing myself daily, monitoring my food intake? High-functioning but often churning inside? It's hard to say.

Am I sorry I devoted so many years to swimming? No. Definitely not. Swimming taught me perseverance and commitment. At twenty-nine, when I found myself in the difficult position of becoming a widow with two young children, it was my experience as a swimmer that gave me the confidence and tools to push ahead every day. I have some regrets, of course. Most of us do. In some ways swimming limited me because it left so little time for other pursuits. People often don't realize that you have to give up a helluva lot—to a point that is dysfunctional—when you go into a sport like swimming. Adolescents need time for reflection and time for connection with peers. I didn't read the books I would've read, or engage in activities I would otherwise have enjoyed in my early years. Even if I had been a part of a typical family, I would not have seen much of them.

Fortunately, my siblings and I developed close bonds during those childhood years when we were left alone to fend for ourselves.

To this day, we cherish and rely on each other. None of us remained swimmers, and though my parents ended up with nineteen grandchildren, none of the grandchildren swam. None of us remained Catholics, either, but the lessons we learned from both swimming and our faith have strengthened and sustained us.

When my father died of cirrhosis of the liver in 2003, the five of us kids gathered around his bed, having made peace with his passing. I had asked him in his final hours if he had regrets and he had said no; my mother said the same before she died ten years later. My reaction with both of them was, "Seriously? No regrets?" I could think of dozens of regrets they *should've* had.

From left to right: Emma Peters, Beejay Peters, Kim, Rick Peters,
Dick Peters, Pam Peters Sprague, Jacquie Peters Hiddink, David Peters.
The family visiting my father in Columbus, Ohio, before his death in 2003.

Still, despite the wild moments and long stretches we kids spent fending for ourselves, I cannot stop loving my parents for the gifts they gave us, especially the encouragement to speak our minds, the humor—which we needed, for sure—and the deep well of material for writing, so profound that I don't think I could ever run out.

For years I was angry. I'm not so angry anymore, though I will forever wish my parents had made different choices and taken more responsibility for our family's dysfunction. I regret that our lives as children had to be the way they were. And yet the thing I've learned about regret is that it follows behind you like a shadow. It can stalk you through life, casting its pall over all you do. But like a shadow, regret can fade. And so can blame.

PAUL BERGEN WENT ON TO COACH the US Olympic Team in 1980, 1984, 1988, and 2000. He was inducted into the International Swimming Hall of Fame in 1998, an honor that remains controversial due to allegations by Deena Deardurff and Melissa Halmi that he molested them while they were swimming for him.

In 2010, in an interview on the television program 20/20, Deena had the courage to speak about her sexual abuse as a swimmer under Paul Bergen, from ages eleven to fourteen, which led directly to the forming of a Safe Sport Program at USA Swimming. Deena coached the swim team at San Diego State University from 1994 to 2007, and after surviving breast cancer served as a national spokesperson for the Susan G. Komen Foundation.

Charles Keating Jr., eventually known as one of the "Keating Five," served time in prison in the 1990s for his role in the national savings and loan debacle. Decades later, he still remains one of the most generous contributors to the sport of swimming in Cincinnati.

Kaia Hedlund devoted much of her life to amateur and intercollegiate athletics as a coach, administrator, and volunteer. Since 2006, she has been a sports consultant.

Mike Bottom earned a spot on the 1980 Olympic team that boycotted the Games; thirty-six years later, he was chosen as Olympic coach for Team USA in Rio de Janeiro. He currently coaches the University of Michigan Swim Team.

John Naber, a five-time Olympic medalist, has supported swimming throughout his life as a popular national sports commentator, motivational speaker, and author. He was inducted into the US Olympic and International Swimming Halls of Fame and was twice elected as president of the US Olympians and Paralympians Associations.

WHILE MY SWIM THAT DAY WHEN MY father was in hospice got me back in the water, some part of me still recoils at the thought of swimming, which I have done only on rare occasions and only for recreation throughout my adulthood. Still, as the weeks pass without my touching the water, there isn't a day that goes by when my mind doesn't drift at least once to swimming.

In a daydream, I am out in the ocean alone, floating on my back in the salt air. My tan shoulders soak up the sun's rays, and waves sweep me up and over as I scull. I hear the muffled squeals of beachgoers along the water's edge, the waves crashing on the shore. I turn over and take a few power strokes toward the beach. With my hands by my sides as rudders, I feel the strength of the water.

As I stand up, a blurry heat rises from the sand, and when I squint, they're both there: Mom seated, her head up in rapt attention, eyes glowing; Dad, with his booming voice, drawing me in with a question: "How did you do, Butch?"

I hesitate for a moment in that space between awake and asleep. Then I smile.

"Great," I tell him. "It was great." And this time, I mean it.

ACKNOWLEDGMENTS

This book has been my capstone project, and many people encouraged and supported me along the way. I want to thank my children, George and Hannah Fairley, my biggest supporters, who were there throughout the process.

I owe an ocean of gratitude to Christi Mersereau, who read through countless drafts and discussed the content over long lunches and phone calls. I also owe a huge thank-you to Mary Eastlake Ferraris, Cindy Schilling Blatt, Deena Deardurff, Barbara McLeroy, Genie Wolfson, Barbara Horwitch, Roxann Howard Keating, and Dan Angress, who waded through early drafts and provided invaluable suggestions and support.

I don't know what I would've done without the Ann Arbor Area Writers, especially Anan Ameri, Michael Andreoni, Elli Andrews, Janet Cannon, Kate Chenli, Bill Feight, Fritz Freiheit, Lois Godel, Pamela Goldstein, Donnelly Haddon, Ellen Halter, Skipper Hammond, Karen Hildebrandt, Yma Johnson, Raymond Juracek, Gayle Keiser, Fartumo Kusow, Lori Lorimer, Leslie McGraw, Don McKay, Beth Neal, Barbara Richstone, Shelley Schanfield, Christina Shannon, Karen Simpson, Pat Tompkins, Elizabeth Van Ark, David

Wanty, Marjorie Winful-Sakyi, and Karen Wolff, who made me believe that any of this was interesting.

Sarah Aschenbach, Christine DeSmet, Jane Ratcliffe, and Zilka Joseph played roles in shaping early drafts. Dorothy Wall helped me expand my story and bring it to life. Her encouragement and expertise have been invaluable. I also feel indebted to Katherine Sharpe, Jill Smolowe, Lorrie Goldensohn, and Mark Haskins for their insight and advice.

I am grateful—extremely grateful—to Samantha Strom, Krissa Lagos, Elizabeth Kauffman, and Tabitha Lahr at She Writes Press for supporting this book in countless ways, and especially to Brooke Warner, whom I admire for her strength and leadership.

A loving thank you to my sisters, Jacqueline Hiddink and Pamela Sprague, and my brothers, Rick and David Peters, who have read excerpts over the phone, offered advice, and trusted me enough to call me out when my account of our childhood wasn't what they remembered. Without their encouragement, I doubt I would have written this book.

And finally, Mom and Dad, if you can hear me, thank you for all of the rich material you provided. Mom, your loving response to my story will forever be one of the greatest gifts you gave me.

ABOUT THE AUTHOR

K im Fairley writes about her May–December marriage, wrestling with secrets, and healing from grief and trauma. She grew up in Cincinnati, Ohio, attended the University of Southern California, and holds an MFA in mixed media from the University of Michigan. She has written two other books, *Shooting out the Lights: A Memoir* and *Boreal Ties: Photographs and Two Diaries of the 1901 Peary Relief Expedition*. She lives in Ann Arbor, Michigan.

kimfairley.com

 twitter.com/kimfairley1

facebook.com/kimfairley11

instagram.com/kimfairleywrites

SELECTED TITLES FROM SHE WRITES PRESS

She Writes Press is an independent publishing company founded to serve women writers everywhere. Visit us at www.shewritespress.com.

Shooting Out the Lights: A Memoir by Kim Fairley. $16.95, 978-1-64742-134-2. After twenty-four-year-old Kim falls in love with and marries fifty-six-year-old Vern, she quickly becomes pregnant—only to have their love tested by the ghosts of Vern's past, his failing health, and the unexpected arrival of a troubled young boy.

Wave Woman: The Life and Struggles of a Surfing Pioneer by Vicky Heldreich Durand. $29.95, 978-1-68463-042-4. The untold story of Betty Pembroke Heldreich—a pioneering champion Hawaii surfer in the mid-1950s, a female athlete and professional who broke glass ceilings and believed anything exciting was worth trying at least once.

The Sportscaster's Daughter: A Memoir by Cindi Michael. $16.95, 978-1-63152-107-2. Despite being disowned by her father—sportscaster George Michael, said to be the man who inspired ESPN's *SportsCenter*—Cindi Michael manages financially and heals emotionally, ultimately finding confidence from within.

Raising Myself: A Memoir of Neglect, Shame, and Growing Up Too Soon by Beverly Engel. $16.95, 978-1-63152-367-0. A powerfully inspiring and unflinchingly honest story of how best-selling author and abuse recovery expert Beverly Engel made her way in the world—in spite of her mother's neglect and constant criticism, undergoing sexual abuse at nine, and being raped at twelve.

Rebellion, 1967: A Memoir by Janet Luongo. $16.95, 978-1-64742-104-5. When spunky seventeen-year-old Janet Duffy's dream of college is dimmed by family neglect, she runs away with a Black musician to become an artist and work for racial equality and peace—a misadventure that brings her heartbreak, poverty, and danger.

Implosion: Memoir of an Architect's Daughter by Elizabeth W. Garber. $16.95, 978-1-63152-351-9. When Elizabeth Garber, her architect father, Woodie, and the rest of their family move into Woodie's modern masterpiece, a glass house, in 1966, they have no idea that over the next few years their family's life will be shattered—both by Woodie's madness and the turbulent 1970s.